ROAD ATLAS

HANDY FRANCE

BELGIUM & THE NETHERLANDS

www.philips-maps.co.uk

First published in 2009 by
Philip's, a division of
Octopus Publishing Group Ltd
www.octopusbooks.co.uk
Carmelite House,
50 Victoria Embankment
London EC4Y 0DZ

An Hachette UK Company
www.hachette.co.uk

The authorised representative in
the EEA is Hachette Ireland,
8 Castlecourt Centre,
Castleknock Road,
Castleknock, Dublin 15,
D15 YF6A, Ireland

Fifth edition 2025
First impression 2025

ISBN 978-1-84907-704-0

Cartography by Philip's
Copyright © Philip's 2025

Printed in China

CONTENTS

II Legend
III Driving regulations, Ski resorts
IV Tourist sights of Belgium, France and The Netherlands

VI Route planning map
VIII Distance table

1 Road maps
1 Key map

39 City plans and approach maps
39 Legends to city plans and approach maps
39 Amsterdam
40 Brussels · Bordeaux · Bordeaux *approaches*
41 Lyon · Lyon *approaches* · Luxembourg · Marseilles
42 Paris *approaches*
43 Paris · Strasbourg · Strasbourg *approaches*

44 Index to road maps

T0342954

Legend

Route planning map pages VI–VII

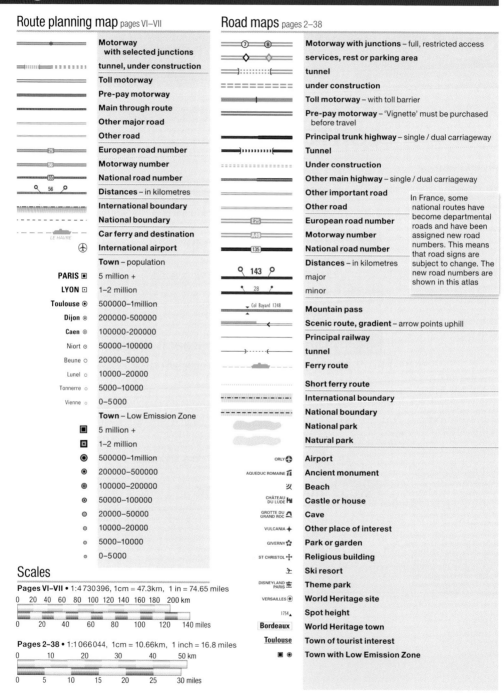

	Motorway with selected junctions
	tunnel, under construction
	Toll motorway
	Pre-pay motorway
	Main through route
	Other major road
	Other road
25	European road number
56	Motorway number
55	National road number
56	Distances – in kilometres
	International boundary
	National boundary
LE HAVRE	Car ferry and destination
✈	International airport
	Town – population
PARIS ■	5 million +
LYON ▣	1–2 million
Toulouse ◉	500000–1million
Dijon ◉	200000–500000
Caen ◉	100000–200000
Niort ◉	50000–100000
Beune ○	20000–50000
Lunel ○	10000–20000
Tonnerre ○	5000–10000
Vienne ○	0–5000
	Town – Low Emission Zone
■	5 million +
▣	1–2 million
◉	500000–1million
◉	200000–500000
◉	100000–200000
◉	50000–100000
○	20000–50000
○	10000–20000
○	5000–10000
○	0–5000

Road maps pages 2–38

⑦ ⑧	**Motorway with junctions** – full, restricted access
◇ ◈	services, rest or parking area
	tunnel
	under construction
	Toll motorway – with toll barrier
	Pre-pay motorway – 'Vignette' must be purchased before travel
	Principal trunk highway – single / dual carriageway
	Tunnel
	Under construction
	Other main highway – single / dual carriageway
	Other important road
	Other road
E25	**European road number**
A49	**Motorway number**
135	**National road number**
143	**Distances** – in kilometres
	major
28	minor
Col Bayard 1248	**Mountain pass**
	Scenic route, gradient – arrow points uphill
	Principal railway
	tunnel
	Ferry route
	Short ferry route
	International boundary
	National boundary
	National park
	Natural park
ORLY 🛫	**Airport**
AQUEDUC ROMAINE 🏛	**Ancient monument**
丛	**Beach**
CHÂTEAU DU LUDE 🏰	**Castle or house**
GROTTE DU GRAND ROC ⌂	**Cave**
VULCANIA ✦	**Other place of interest**
GIVERNY ❀	**Park or garden**
ST CHRISTOL ✝	**Religious building**
峰	**Ski resort**
DISNEYLAND PARIS 🎡	**Theme park**
VERSAILLES ◉	**World Heritage site**
1754 ▲	**Spot height**
Bordeaux	**World Heritage town**
Toulouse	**Town of tourist interest**
■ ◉	**Town with Low Emission Zone**

> In France, some national routes have become departmental roads and have been assigned new road numbers. This means that road signs are subject to change. The new road numbers are shown in this atlas

Scales

Pages VI–VII • 1:4 730396, 1cm = 47.3km, 1 in = 74.65 miles

0 20 40 60 80 100 120 140 160 180 200 km

0 20 40 60 80 100 120 140 miles

Pages 2–38 • 1:1 066044, 1cm = 10.66km, 1 inch = 16.8 miles

0 10 20 30 40 50 km

0 5 10 15 20 25 30 miles

Belgium Ⓑ

⏱	🏛 120[1]	⚠ 120[1]	⚠ 90[2]	🛏 50[3]
Over 3.5 tonnes				
⏱	90	90	70[2]–90	50[3]

[1]Minimum speed of 70 kph may be applied in certain conditions on motorways and some dual carriageways. [2]70 kph in Flanders. [3]20 kph in residential areas, 30 kph near some schools, hospitals and churches, and in designated cycle zones.

🛡 Compulsory

🔔 All under 18s under 135 cm must wear an appropriate child restraint. Airbags must be deactivated if a rear-facing child seat is used in the front.

🍷 0.05% • 0.02% professional drivers

△ Compulsory

📇 Recommended (compulsory for vehicles registered in Belgium) 💡 Recommended

🔦 Recommended (compulsory for vehicles registered in Belgium) ⊖ 18

📱 Only allowed with a hands-free kit

LEZ LEZs in operation in Antwerp, Brussels and Ghent. Preregistration necessary and fees payable for most vehicles.

◎ꜜ Mandatory at all times for motorcycles and during the day in poor conditions for other vehicles

❄ Winter tyres permitted 1 Oct to 31 Apr. Snow chains only permitted if road is fully covered by snow or ice. Vehicles with studded tyres restricted to 90 kph on motorways/dual carriageways and 60 kph on other roads.

★ If a tram or bus stops to allow passengers on or off, you must not overtake ★ Motorcyclists must wear fully protective clothing ★ On-the-spot fines imposed ★Radar detectors prohibited ★ Sticker indicating maximum recommended speed for winter tyres must be displayed on dashboard if using them ★Visibility vest compulsory ★When a traffic jam occurs on a road with two or more lanes in the direction of travel, motorists should move aside to create a path for emergency vehicles between the lanes.

France Ⓕ

⏱	🏛 130	⚠ 110	⚠ 80	🛏 50
On wet roads or if full driving licence held for less than 3 years				
⏱	110	100	70	50
above 3.5 tonnes gross				
⏱	90	80	80	50

50kph on all roads if fog reduces visibility to less than 50m

🛡 Compulsory in front seats and, if fitted, in rear

🔔 Children up to age 10 must use suitable child seat or restraint and may only travel in the front if: • the vehicle has no rear seats • no rear seatbelts • the rear seats are already occupied by children up to age 10 • the child is a baby in a rear facing child seat and the airbag is deactivated.

🍷 0.05% • 0.02% if full driving licence held for less than 3 years • All drivers/motorcyclists are required to carry an unused breathalyser though this rule is not currently enforced.

△ Compulsory 📇 Recommended

💡 Recommended

⊖ 18 (16 for motorbikes up to 125cc)

📱 Use permitted only with hands-free kit. Must not be used with headphones or earpieces

LEZ An LEZ operates in the Mont Blanc tunnel and such zones are being progressively introduced across French cities. Non-compliant vehicles are banned during operating hours. Crit'Air stickers must be displayed by compliant vehicles. See http://certificat-air.gouv.fr/en

◎ꜜ Compulsory in poor daytime visibility and at all times for motorcycles

❄ In mountainous areas (marked by signs), winter tyres must be fitted or snow chains available 1 Nov to 31 March

★ GPS must have fixed speed camera function

Driving regulations

deactivated; radar-detection equipment is prohibited ★Headphones or earpieces must not be used for listening to music or making phone calls while driving. ★ Motorcyclists and passengers must have four reflective stickers on their helmets (front, back and both sides) and wear CE-certified gloves. ★On-the-spot fines imposed ★Tolls on motorways. Electronic tag needed if using automatic tolls. ★ Visibility vests, to be worn on the roadside in case of emergency or breakdown, must be carried for all vehicle occupants and riders. ★Wearers of contact lenses or spectacles should carry a spare pair

Netherlands ⓃⓁ

⏱	🏛 100–130	⚠ 80/100	⚠ 80/100	🛏 50

🛡 Compulsory

🔔 Under 3 must travel in the back, using an appropriate child restraint; 3–18 and under 135cm must use an appropriate child restraint. A rear-facing child seat may only be used in front if airbags are deactivated.

🍷 0.05% • 0.02% if full licence held less than 5 years and for moped riders under 24.

△ Compulsory

📇 Recommended 💡 Recommended

🔦 Recommended ⊖ 18

📱 Only allowed with a hands-free kit

LEZ LEZs for diesel vehicles operate in many Dutch cities. Restrictions depend on vehicle's Euro emissions standard. For information see https://www.milieuzones.nl/english

◎ꜜ Recommended in poor visibility and on open roads. Compulsory for motorcycles.

★ On-the-spot fines imposed ★ Radar-detection equipment is prohibited ★ Trams have priority over other traffic. You must wait if a bus or tram stops in the middle of the road to allow passengers on or off.

Ski resorts

Alps

Alpe d'Huez 26 B3 ❄ 1860–3330m • 85 lifts • Dec–Apr 🖥 www.alpedhuez.com/en

Avoriaz 26 A3 ❄ 1800/1100–2280m • 36 lifts • Dec–Apr 🖥 www.avoriaz.com/en

Chamonix-Mont-Blanc 27 B3 ❄ 1035–3840m • 49 lifts • Dec–Apr 🖥 https://en.chamonix.com/

Chamrousse 26 B2 ❄ 1700/1420–2250m • 15 lifts • Dec–Apr 🖥 https://en.chamrousse.com/

Châtel 27 A3 ❄ 1200/1110–2200m • 41 lifts • Dec–Apr 🖥 https://en.chatel.com/ete

Courchevel 26 B3 ❄ 1300–2470m • 67 lifts • Dec–Apr 🖥 https://courchevel.com/en/

Flaine 26 A3 ❄ 1600–2500m • 24 lifts • Dec–Apr 🖥 https://en.flaine.com/

La Clusaz 26 B3 ❄ 1100–2600m • 49 lifts • Dec–Apr 🖥 https://en.laclusaz.com/

La Plagne 26 B3 ❄ 2500/1250–3250m • 75 lifts • Dec–Apr 🖥 https://en.la-plagne.com/

Les Arcs 27 B3 ❄ 1600/1200–3230m • 77 lifts • Dec–Apr 🖥 https://www.lesarcs.com/

Les Carroz d'Araches 26 A3 ❄ 1140–2500m • 80 lifts • Dec–Apr 🖥 www.lescarroz.com/en

Les Deux-Alpes 26 C3 ❄ 1650/1300–3600m • 49 lifts • Dec–Apr & Jun–Aug 🖥 www.les2alpes.com/en

Les Gets 26 A3 ❄ 1170/1000–2000m • 47 lifts • Dec–Apr 🖥 www.lesgets.com/en

Les Ménuires 26 B3 ❄ 1815/1850–3200m • 39 lifts • Dec–Apr 🖥 www.lesmenuires.com

Les Sept Laux Prapoutel 26 B3 ❄ 1350–2400m, • 24 lifts • Dec–Apr 🖥 www.les7laux.com/winter

Megève 26 B3 ❄ 1100/1050–2350m • 79 lifts • Dec–Apr 🖥 www.megeve.com/en

Méribel 26 B3 ❄ 1400/1100–2950m • 61 lifts • Dec–Apr 🖥 www.meribel.net/en

Morzine 26 A3 ❄ 1000–2460m • 46 lifts • Dec–Apr 🖥 http://en.morzine-avoriaz.com

Pra Loup 32 A2 ❄ 1500–2600m • 20 lifts • Dec–Apr 🖥 www.praloup.com

Risoul 26 C3 ❄ 1850/1650–2750m • 59 lifts • Dec–Apr 🖥 https://en.risoul.com

St-Gervais Mont-Blanc 26 B3 ❄ 850/1150–2350m • 27 lifts • Dec–Apr 🖥 www.ski-saintgervais.com/en

Serre Chevalier 26 C3 ❄ 1350/1200–2800m • 68 lifts • Dec–Apr 🖥 www.serre-chevalier.com/en

Tignes 27 B3 ❄ 2100/1550–3450m • 78 lifts • Jan–Dec 🖥 https://en.tignes.net/

Val d'Isère 27 B3 ❄ 1850/1550–3450m • 78 lifts • Dec–May, possibly until Jul 🖥 www.valdisere.com/en/

Val Thorens 26 B3 ❄ 2300/1850–3200m • 31 lifts • Nov–May 🖥 www.les3vallees.com/en/ski-resort/val-thorens

Valloire 26 B3 ❄ 1430–2750m • 35 lifts • Dec–Apr 🖥 https://tourism.valloire.net

Valmeinier 26 B3 ❄ 1500–2750m • 35 lifts • Dec–Apr 🖥 www.valmeinier.com/en

Valmorel 26 B3 ❄ 1400–2550m • 50 lifts • Dec–Apr 🖥 www.valmorel.com/en/

Vars Les Claux 26 C3 ❄ 1850/1650–2750m • 59 lifts • Dec–Apr 🖥 www.vars.com

Villard de Lans 26 B2 ❄ 1050/1160–2170m • 21 lifts • Dec–Apr 🖥 https://uk.villarddelans-correnconenvercors.com

Pyrenees

Font-Romeu 36 B3 ❄ 1800/1600–2200m • 23 lifts • Nov–Mar 🖥 https://font-romeu.fr/en/

Saint-Lary Soulan 35 B4 ❄ 830/1650/1700–2515m • 31 lifts • Dec–Apr 🖥 www.saintlary.com

Vosges

La Bresse-Hohneck 20 A1 ❄ 600–1370m • 33 lifts • Dec–Mar 🖥 www.labresse.net

❄ = resorts with snow cannon

Tourist sights of Belgium, France and The Netherlands

Belgium Belgique

http://walloniabelgiumtourism.co.uk

Antwerp *Antwerpen* City with many tall gabled Flemish houses on the river. Heart of the city is Great Market with 16–17c guildhouses and Town Hall. Charles Borromeus Church (Baroque). 14–16c Gothic cathedral has Rubens paintings. Rubens also at the Rubens House and his burial place in St Jacob's Church. Excellent museums: Mayer van den Bergh Museum (applied arts); Koninklijk Museum of Fine Arts (Flemish, Belgian); MAS (ethnography, folklore, shipping); Muhka (modern art). www.visitantwerpen.be 5 A4

Bruges *Brugge* Well-preserved medieval town with narrow streets and canals. Main squares: the Market with 13c Belfort and covered market; the Burg with Basilica of the Holy Blood and Town Hall. The collections of Groeninge Museum and Memling museum in St Jans Hospital include 15c Flemish masters. The Onze Lieve Vrouwekerk has a famous *Madonna and Child* by Michelangelo www.visitbruges.be 4 A3

Brussels *Bruxelles* Capital of Belgium. The Lower Town is centred on the enormous Grand Place with Hôtel de Ville and rebuilt guildhouses. Symbols of the city include the 'Manneken Pis' and Atomium (giant model of a molecule). The 13c Notre Dame de la Chapelle is the oldest church. The Upper Town contains: Gothic cathedral; Neoclassical Place Royale; 18c King's Palace; Royal Museums of Fine Arts (old and modern masters) Magritte Museum; MRAH (art and historical artefacts); BELvue museum (in the Bellevue Residence). Also: much Art Nouveau (Horta Museum, Hôtel Tassel, Hôtel Solvay); Place du Petit Sablon and Place du Grand Sablon; 19c Palais de Justice. https://visit.brussels/en 5 B4

Ghent *Gent* Medieval town built on islands surrounded by canals and rivers. Views from Pont St-Michel. The Graslei and Koornlei quays have Flemish guild houses. The Gothic cathedral has famous Van Eyck altarpiece. Also: Belfort; Cloth Market; Gothic Town Hall; Gravensteen. Museums: STAM Museum in Bijloke Abbey (provincial and applied art); Museum of Fine Arts (old masters). https://visit.gent.be/en 5 A3

Namur Reconstructed medieval citadel is the major sight of Namur, which also has a cathedral and provincial museums. www.namurtourisme.be/index.php 5 B4

Tournai The Romanesque-Gothic cathedral is Belgium's finest (much excellent art). Fine Arts Museum has a good collection (15–20c). https://en.visittournai.be 4 B3

France

https://uk.france.fr/en

Albi Old town with rosy brick architecture. The vast Cathédrale Ste-Cécile (begun 13c) holds some good art. The Berbie Palace houses the Toulouse-Lautrec Museum. www.albi-tourisme.fr/en 30 B1

Alps Grenoble capital of the French Alps, has a good 20c collection in the Museum of Grenoble. The Vanoise Massif has the greatest number of resorts (Val d'Isère, Courchevel). Chamonix has spectacular views of Mont Blanc, France's and Europe's highest peak. www.grenoble-tourisme.com/en 26 B2

Amiens France's largest Gothic cathedral has beautiful decoration. The Museum of Picardy has unique 16c panel paintings. Also: Jules Verne House. www.visit-amiens.com 10 B2

Arles Ancient, picturesque town with Roman relics (1c amphitheatre), 11c St Trophime church, Archaeological Museum (Roman art), Van Gogh centre. www.arlestourisme.com/en/ 31 B3

Avignon Medieval papal capital (1309–77) with 14c walls and many ecclesiastical buildings. Vast Palace of the Popes has stunning frescoes. The Little Palace has fine Italian Renaissance painting. The 12–13c Bridge of St Bénézet is famous. https://avignon-tourisme.com/en/ 31 B3

Bourges The Gothic Cathedral of St Etienne, one of the finest in France, has a superb sculptured choir. Also notable is the House of Jacques Coeur. www.bourgesberrytourisme.com 17 B4

Brittany *Bretagne* Brittany is famous for cliffs, sandy beaches and wild landscape. It is also renowned for megalithic monuments (Carnac) and Celtic culture. Its capital, Rennes, has the Parlement de Bretagne and good collections in the Museum of Brittany (history) and Museum of Fine Arts. Also: Nantes; St-Malo. www.brittanytourism.com

Burgundy *Bourgogne* Rural wine region with a rich Romanesque, Gothic and Renaissance heritage. The 12c cathedral in Autun and 12c basilica in Vézelay have fine Romanesque sculpture. Monasteries include 11c Abbaye de Cluny (ruins) and Abbaye de Fontenay. Beaune has beautiful Gothic Hôtel-Dieu and 15c Nicolas Rolin hospices. www.burgundy-tourism.com 18 B3

Caen City with two beautiful Romanesque buildings: Abbaye aux Hommes; Abbaye aux Dames. The château has two museums (16–20c painting; history). The *Bayeux Tapestry* is displayed in nearby Bayeux. www.caenlamer-tourisme.com 9 A3

Carcassonne Unusual double-walled fortified town of narrow streets with an inner fortress. The fine Romanesque Church of St Nazaire has superb stained glass. www.tourisme-carcassonne.fr/en 30 B1

Chartres The 12–13c cathedral is an exceptionally fine example of Gothic architecture (Royal Doorway, stained glass, choir screen). The Fine Arts Museum has a good collection. www.chartres.com 10 C1

Clermont-Ferrand The old centre contains the cathedral built out of lava and Romanesque basilica. The Puy de Dôme and Puy de Sancy give spectacular views over some 60 extinct volcanic peaks (*puys*). www.clermontauvergnetourisme.com/en/ 24 B3

Colmar Town characterised by Alsatian half-timbered houses. The Unterlinden Museum has excellent German religious art including the famous Isenheim Altarpiece. Also: Espace André Malraux (contemporary arts). www.tourisme-colmar.com/en/ 20 A2

Corsica *Corse* Corsica has a beautiful rocky coast and mountainous interior. Napoleon's birthplace of Ajaccio has: Fesch Museum with Imperial Chapel and a large collection of Italian art; Maison Bonaparte; cathedral. Bonifacio, a medieval town, is spectacularly set on a rock over the sea. www.visit-corsica.com/en

Côte d'Azur The French Riviera is best known for its coastline and glamorous resorts. There are many relics of artists who worked here: St-Tropez has Musée de l'Annonciade; Antibes has 12c Château Grimaldi with the Picasso Museum; Cagnes has the Renoir Museum; Le Cannet has the Bonnard Museum; St-Paul-de-Vence; St-Paul-de-Vence has the excellent Maeght Foundation; and nearby Vence has Matisse's Chapelle du Rosaire. Cannes is famous for its film festival. Also: Marseille, Monaco, Nice. www.provence-alpes-cotedazur.com 33 B3

Dijon Great 15c cultural centre. The Palais des Ducs et des Etats is the most notable monument and contains the Museum of Fine Arts. Also: the Charterhouse of Champmol. https://en.destinationdijon.com 19 B4

Disneyland Paris Europe's largest theme park follows in the footsteps of its famous predecessors in the United States. www.disneylandparis.com 10 C2

Le Puy-en-Velay Medieval town bizarrely set on the peaks of dead volcanoes. It is dominated by the Romanesque cathedral (cloisters). The Romanesque chapel of St-Michel is dramatically situated on the highest rock. www.lepuyenvelay-tourisme.co.uk 25 B3

Loire Valley The Loire Valley has many 15–16c châteaux built amid beautiful scenery by French monarchs and members of their

courts. Among the most splendid are Azay-le-Rideau, Chambord, Chenonceau and Loches. Also: Abbaye de Fontévraud. www.loirevalley-france.co.uk 16 B2

Lyon France's third largest city has an old centre and many museums including the Museum of Fine Arts (old masters) and the modern Musée des Confluences. https://en.lyon-france.com/ 25 B4

Marseilles *Marseille* Second largest city in France. Spectacular views from the 19c Notre-Dame de la Garde. The Old Port has 11–12c Basilique St Victor (crypt, catacombs). Cantini Museum has major collection of 20c French art, and the Mucem tells the history of Mediterranean civilizations. Château d'If was the setting of Dumas' *The Count of Monte Cristo*. www.marseille-tourisme.com/en/ 31 B4

Mont-St-Michel Gothic pilgrim abbey (11–12c) set dramatically on a steep rock island rising from mud flats and connected to the land by a road covered by the tide. The abbey is made up of a complex of buildings. www.ot-montsaintmichel.com/ 15 A4

Nancy A centre of Art Nouveau. The 18c Place Stanislas was constructed by dethroned Polish king Stanislas. Museums: School of Nancy Museum (Art Nouveau furniture); Fine Arts Museum. www.nancy-tourisme.fr/en/ 12 C2

Nantes Former capital of Brittany, with the 15c Château des ducs de Bretagne. The cathedral has a striking interior. www.nantes-tourisme.com/en 15 B4

Nice Capital of the Côte d'Azur, the old town is centred on the old castle on the hill. The seafront includes the famous 19c Promenade des Anglais. The aristocratic quarter of the Cimiez Hill has the Marc Chagall Museum and the Matisse Museum. Also: Museum of Modern and Contemporary Art (especially neo-Realism and Pop Art). http://en.nicetourisme.com/ 33 B3

Paris Capital of France, one of Europe's most interesting cities. The Île de la Cité area, an island in the River Seine, has the 12–13c Notre Dame, devastated by fire in 2019 and undergoing major restoration, and La Sainte Chapelle (1240–48), one of the jewels of Gothic art. The Left Bank area: Latin Quarter with the famous Sorbonne university; Museum of Cluny housing medieval art; the Panthéon; Luxembourg Palace and Gardens; Montparnasse, inter-war artistic and literary centre; Eiffel Tower; Hôtel des Invalides with Napoleon's tomb. Right Bank: the great boulevards (Avenue des Champs-Élysées joining the Arc de Triomphe and Place de la Concorde); 19c Opéra Quarter; Marais, former aristocratic quarter of elegant mansions (Place des Vosges); Bois de Boulogne, the largest park in Paris; Montmartre, centre of 19c bohemianism, with the Basilique Sacré-Coeur. The Church of St Denis is the first Gothic church and the mausoleum of the French monarchy. Paris has three of the world's greatest art collections: The Louvre (to 19c, *Mona Lisa*), Musée d'Orsay (19–20c) and National Modern Art Museum in the Pompidou Centre. Other major museums include: Orangery Museum; Paris Museum of Modern Art; Rodin Museum; Picasso Museum; Atelier des Lumières. Notable cemeteries with graves of the famous: Père-Lachaise, Montmartre, Montparnasse. Near Paris are the royal residences of Fontainebleau and Versailles. https://en.parisinfo.com 10 C2

Pyrenees Beautiful unspoiled mountain range. Towns include: delightful sea resorts of St-Jean-de-Luz and Biarritz; Pau, with access to the Pyrenees National Park; pilgrimage centre Lourdes.

Reims Together with nearby Épernay, the centre of champagne production. The 13c Gothic cathedral is one of the greatest architectural achievements in France (stained glass by Chagall). Other sights: Palais du Tau with cathedral sculpture, 11c Basilica of St Rémi; cellars on Place St-Niçaise and Place des Droits de l'Homme. https://en.reims-tourisme.com 11 B4

Rouen Old centre with many half-timbered houses and 12–13c Gothic cathedral and the Gothic Church of St Maclou with its fascinating remains of a danse macabre on the former cemetery of Aître St-Maclou. The Fine Arts Museum has a good collection. https://en.rouentourisme.com/ 9 A5

St-Malo Fortified town (much rebuilt) in a fine coastal setting. There is a magnificent boat trip along the river Rance to Dinan, a splendid well-preserved medieval town. www.saint-malo-tourisme.co.uk 15 A3

Strasbourg Town whose historic centre includes a well-preserved quarter of medieval half-timbered Alsatian houses, many of them set on the canal. The cathedral is one of the best in France. The Palais Rohan contains several museums. www.visitstrasbourg.fr/en/welcome-in-strasbourg 13 C3

Toulouse Medieval university town characterised by flat pink brick (Hôtel Assézat). The Basilique St Sernin, the largest Romanesque church in France, has many art treasures. Marvellous Church of the Jacobins holds relics of St Thomas Aquinas. www.toulouse-visit.com 29 C4

Tours Historic town centred on Place Plumereau. Good collections in the Guilds Museum and Fine Arts Museum. Also: cathedral (predominantly Gothic). www.tours-tourism.com/ 16 B2

Versailles Vast royal palace built for Louis XIV, primarily by Mansart, set in large formal gardens with magnificent fountains. The extensive and much-imitated state apartments include the famous Hall of Mirrors and the exceptional Baroque chapel. http://en.chateauversailles.fr/ 10 C2

Vézère Valley Caves A number of prehistoric sites, most notably the cave paintings of Lascaux (some 17,000 years old), now only seen in a duplicate cave, and the cave of Font de Gaume. The National Museum of Prehistory is in Les Eyzies. www.lascaux-dordogne.com/en 29 B4

Netherlands Nederland
www.holland.com

Amsterdam Capital of the Netherlands. Old centre has picturesque canals lined with distinctive elegant 17–18c merchants' houses. Dam Square has 15c New Church and Royal Palace. Other churches include Westerkerk. The Museumplein has three world-famous museums: the Rijksmuseum (several art collections including 15–17c painting); Van Gogh Museum; Municipal Museum (art from 1850 on). Other museums: Anne Frank House; Jewish Historical Museum; Rembrandt House; Hermitage Museum (exhibitions). 2 B1

Delft Well-preserved old Dutch town with gabled red-roofed houses along canals. Gothic churches: New Church; Old Church. Famous for Delftware (two museums). www.delft.nl 2 B1

Haarlem Many medieval gabled houses centred on the Great Market with 14c Town Hall and 15c Church of St Bavon. Museums: Frans Hals Museum; Teylers Museum. www.visithaarlem.com/en/ 2 B1

The Hague *Den Haag* Seat of Government and of the royal house of the Netherlands. The 17c Mauritshuis houses the Royal Picture Gallery (excellent 15–18c Flemish and Dutch). Other museums: Escher Museum; Meermanno Museum (books); Municipal Museum. 2 B1

Het Loo Former royal palace and gardens set in a vast landscape (commissioned by the future King and Queen of England, William and Mary). www.paleishetloo.nl 2 B2

Keukenhof In spring, landscaped gardens, planted with bulbs of many varieties, are the largest flower gardens in the world. www.keukenhof.nl 2 B1

Leiden University town of beautiful gabled houses set along canals. The Rijksmuseum Van Oudheden is Holland's most important home to archaeological artefacts from the Antiquity. The 16c Hortus Botanicus is one of the oldest botanical gardens in Europe. The Cloth Hall with van Leyden's *Last Judgement*. http://leidenholland.com 2 B1

Rotterdam The largest port in the Europe. The Boymans-van Beuningen Museum has a huge and excellent decorative and fine art collection (old and modern). Nearby: 18c Kinderdijk with 19 windmills. https://en.rotterdam.info 5 A4

Utrecht Delightful old town centre along canals with the Netherlands' oldest university and Gothic cathedral. Good art collections: Central Museum; National Museum. www.utrecht.nl 2 B2

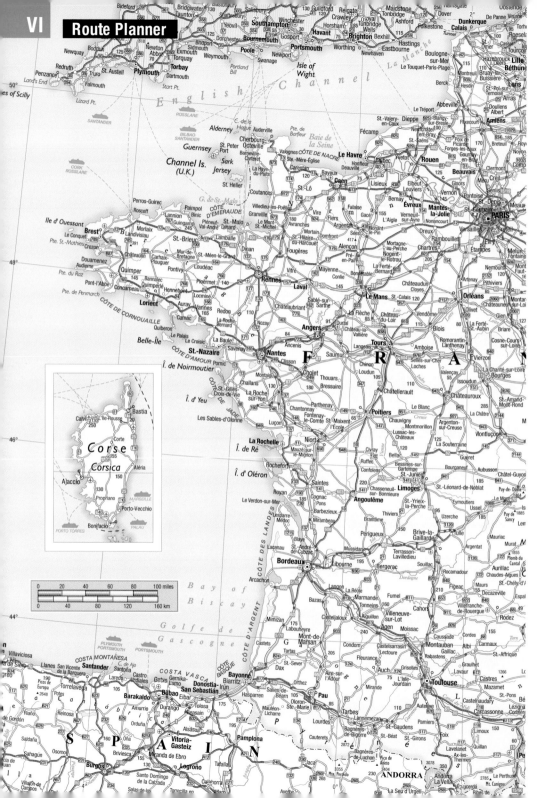

Distances

Amsterdam

99
159 **Antwerp**

662 573
1065 922 **Bordeaux**

242 145 539
390 233 867 **Boulogne**

646 547 398 421
1040 881 641 678 **Brest**

127 28 545 140 525
205 45 877 226 845 **Brussels**

227 126 533 22 442 122
366 203 857 35 712 196 **Calais**

505 388 431 273 262 370 291
812 624 694 439 422 596 468 **Cherbourg-Octeville**

574 474 230 422 513 447 442 446
924 763 370 679 825 720 711 717 **Clermont-Ferrand**

334 232 439 85 339 180 109 184 344
538 374 706 137 545 290 176 296 554 **Dieppe**

77 55 607 199 595 79 181 441 516 247
124 89 977 321 958 127 291 709 831 397 **Eindhoven**

641 495 419 513 678 500 530 575 185 474 539
1032 797 674 826 1091 804 853 926 297 763 867 **Grenoble**

604 511 113 413 273 478 431 293 295 337 560 462
972 823 182 665 439 769 694 472 475 543 902 743 **La Rochelle**

375 275 418 151 288 250 172 135 366 68 328 478 314
604 442 673 243 463 402 277 217 589 110 528 770 506 **Le Havre**

438 341 269 244 243 314 267 176 270 169 395 446 178 153
705 548 433 392 391 505 430 283 435 272 636 717 286 246 **Le Mans**

152 77 566 194 559 60 185 402 478 239 67 489 519 288 350
244 124 911 313 899 96 297 647 770 385 108 787 835 464 564 **Liege**

176 78 488 71 460 68 69 305 398 115 130 493 425 132 263 126
283 125 786 115 741 109 111 491 640 185 210 793 684 213 423 202 **Lille**

542 463 137 401 373 434 421 371 113 341 508 330 137 334 184 469 375
872 745 221 646 600 699 678 597 182 549 817 531 220 537 296 755 604 **Limoges**

233 159 544 252 612 132 249 426 367 264 166 371 485 321 88 87 174 473
375 256 875 405 985 212 401 686 590 425 267 597 781 516 142 140 280 762 **Luxembourg**

575 473 347 442 629 446 464 493 106 389 492 66 459 411 331 413 426 260 318
925 761 558 712 1013 717 746 794 170 626 792 106 739 662 533 665 685 418 511 **Lyon**

768 670 393 640 786 643 581 700 255 600 699 180 516 595 546 615 609 366 518 187
1236 1079 632 1030 1265 1035 935 1127 410 966 1125 290 830 958 878 990 980 589 833 301 **Marseilles**

760 662 303 626 696 641 643 643 207 548 678 183 413 564 470 609 606 270 506 188 103
1223 1066 488 1008 1120 1031 1034 1035 333 882 1091 295 665 908 756 980 975 434 814 302 165 **Montpellier**

327 228 547 324 598 203 321 460 342 321 249 318 491 357 362 175 260 409 72 254 445 439
527 367 880 521 962 326 517 740 550 517 401 512 790 574 582 282 418 659 116 409 716 707 **Nancy**

548 449 219 353 185 428 373 211 333 278 115 465 374 217 465 451 613 511 469
882 723 352 568 297 688 601 339 536 448 813 815 140 385 185 749 602 350 748 725 987 823 755 **Nantes**

865 767 499 737 894 743 761 798 393 698 784 204 608 699 652 713 716 527 611 293 127 202 542 710
1392 1235 803 1186 1438 1195 1225 1284 633 1124 1261 328 979 1125 1050 1148 1153 848 984 471 204 325 872 1142 **Nice**

175 75 550 78 501 70 60 347 452 172 128 551 481 227 321 131 55 432 207 484 677 670 278 429 774
282 121 885 126 807 113 97 558 727 277 206 886 774 365 516 211 89 695 333 779 1090 1079 447 690 1245 **Oostende**

312 212 364 190 120 180 122 129 228 137 244 232 289 482 466 240 240 579 191
502 341 585 255 591 305 290 355 423 195 427 571 471 196 208 367 220 392 373 465 775 750 386 386 932 307 **Paris**

296 199 447 171 451 167 166 313 331 176 241 373 377 217 213 164 126 327 145 303 496 489 129 323 593 180 89
477 321 720 275 726 269 267 503 532 284 388 600 606 349 342 264 202 526 233 488 799 787 208 520 955 289 143 **Reims**

532 432 289 309 150 409 329 145 368 230 485 546 158 174 96 449 356 287 444 478 652 570 451 67 749 387 219 302
856 695 465 498 241 659 530 234 592 370 781 878 255 280 155 722 573 462 715 770 1050 918 725 108 1206 622 352 486 **Rennes**

46 62 635 210 612 94 193 454 537 294 69 606 568 337 404 135 142 519 215 538 731 724 290 514 829 139 279 261 496
74 99 1022 338 985 151 310 731 864 473 111 976 914 543 650 218 228 835 346 866 1177 1165 466 827 1334 223 449 420 799 **Rotterdam**

378 293 593 387 666 268 385 528 375 392 301 330 584 432 426 240 342 457 137 308 500 493 97 536 489 342 303 216 515 357
608 472 954 623 1071 432 620 850 604 631 484 531 940 696 686 386 550 735 220 495 805 793 156 863 787 550 487 347 828 575 **Strasbourg**

732 632 152 579 548 609 601 578 232 534 685 330 262 536 378 647 556 179 654 334 252 150 585 364 349 610 422 505 434 696 639
1178 1017 244 932 882 979 967 930 346 860 1103 531 421 863 608 1041 894 288 1052 538 405 241 941 585 562 982 679 812 699 1120 1028 **Toulouse**

459 359 216 305 308 336 325 237 210 230 413 384 146 211 63 375 283 140 378 328 496 413 346 134 593 337 149 232 157 423 430 318
738 577 347 491 496 541 523 382 339 370 664 618 235 340 102 603 456 225 609 528 799 664 557 215 955 543 239 374 253 681 692 511 **Tours**

How to use this table

Distances are shown in miles and, in light type, kilometres.
For example, the distance between Antwerp and Dieppe is
232 miles or 374 kilometres.

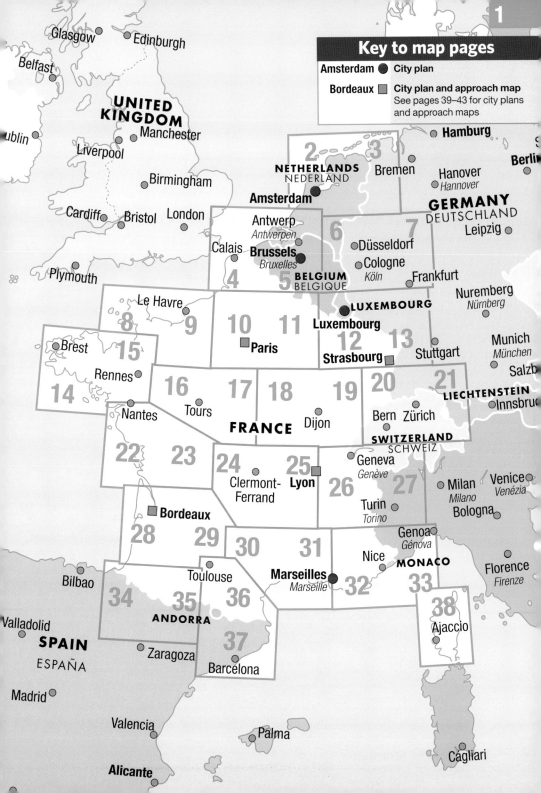

1

Key to map pages

Amsterdam ● City plan

Bordeaux ■ City plan and approach map
See pages 39–43 for city plans
and approach maps

Glasgow
Edinburgh
Belfast
**UNITED
KINGDOM**
ublin
Manchester
Liverpool
Birmingham
Cardiff
Bristol
London
Plymouth

Hamburg
2   **3**
NETHERLANDS
NEDERLAND
Bremen
Hanover
Hannover
Berli
GERMANY
DEUTSCHLAND
Leipzig
Amsterdam
Antwerp
Antwerpen
6   **7**
Düsseldorf
Calais
Brussels
Bruxelles
Cologne
Köln
Frankfurt
4   **5**   **BELGIUM**
BELGIQUE
LUXEMBOURG
Nuremberg
Nürnberg
Le Havre
8   **9**
10   **11**
Luxembourg
Munich
München
Salzb
Brest
15
Paris
12   **13**
Strasbourg
Stuttgart
Rennes
14
16   **17**   **18**   **19**   **20**   **21**
LIECHTENSTEIN
Innsbruc
Nantes
Tours
FRANCE
Dijon
Bern   Zürich
SWITZERLAND
SCHWEIZ
22   **23**
24   **25**   **26**
Geneva
Genève
27
Milan
Milano
Venice
Venézia
Clermont-
Ferrand
Lyon
Turin
Torino
Bologna
Bordeaux
Genoa
Génova
28   **29**
30   **31**
Nice
MONACO
Florence
Firenze
Bilbao
Toulouse
Marseilles
Marseille
32   **33**
34   **35**   **36**
ANDORRA
38
Ajaccio
Valladolid
SPAIN
ESPAÑA
Zaragoza
37
Madrid
Barcelona
Valencia
Palma
Alicante
Cagliari

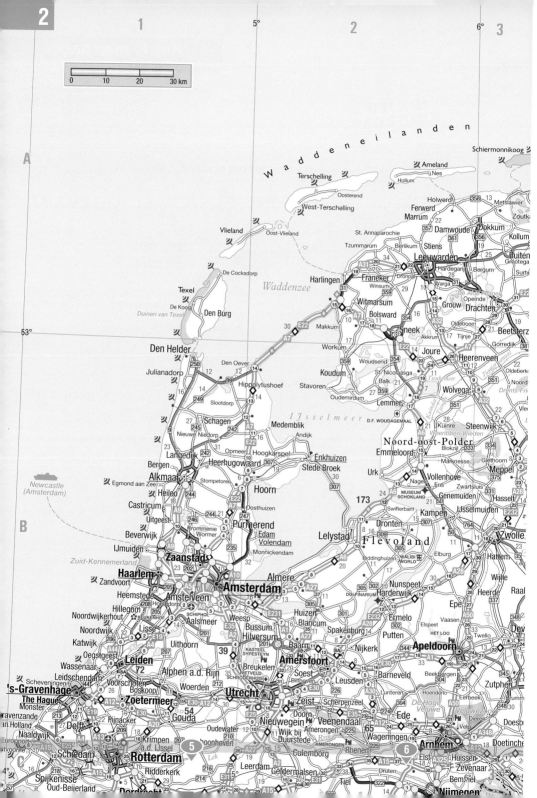

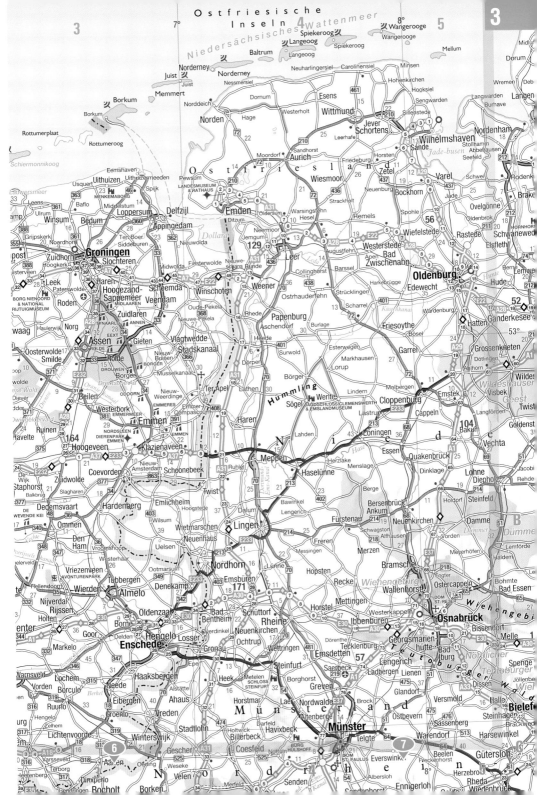

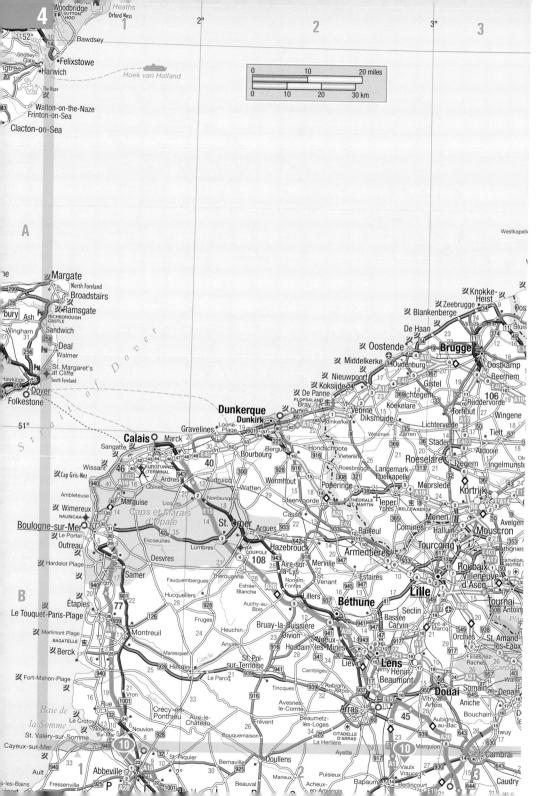

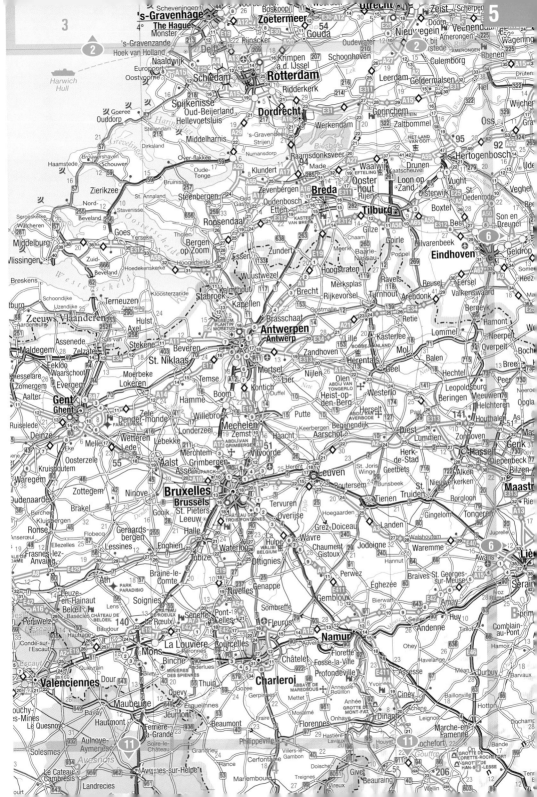

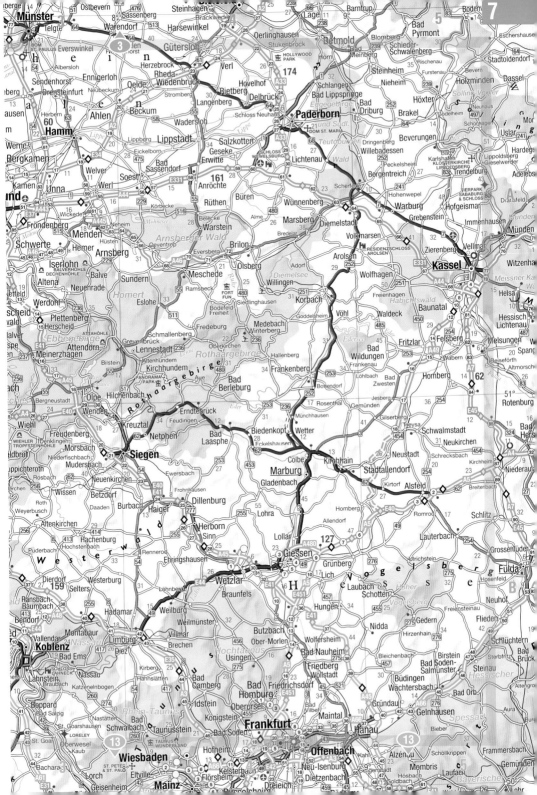

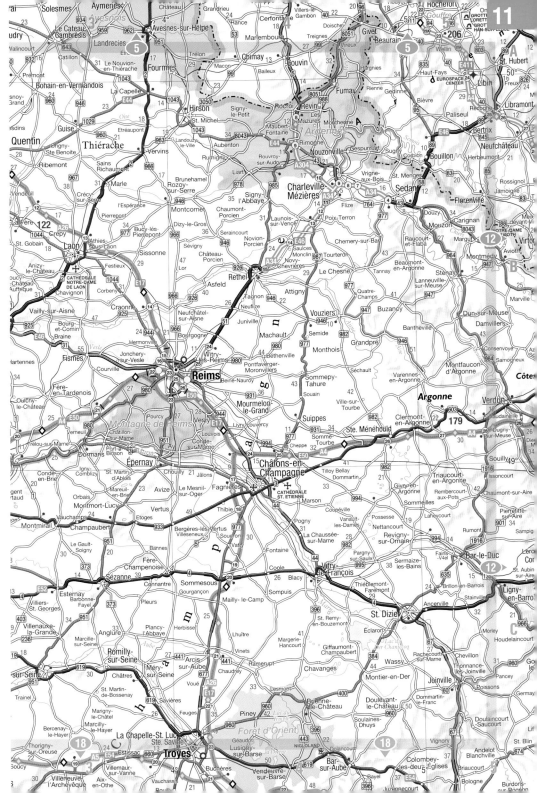

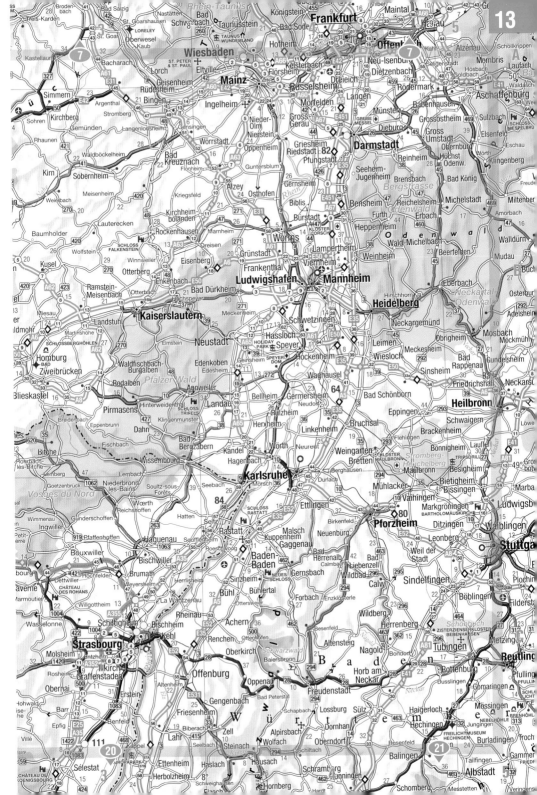

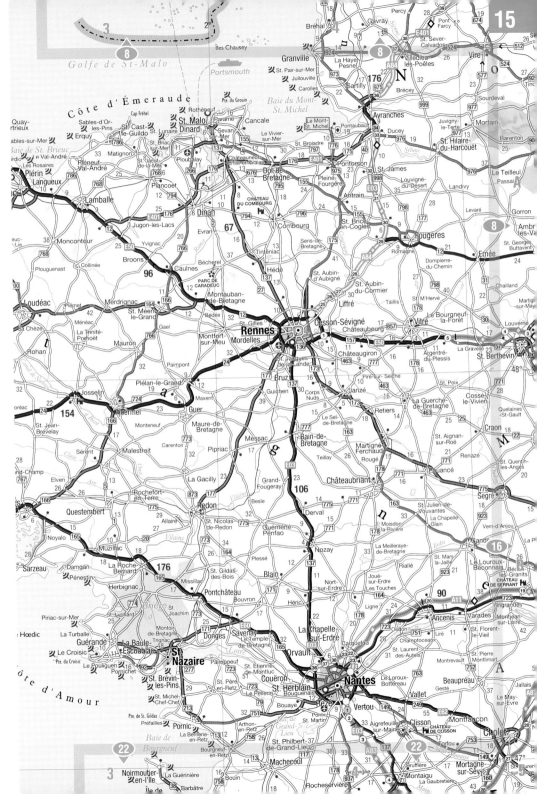

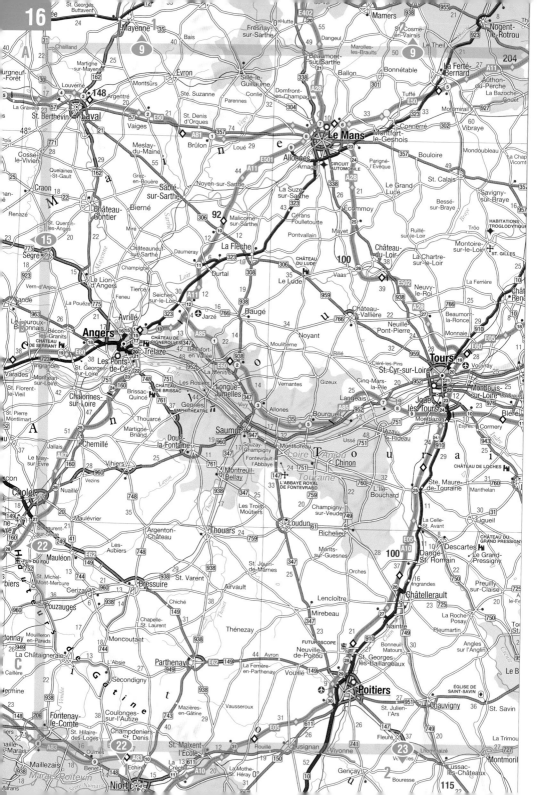

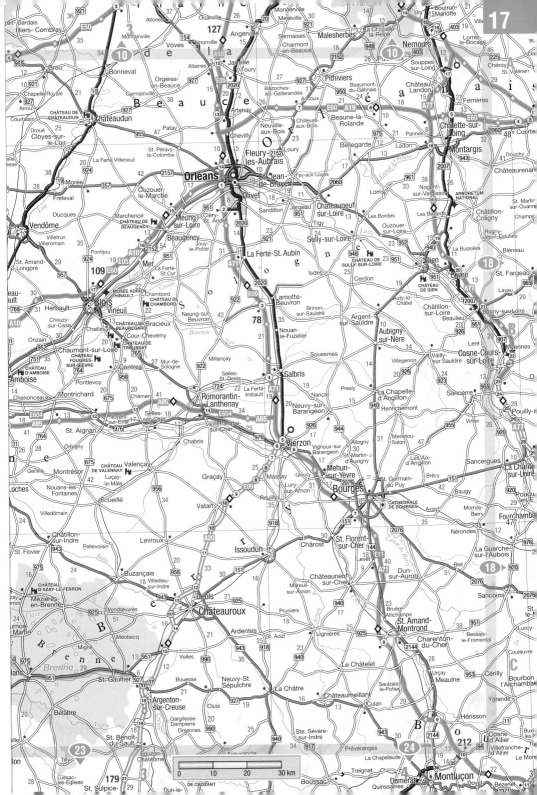

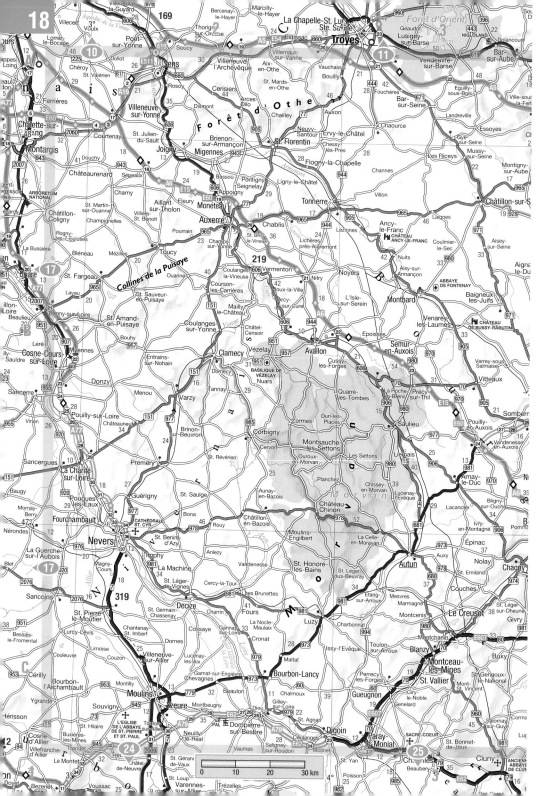

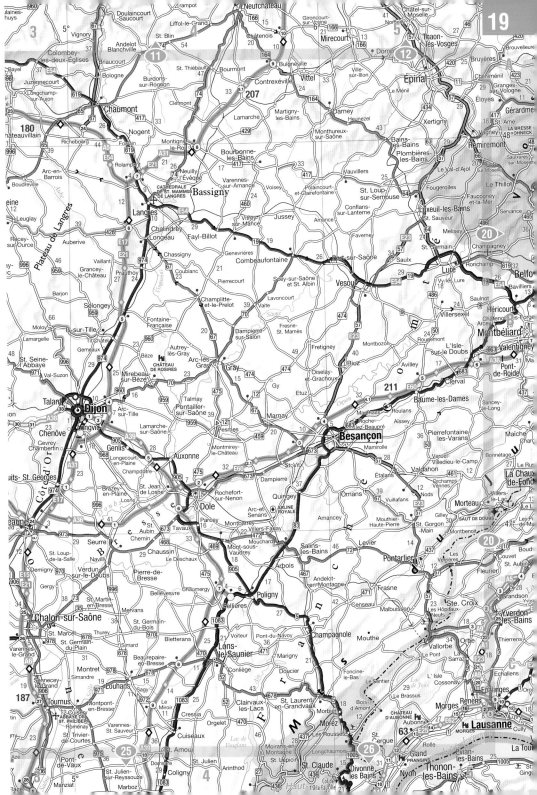

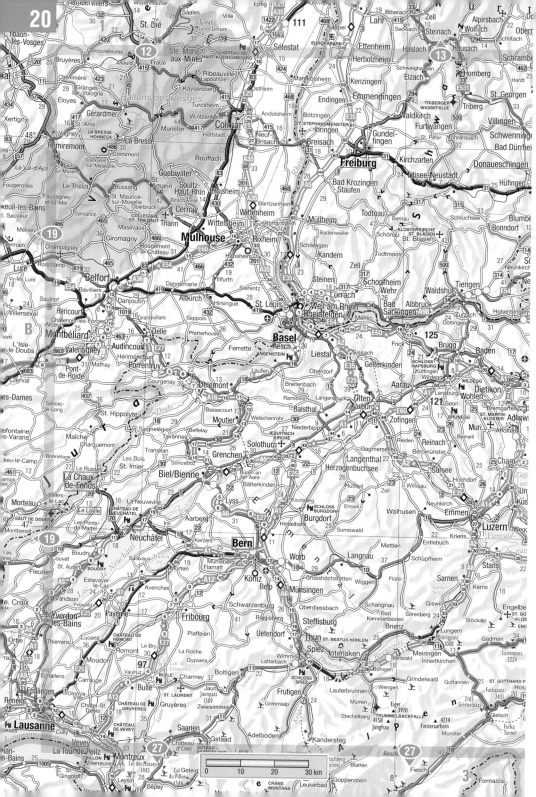

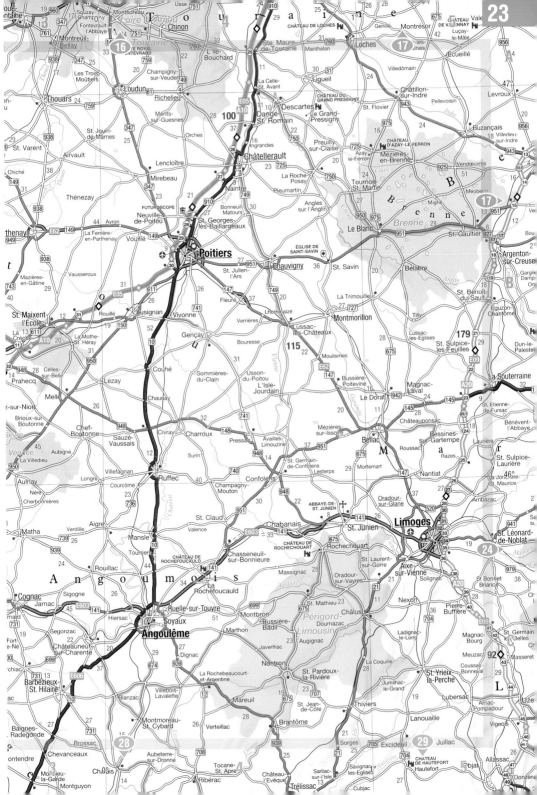

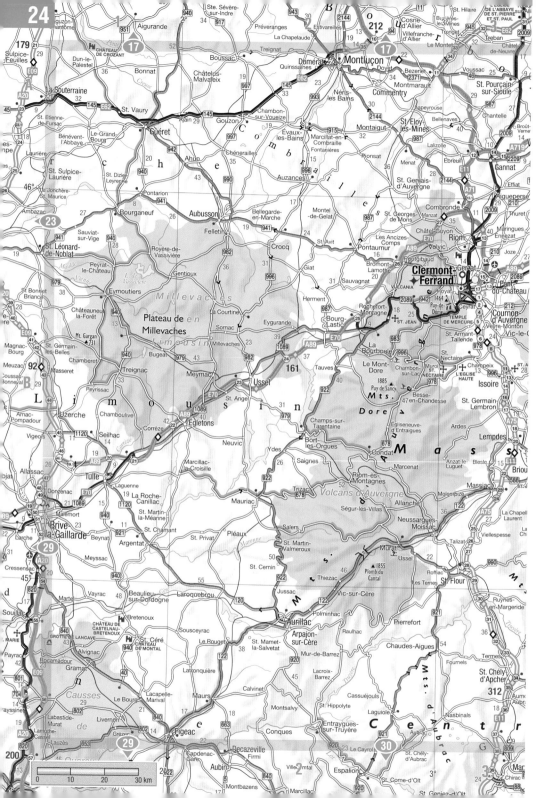

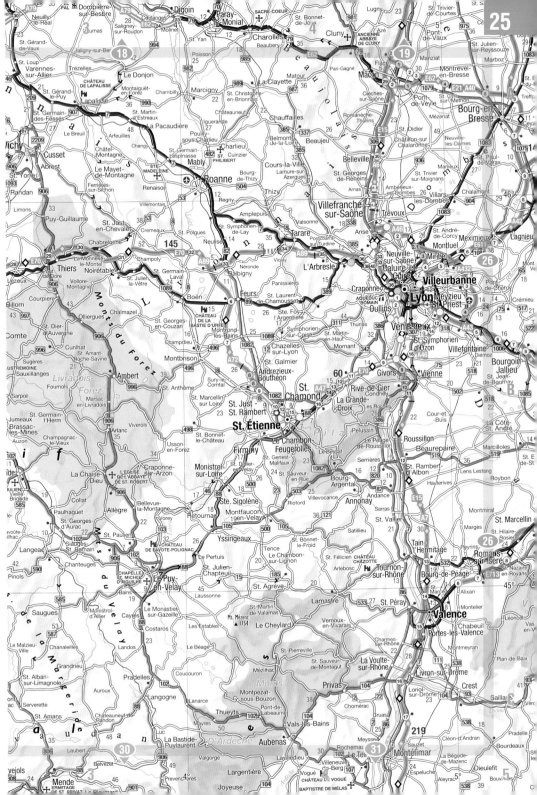

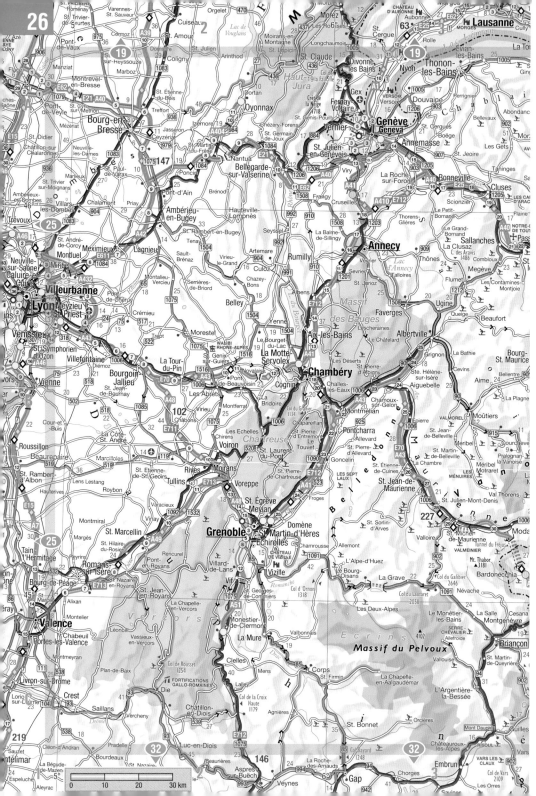

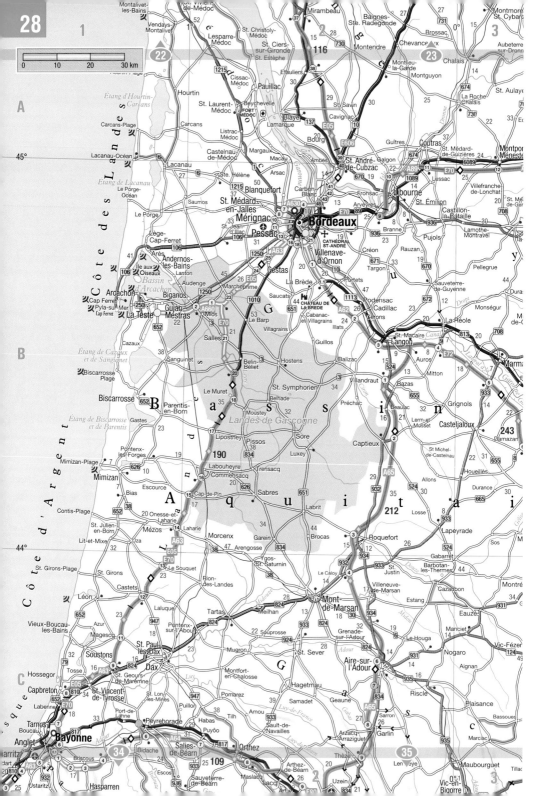

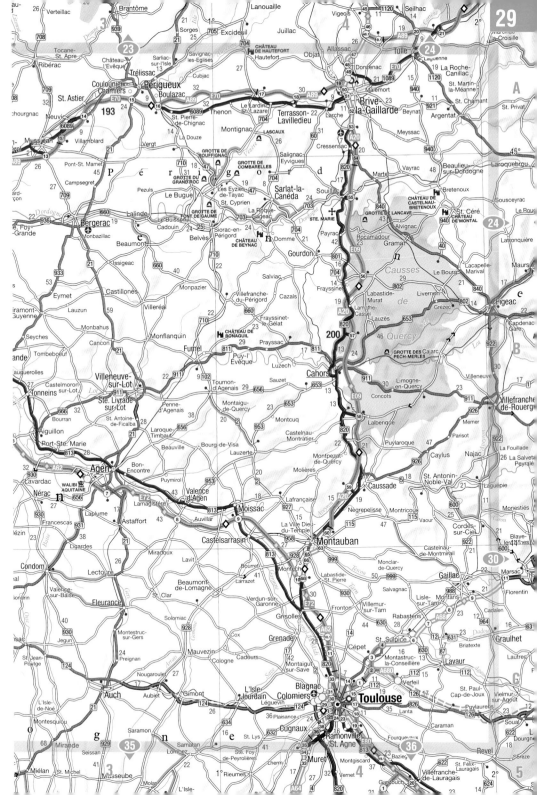

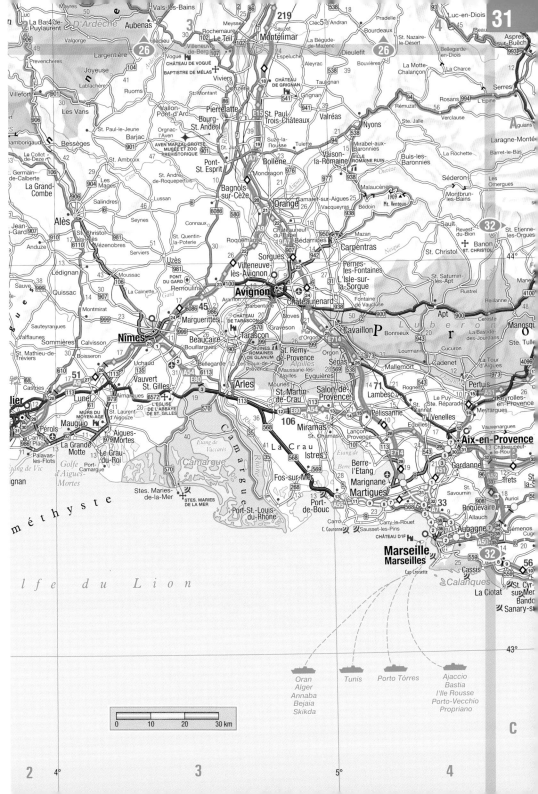

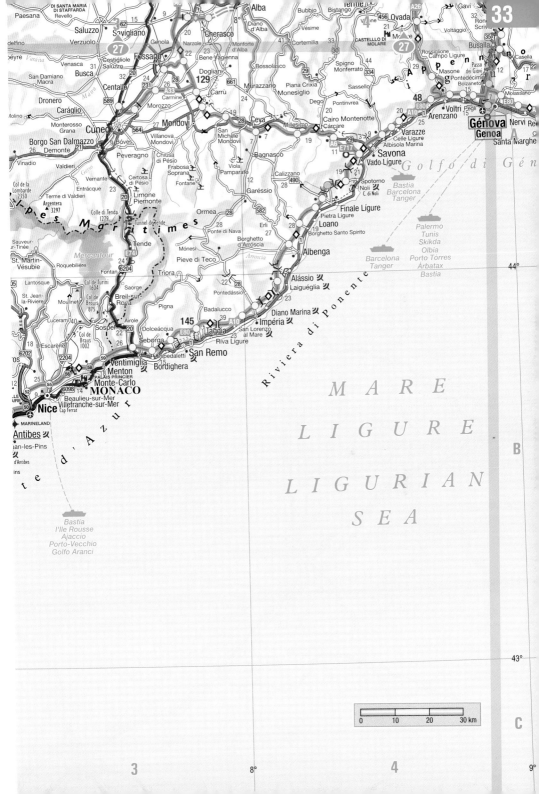

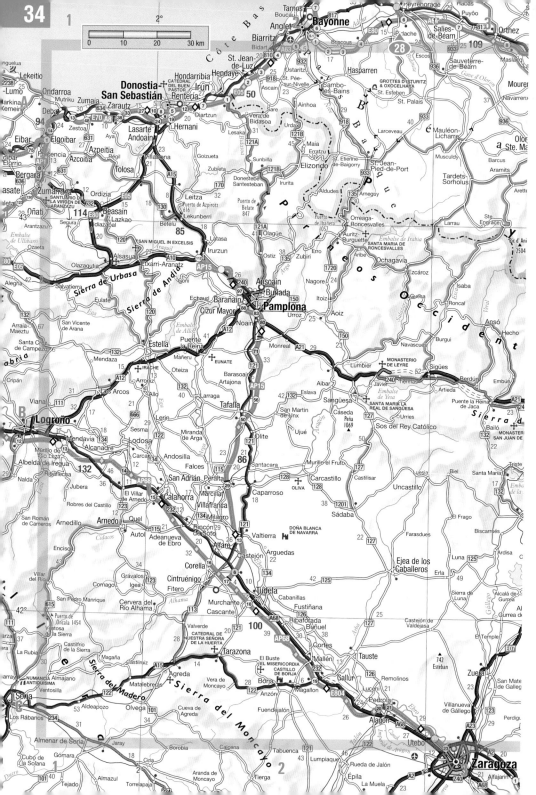

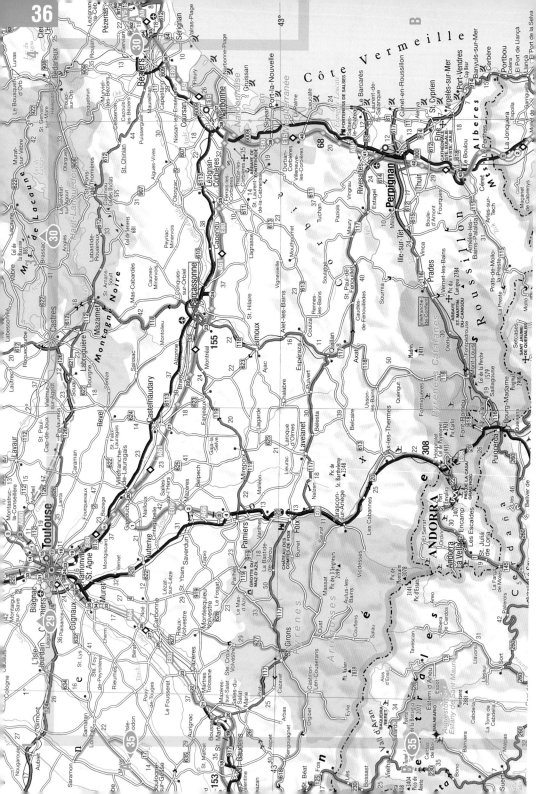

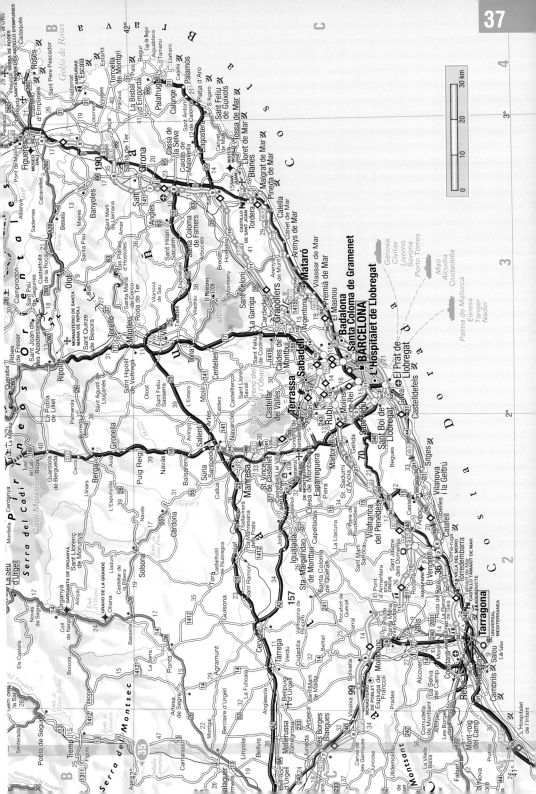

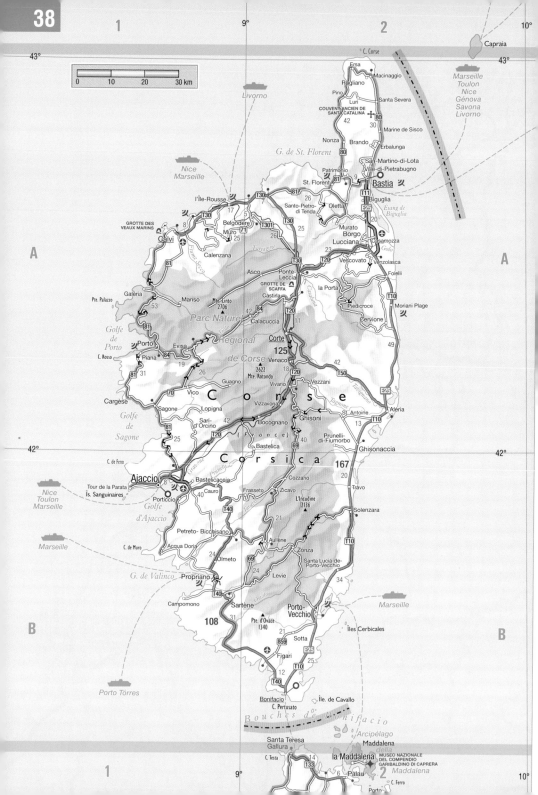

City plans

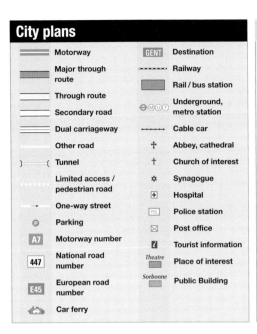

	Motorway	GENT	Destination
	Major through route		Railway
	Through route		Rail / bus station
	Secondary road	Ⓜ Ⓝ Ⓤ Ⓣ	Underground, metro station
	Dual carriageway		Cable car
	Other road	✝	Abbey, cathedral
)⸺(	Tunnel	✝	Church of interest
	Limited access / pedestrian road	✡	Synagogue
→	One-way street	✚	Hospital
Ⓟ	Parking	POL	Police station
A7	Motorway number	✉	Post office
447	National road number	ⓘ	Tourist information
E45	European road number	Theatre	Place of interest
🚗	Car ferry	Sorbonne	Public Building

Approach maps

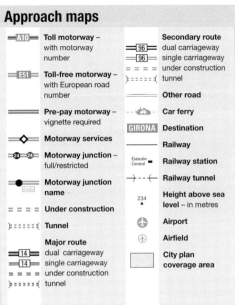

A10	Toll motorway – with motorway number	96	Secondary route dual carriageway
E51	Toll-free motorway – with European road number	96	single carriageway
			under construction
		)⸺(	tunnel
	Pre-pay motorway – vignette required		Other road
◇	Motorway services	🚗	Car ferry
24 24	Motorway junction – full/restricted	GIRONA	Destination
●	Motorway junction name		Railway
Emilia		Estación Central ▬	Railway station
≡ ≡ ≡	Under construction	)⸺(	Railway tunnel
)⸺(	Tunnel	234 ▲	Height above sea level – in metres
	Major route dual carriageway	✈	Airport
14	single carriageway	⊕	Airfield
14	under construction		City plan coverage area
)⸺(	tunnel		

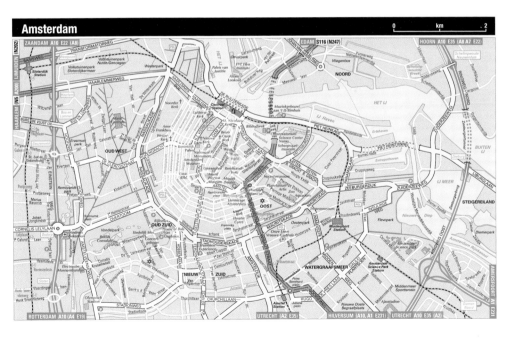

Amsterdam

0   km   2

Bruxelles Brussels

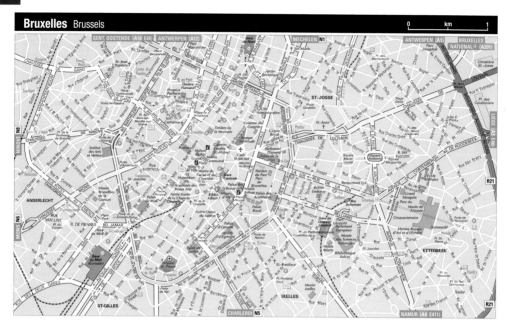

Bordeaux

Bordeaux

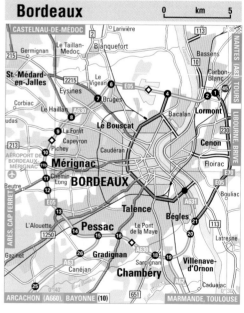

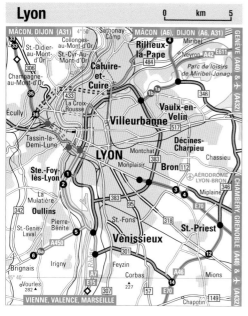

Lyon

0 km 5

MÂCON, DIJON (A31) • MÂCON (A6), DIJON (A6, A31) • GENÈVE (A40) & (A432)

St-Didier-au-Mont-d'Or
St-Cyr-Au-Mont-d'Or
Collonges-au-Mont-d'Or
Sathonay Camp
Rillieux-la-Pape
Miribel
Neyron
Parc de loisirs de Miribel-Jonage
Champagne-au-Mont-d'Or
Cahuire-et-Cuire
La Croix-Rousse
Vaulx-en-Velin
Écully
Villeurbanne
Décines-Charpieu
Chassieu
Tassin-la-Demi-Lune
Montchat
Monplaisir
LYON
Bron
AÉRODROME LYON-BRON
Ste-Foy-lès-Lyon
Miplaine
La Mulatière
Oullins
St-Fons
St-Genis-Laval
Pierre-Bénite
Vénissieux
St.-Priest
Brignais
Irigny
Feyzin
Corbas
Mions
Vourles
Chapotin

VIENNE, VALENCE, MARSEILLE • CHAMBERY GRENOBLE (A48) & (A43)

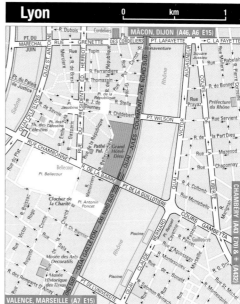

Lyon

0 km 1

MÂCON, DIJON (A46, A6 E15) • CHAMBERY (A43 E70) & (A432)

PT. DU MARECHAL JUIN
R. Dubois
Cordeliers
DES CORDELIERS
PT. LAFAYETTE
C. LA FAYETTE
Square Jussieu
Préfecture du Rhône
Pl. Bellecour
Bellecour
Grand Hôtel Dieu
Clocher de la Charité
Pl. Antonin Poncet
Musée des Arts Decoratifs
Musée Historique des Tissus
Piscine

VALENCE, MARSEILLE (A7 E15)

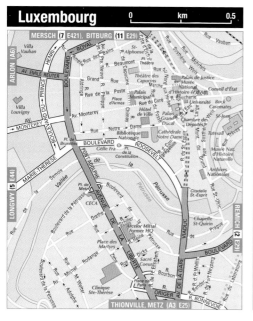

Luxembourg

0 km 0.5

MERSCH (7) E421, BITBURG (11) E29 • ARLON (A6) • REMICH (2) E29

Villa Vauban
St-Alphonse
Théâtre des Capucins
Palais de Justice
Conseil d'Etat
Palais Municipal
Musée National d'Histoire et d'Art
Villa Louvigny
Hôtel de Ville
Chambre des Députés
Cathédrale Notre-Dame
Pl. de Bruxelles
Gëlle Fra
Pl. de la Constitution
Bibliothèque Nationale
Musée Nat. d'Histoire Naturelle
Archives Nationales
Citadelle St-Esprit
Chapelle St-Quirin
Arcelor Mittal Former HQ
Place des Martyrs
Sacré Coeur
Clinique Ste-Thérèse

THIONVILLE, METZ (A3 E25) • LONGWY (5 E44)

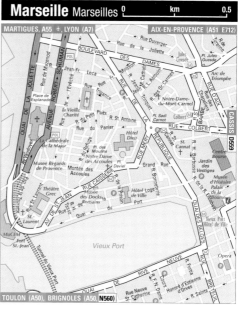

Marseille Marseilles

0 km 0.5

MARTIGUES, A55 + LYON (A7) • AIX-EN-PROVENCE (A51 E712)

La Joliette
Arc de Triomphe
Notre-Dame-du-Mont-Carmel
La Vieille Charité
Hôtel Dieu
La Cathédrale de la Major
Musée Regards de Provence
Notre Dame des Accoules
Montée des Accoules
Théâtre Grec
Hôtel de Ville
Centre Bourse
Jardin des Vestiges
Musée d'Histoire de Marseille
Musée des Docks Romains
MuCEM
Fort St-Jean
Vieux Port
Opéra

TOULON (A50), BRIGNOLES (A50, N560) • CASSIS D559

Paris

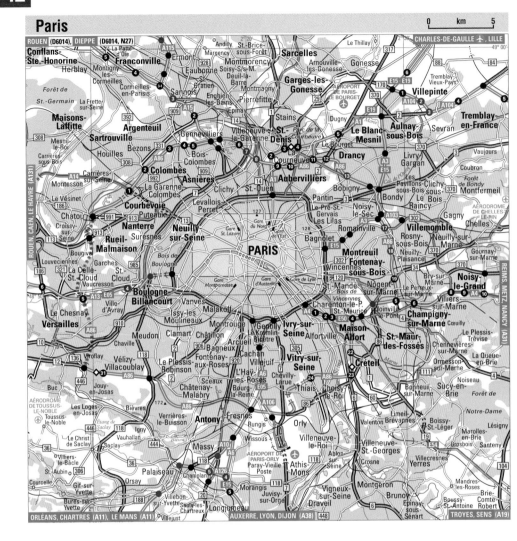

0   km   5

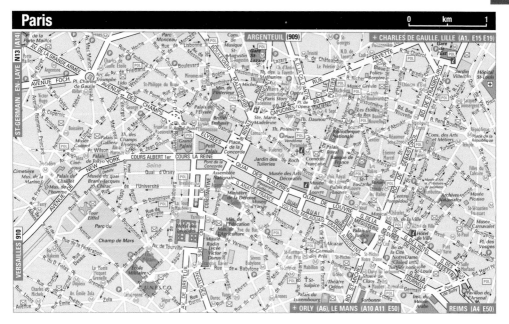

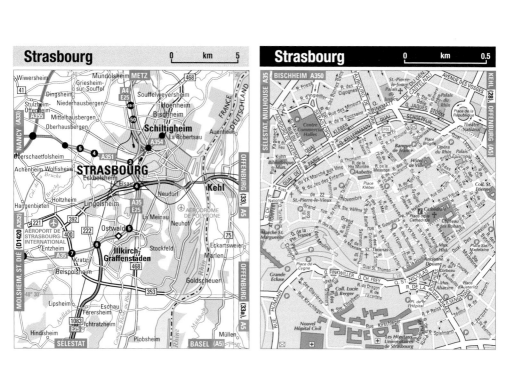

Index to road maps

Ⓐ Austria — Ⓑ Belgium — Ⓓ Germany — Ⓕ France — Ⓘ Italy — (MC) Monaco
(AND) Andorra — (CH) Switzerland — Ⓔ Spain — (FL) Liechtenstein — Ⓛ Luxembourg — (NL) Netherlands

Aac – Bai

A

Aach D 21 B4
Aachen D 6 B2
Aalsmeer NL 2 B1
Aalst B 5 B4
Aalten NL 3 C3
Aalter B 5 A3
Aarau CH 20 B3
Aarberg CH 20 B2
Aarburg CH 20 B2
Aardenburg NL 5 A3
Aarschot B 5 B4
Abbeville F 10 A1
Abiego E 35 B3
Ablis F 10 C1
Abondance F 26 A3
Abreschviller F 12 C3
Abrest F 25 A3
Abriès F 27 C3
Accéglio I 32 A2
Accous F 35 A3
Achene B 5 B5
Achern D 13 C4
Acheux-en-Amienois F 10 A2
Acqua Doria F 38 B1
Acquigny F 9 A5
Ácqui Terme I 27 C5
Acy-en-Multien F 10 B2
Adeanueva de Ebro E 34 B2
Adelboden CH 20 C2
Adenau D 6 B2
Adinkerke B 4 A2
Adliswil CH 21 B3
Adorf D 7 A4
Adrall E 37 B2
Aesch CH 20 B2
Affoltern CH 20 B3
Agay F 32 B2
Agde F 30 B2
Agen F 29 B3
Ager E 35 C4
Agnières F 26 C2
Agon Coutainville F 8 A2
Agramunt E 37 C2
Agreda E 34 C2
Aguas E 35 B3
Aguessac F 30 A2
Ahaus D 3 B3
Ahlen D 7 A3
Ahlhorn D 3 B5
Ahun F 24 A2
Aibar E 34 B2
Aigle CH 27 A3
Aignan F 28 C3
Aignay-le-Duc F 18 B3
Aigre F 23 C4
Aigrefeuille-d'Aunis F 22 B3
Aigrefeuille-sur-Maine F 15 B4
Aiguablava E 37 C4
Aiguebelle F 26 B3
Aigueperse F 24 A3
Aigues-Mortes F 31 B3
Aigues-Vives F 30 B1
Aiguilles F 27 C3
Aiguillon F 29 B3
Aigurande F 17 C3
Ailefroide F 26 C3
Aillant-sur-Tholon F 18 B2
Ailly-sur-Noye F 10 B2
Ailly-sur-Somme F 10 B2
Aimargues F 31 B3
Aime F 26 B3
Ainhoa F 34 A2
Ainsa E 35 B4
Airaines F 10 B1
Aire-sur-l'Adour F 28 C2
Aire-sur-la-Lys F 4 B2
Airole I 33 B3
Airolo CH 21 C3
Airvault F 16 C1
Aisey-sur-Seine F 18 B3
Aïssey F 19 B5
Aisy-sur-Armançon F 18 B3
Aitrach D 21 B5
Aix-en-Othe F 18 A2
Aix-en-Provence F 31 B4
Aixe-sur-Vienne F 23 C5
Aix-les-Bains F 26 B2
Aizenay F 22 B2
Ajac F 36 A3
Ajaccio F 38 B1
Ajain F 24 A1
Akkrum NL 2 A2
Ala di Stura I 27 B4
Alagna Valsésia I 27 B4
Alagón E 34 C2
Alássio I 33 A4
Alba I 27 C5
Albalate de Cinca E 35 C4
Alban F 30 B1
Albanyà E 37 B3
Albbruck D 20 B3
Albenga I 33 A4
Albens F 26 B2
Albersloh D 7 A3
Albert F 10 A2
Albertville F 26 B3
Alberuela de Tubo E 35 C3
Albi F 30 B1
Albisola Marina I 33 A4
Albstadt D 21 A4
Alcaláde Gurrea E 34 B3
Alcampell E 35 C4
Alcanadre E 34 B1
Alcolea de Cinca E 35 C4
Alcover E 37 C2
Alcubierre E 35 C3
Aldeapozo E 34 C1
Aldenhoven D 6 B2
Aldudes F 34 A2
Alençon F 9 B4
Alenya F 36 B3
Aléria F 38 A2
Alès F 31 A3
Alet-les-Bains F 36 B3
Aleyrac F 31 A3
Alfaro E 34 B2
Alfarrás E 35 C4
Alfhausen D 3 B4
Alforja E 37 C1
Alguaire E 35 C4
Alinyà E 37 B2
Alixan F 25 C5
Alken B 5 B5
Alkmaar NL 2 B1
Allaines F 17 A3
Allaire F 15 B3
Allanche F 24 B2
Allassac F 29 A4
Allauch F 31 B4
Allègre F 25 B3
Allemont F 26 B3
Allendorf D 7 B4
Allevard F 26 B3
Allmannsdorf D 21 B4
Allo E 34 B1
Allogny F 17 B4
Allones
Eure et Loire F 10 C1
Maine-et-Loire F 16 B2
Allonnes F 16 B2
Allons F 28 B2
Allos F 32 A2
Almacelles E 35 C4
Almajano E 34 C1
Alme D 7 A4
Almelo NL 3 B3
Almenar E 35 C4
Almere NL 2 B2
Almese I 27 B4
Almudévar E 35 B3
Alos d'Ensil E 36 B2
Alpen D 6 A2
Alphen aan de Rijn NL 2 B1
Alpignano I 27 B4
Alpirsbach D 13 C4
Alquézar E 35 B4
Alsasua E 34 B1
Alsdorf D 6 B2
Alsfeld D 7 B5
Alstätte D 3 B3
Altdorf CH 21 C3
Altena D 7 A3
Altenberge D 3 B4
Altenheim D 13 C3
Altenhundem D 7 A4
Altenkirchen D 7 B3
Altensteig D 13 C4
Altkirch F 20 B2
Altshausen D 21 B4
Altstätten CH 21 B4
Altusried D 21 B5
Alvignac F 29 B4
Alvimare F 9 A4
Alzénau D 13 A5
Alzey D 13 B4
Alzonne F 36 A3
Amance F 19 B5
Amancey F 19 B5
Amay B 5 B5
Ambazac F 23 C5
Ambérieu-en-Bugey F 26 B2
Ambérieux-en-Dombes F 25 A4
Ambert F 25 B3
Ambés F 28 A2
Ambleteuse F 4 B1
Amboise F 16 B2
Ambrières-les-Vallées F 8 B3
Amden CH 21 B4
Amel B 6 B2
Amélie-les-Bains-Palalda F 36 B3
Amer E 37 B3
Amerongen NL 2 B2
Amersfoort NL 2 B2
Amiens F 10 B2
Amou F 28 C2
Amplepuis F 25 B4
Amriswil CH 21 B4
Amstelveen NL 2 B1
Amsterdam NL 2 B1
Amtzell D 21 B4
Ancenis F 15 B4
Ancerville F 11 C5
Ancy-le-Franc F 18 B3
Andance F 25 B4
Andeer CH 21 C4
Andelfingen CH 21 B3
Andelot-Blanchville F 19 A4
Andelot-en-Montagne F 19 C4
Andenne B 5 B5
Anderlues B 5 B4
Andermatt CH 21 C3
Andernach D 6 B3
Andernos-les-Bains F 28 B1
Andijk NL 2 B2
Andoain E 34 A1
Andolsheim F 20 A2
Andorra La Vella AND 36 B2
Andosilla E 34 B2
Andrest F 35 A4
Andrezieux-Bouthéon F 25 B4
Anduze F 31 A2
Anet F 10 C1
Angaïs F 35 A3
Angers F 16 B1
Angerville F 10 C2
Anglès E 37 C3
Anglés F 30 B1
Angles F 22 B2
Anglesola E 37 C2
Angles sur l'Anglin F 23 B4
Anglet F 28 C1
Anglure F 11 C3
Angoulême F 23 C4
Angoulins F 22 B2
Angües E 35 B3
Anhée B 5 B4
Aniane F 30 B2
Aniche F 4 B3
Anizy-le-Château F 11 B3
Ankum D 3 B4
Anlezy F 18 C2
Annecy F 26 B3
Annemasse F 26 A3
Annevoie-Rouillon B 5 B4
Annonay F 25 B4
Annot F 32 B2
Annweiler D 13 B3
Anould F 20 A1
Anröchte D 7 A4
Anse F 25 B4
Anseroeul B 5 B3
Ansó E 34 B3
Ansoain E 34 B2
Antibes F 32 B3
Antoing B 5 B3
Antrain F 8 B2
Antronapiana I 27 A5
Antwerp = Antwerpen B 5 A4
Antwerpen = Antwerp B 5 A4
Anvin F 4 B2
Anzat-le-Luguet F 24 B3
Anzón E 34 C2
Aoiz E 34 B2
Aosta I 27 B4
Apeldoorn NL 2 B2
Apen D 3 A4
Appenzell CH 21 B4
Appingedam NL 3 A3
Appoigny F 18 B2
Apremont-la-Forêt F 12 C1
Apt F 31 B4
Aragnouet F 35 B4
Aramits F 34 A3
Aramon F 31 B3
Arbas F 35 B4
Arbeca E 37 C1
Arbois F 19 C4
Arbon CH 21 B4
Arbório I 27 B5
Arbùcies E 37 C3
Arcachon F 28 B1
Arcen NL 6 A2
Arc-en-Barrois F 19 B3
Arces-Dilo F 18 A2
Arc-et-Senans F 19 B4
Arcey F 20 B1
Archiac F 23 C3
Arcis-sur-Aube F 11 C4
Arc-lès-Gray F 19 B4
Arc-sur-Tille F 19 B4
Arcusa E 35 B4
Arcy-sur-Cure F 18 B2
Ardentes F 17 C3
Ardes F 24 B3
Ardez CH 21 C5
Ardisa E 34 B3
Ardooie B 4 B3
Ardres F 4 B1
Arendonk B 5 A5
Arengosse F 28 B2
Arenys de Mar E 37 C3
Arenys de Munt E 37 C3
Arenzano I 33 A4
Areo E 36 B2
Arès F 28 B1
Arette F 34 A3
Arfeuilles F 25 A3
Argelès-Gazost F 35 A3
Argelès-sur-Mer F 36 B4
Argentan F 9 B3
Argentat F 24 B1
Argentera I 32 A2
Argenteuil F 10 C2
Argenthal D 13 B3
Argentona E 37 C3
Argenton-Château F 16 C1
Argenton-sur-Creuse F 17 C3
Argentré F 16 A1
Argentré-du-Plessis F 15 A4
Argent-sur-Sauldre F 17 B4
Arguedas E 34 B2
Argueil F 10 B1
Aribe E 34 B2
Arinthod F 26 A2
Arlanc F 25 B3
Arlebosc F 25 B4
Arles F 31 B3
Arles-sur-Tech F 36 B3
Arlon B 12 B1
Armeno I 27 B5
Armentières F 4 B2
Arnac-Pompadour F 23 C5
Arnage F 16 B2
Arnas F 25 A4
Arnay-le-Duc F 18 B3
Arnedillo E 34 B1
Arnedo E 34 B1
Arneguy F 34 A2
Arnhem NL 2 C2
Arnsberg D 7 A4
Arolla CH 27 A4
Arolsen D 7 A5
Arona I 27 B5
Arosa CH 21 C4
Arpajon F 10 C2
Arpajon-sur-Cère F 24 C2
Arques F 4 B2
Arques-la-Bataille F 9 A5
Arrancourt F 12 C2
Arras F 4 B2
Arreau F 35 B4
Arrens-Marsous F 35 B3
Arromanches-les-Bains F 8 A3
Arroniz E 34 B1
Arrou F 17 A3
Arsac F 28 B2
Ars-en-Ré F 22 B2
Ars-sur-Moselle F 12 B2
Artajona E 34 B2
Artemare F 26 B2
Artenay F 17 A3
Artés E 37 C2
Artesa de Segre E 37 C2
Arth CH 21 B3
Arthez-de-Béarn F 35 A3
Arthon-en-Retz F 15 B4
Artieda E 34 B3
Artix F 35 A3
Arudy F 35 A3
Arveyres F 28 B2
Arvieux F 26 C3
Arzacq-Arraziguet F 28 C2
Arzano F 14 B2
As B 6 A1
Asasp F 35 A3
Ascain F 34 A2
Aschaffenburg D 13 B5
Ascheberg D 7 A3
Aschendorf D 3 A4
Asco F 38 A2
Ascoux F 17 A4
Asfeld F 11 B4
Aspet F 35 A4
Aspres-sur-Buëch F 32 A1
Asse B 5 B4
Asselborn L 12 A1
Assen NL 3 B3
Assenede B 5 A3
Assesse B 5 B5
Asson F 35 A3
Astaffort F 29 B3
Asten NL 6 A1
Asti I 27 C5
Ath B 5 B3
Athies F 10 B2
Athies-sous-Laon F 11 B3
Attendorn D 7 A3
Attichy F 10 B3
Attigny F 11 B4
Au A 21 B4
Aubagne F 32 B1
Aubange B 12 B1
Aubel B 6 B1
Aubenas F 25 C4
Aubenton F 11 B4
Auberive F 19 B4
Aubeterre-sur-Dronne F 28 A3
Aubiet F 29 C3
Aubigné F 23 B3
Aubigny F 22 B2
Aubigny-au-Bac F 4 B3
Aubigny-en-Artois F 4 B2
Aubigny-sur-Nère F 17 B4
Aubin F 30 A1
Aubonne CH 19 C5
Aubrac F 24 C2
Aubusson F 24 B2
Auch F 29 C3
Auchy-au-Bois F 4 B2
Audenge F 28 B1
Auderville F 8 A2
Audierne F 14 A1
Audincourt F 20 B1
Audruicq F 4 B2
Audun-le-Roman F 12 B1
Audun-le-Tiche F 12 B1
Aue D 7 A4
Augignac F 23 C4
Augustfehn D 3 A4
Aulendorf D 21 B4
Aullène F 38 B2
Aulnay F 23 B3
Aulnoye-Aymeries F 5 B3
Ault F 10 A1
Aulus-les-Bains F 36 B2
Aumale F 10 B1
Aumetz F 12 B1
Aumont-Aubrac F 24 C3
Aunay-en-Bazois F 18 B2
Aunay-sur-Odon F 8 A3
Auneau F 10 C1
Auneuil F 10 B1
Aups F 32 B2
Auray F 14 B3
Aurich D 3 A4
Aurignac F 35 A4
Aurillac F 24 C2
Auriol F 32 B1
Auritz-Burguette E 34 B2
Auros F 28 B2
Auroux F 25 C3
Auterive F 36 A2
Autheuil-Authouillet F 9 A5
Authon F 32 A2
Authon-du-Perche F 16 A2
Autol E 34 B2
Autreville F 12 C1
Autrey-lès-Gray F 19 B4
Autun F 18 C3
Auty-le-Châtel F 17 B4
Auvelais B 5 B4
Auvillar F 29 B3
Auxerre F 18 B2
Auxi-le-Château F 4 B2
Auxon F 18 A2
Auxonne F 19 B4
Auxy F 18 C3
Auzances F 24 A2
Auzon F 25 B3
Availles-Limouzine F 23 B4
Avallon F 18 B2
Avelgem B 5 B3
Avenches CH 20 C2
Avesnes-le-Comte F 4 B2
Avesnes-sur-Helpe F 11 A3
Avià E 37 B2
Avigliana I 27 B4
Avignon F 31 B3
Avilley F 19 B5
Avinyo E 37 C2
Avioth F 12 B1
Avize F 11 C4
Avon F 10 C2
Avord F 17 B4
Avranches F 8 B2
Avril F 12 B1
Avrillé F 16 B1
Awans B 5 B5
Axat F 36 B3
Axel NL 5 A3
Ax-les-Thermes F 36 B2
Ay F 11 B4
Aya E 34 A1
Ayer CH 27 A4
Ayerbe E 34 B3
Ayette F 4 B2
Ayron F 23 B4
Aywaille B 6 B1
Azannes-et-Soumazannes F 12 B1
Azanúy-Alins E 35 C4
Azay-le-Ferron F 23 B5
Azay-le-Rideau F 16 B2
Azé F 25 A4
Azpeitia E 34 A1
Azur F 28 C1

B

Baad A 21 B5
Baar CH 21 B3
Baarle-Nassau B 5 A4
Baarn NL 2 B2
Babenhausen
Bayern D 21 A5
Hessen D 13 B4
Baccarat F 12 C2
Bacharach D 13 A3
Bacqueville-en-Caux F 9 A5
Badalona E 37 C3
Badalucco I 33 B3
Bad Bentheim D 3 B4
Bad Bergzabern D 13 B3
Bad Berleburg D 7 A4
Bad Breisig D 6 B3
Bad Buchau D 21 A4
Bad Camberg D 7 B4
Bad Driburg D 7 A5
Bad Dürkheim D 13 B4
Bad Dürrheim D 21 A3
Bad Ems D 7 B3
Baden CH 20 B3
Baden-Baden D 13 C4
Badenweiler D 20 B2
Bad Essen D 3 B5
Bad Friedrichshall D 13 B5
Bad Herrenalb D 13 C4
Bad Homburg D 7 B4
Bad Honnef D 6 B3
Bad Hönningen D 6 B3
Bad Iburg D 3 B5
Bad Innerlaterns A 21 B4
Bad Karlshafen D 7 A5
Bad Kemmeriboden CH 20 C2
Bad König D 13 B5
Bad Kreuznach D 13 B3
Bad Krozingen D 20 B2
Bad Laasphe D 7 B4
Bad Liebenzell D 13 C4
Bad Lippspringe D 7 A4
Bad Meinberg D 7 A4
Bad Münstereifel D 6 B2
Bad Nauheim D 7 B4
Bad Neuenahr-Ahrweiler D 6 B3
Badonviller F 12 C2
Bad Orb D 7 B5
Bad Peterstal D 13 C4
Bad Ragaz CH 21 C4
Bad Rappenau D 13 B5
Bad Säckingen D 20 B2
Bad Salzig D 7 B3
Bad Sassendorf D 7 A4
Bad Schönborn D 13 B4
Bad Schussenried D 21 A4
Bad Schwalbach D 7 B4
Bad Soden D 7 B4
Bad Soden-Salmünster D 7 B5
Bad Vilbel D 7 B4
Bad Waldsee D 21 B4
Bad Wildungen D 7 A5
Bad Wurzach D 21 B4
Bad Zwesten D 7 A5
Bad Zwischenahn D 3 A5
Baells E 35 C4
Baesweiler D 6 B2
Baflo NL 3 A3
Baga E 37 B2
Bagnasco I 33 A4
Bagnères-de-Bigorre F 35 A4
Bagnères-de-Luchon F 35 B4
Bagnoles-de-l'Orne F 9 B3
Bagnols-en-Forêt F 32 B2
Bagnols-sur-Cèze F 31 A3
Baiersbronn D 13 C4

Baignes-Ste Radegonde F 23 C3
Baigneux-les-Juifs F 18 B3
Baileux B 11 A4
Bailleul F 4 B2
Baillonville B 5 B5
Bailó E 34 B3
Bain-de-Bretagne F 15 B4
Bains F 25 B3
Bains-les-Bains F 19 A5
Bais F 9 B3
Bakum D 3 B5
Balaguer E 35 C4
Balbigny F 25 B4
Balen B 5 A5
Balingen D 21 A3
Balizac F 28 B2
Balk NL 2 B2
Balkbrug NL 3 B3
Ballancourt-sur-Essonne F 10 C2
Ballerias E 35 C3
Balleroy F 8 A3
Ballon F 16 A2
Balme I 27 B4
Balmuccia I 27 B5
Balneario de Panticosa E 35 B3
Balsareny E 37 C2
Balsthal CH 20 B2
Balve D 7 A3
Bande B 5 B5
Bandol F 32 B1
Bangor F 14 B2
Bannalec F 14 B2
Bannes F 11 C3
Banon F 32 A1
Bantheville F 11 B5
Bantzenheim F 20 B2
Banyoles E 37 B3
Banyuls-sur-Mer F 36 B4
Bapaume F 10 A2
Barañain E 34 B2
Baraqueville F 30 A1
Barasoain E 34 B2
Barbastro E 35 B4
Barbâtre F 22 B1
Barbazan F 35 A4
Barbentane F 31 B3
Barbezieux-St Hilaire F 23 C3
Barbonne-Fayel F 11 C3
Barbotan-les-Thermes F 28 C2
Bárcabo E 35 B4
Barcelona E 37 C3
Barcelonette F 32 A2
Barcus F 34 A3
Bardonécchia I 26 B3
Barèges F 35 B4
Barentin F 9 A4
Barenton F 8 B3
Barfleur F 8 A2
Barge I 27 C4
Bargemon F 32 B2
Barjac F 31 A3
Barjols F 32 B1
Barjon F 19 B3
Bar-le-Duc F 11 C5
Barles F 32 A2
Barneveld NL 2 B2
Barneville-Carteret F 8 A2
Baron F 10 B2
Barr F 13 C3
Barre-des-Cevennes F 30 A2
Barrême F 32 B2
Barret-le-Bas F 32 A1
Barruera E 35 B4
Barssel D 3 A4
Bar-sur-Aube F 18 A3
Bar-sur-Seine F 18 A3
Barvaux B 6 B1
Bas E 37 B3
Basécles B 5 B3
Basel CH 20 B2
Bassecourt CH 20 B2
Bassella E 37 B2
Bassou F 18 B2
Bassoues F 28 C3
Bastelica F 38 A2
Bastelicaccia F 38 B1
Bastia F 38 A2
Bastogne B 12 A1
Bätterkinden CH 20 B2
Battice B 6 B1
Baud F 14 B2
Baudour B 5 B3
Baugé F 16 B1
Baugy F 17 B4
Bauma CH 21 B3
Baume-les-Dames F 19 B5
Baumholder D 13 B3
Baunatal D 7 A5
Bavay F 5 B3
Bavilliers F 20 B1
Bawinkel D 3 B4
Bayel F 19 A3
Bayeux F 8 A3
Bayon F 12 C2
Bayonne F 28 C1
Bayons F 32 A2
Bazas F 28 B2
Baziege F 36 A2
Bazoches-les-Gallerandes F 17 A4
Bazoches-sur-Hoëne F 9 B4
Beasain E 34 A1
Beaubery F 25 A4
Beaucaire F 31 B3
Beaufort F 26 B3
Beaufort-en Vallée F 16 B1
Beaugency F 17 B3
Beaujeu
Alpes-de-Haute-Provence F 32 A2
Rhône F 25 A4
Beaulac F 28 B2
Beaulieu F 17 B4
Beaulieu-sous-la-Roche F 22 B2
Beaulieu-sur-Dordogne F 29 B4
Beaulieu-sur-Mer F 33 B3
Beaulon F 18 C2
Beaumesnil F 9 A4
Beaumetz-lès-Loges F 4 B2
Beaumont
B 5 B4
F 29 B3
Beaumont-de-Lomagne F 29 C3
Beaumont-du-Gâtinais F 17 A4
Beaumont-en-Argonne F 11 B5
Beaumont-Hague F 8 A2
Beaumont-la-Ronce F 16 B2
Beaumont-le-Roger F 9 A4
Beaumont-sur-Oise F 10 B2
Beaumont-sur-Sarthe F 16 A2
Beaune F 19 B3
Beaune-la-Rolande F 17 A4
Beaupréau F 15 B5
Beauraing B 11 A4
Beaurepaire F 25 B5
Beaurepaire-en-Bresse F 19 C4
Beaurières F 32 A1
Beauvais F 10 B2
Beauval F 10 A2
Beauville F 29 B3
Beauvoir-sur-Mer F 22 B1
Beauvoir-sur-Niort F 22 B3
Bécherel F 15 A4
Beckum D 7 A4
Bécon-les-Granits F 16 B1
Bédarieux F 30 B2
Bédarrides F 31 A3
Bedburg D 6 B2
Bédée F 15 A4
Bédoin F 31 A4
Bedretto CH 21 C3
Bedum NL 3 A3
Beekbergen NL 2 B2
Beek en Donk NL 6 A1
Beelen D 3 C5
Beerfelden D 13 B4
Beernem B 4 A3
Beetsterzwaag NL 2 A3
Beflelay CH 20 B2
Bégard F 14 A2
Begijnendijk B 5 A4
Begues E 37 C2
Begur E 37 C4
Beho B 6 B1
Beilen NL 3 B3
Beine-Nauroy F 11 B4
Beinwil CH 20 B3
Bélâbre F 23 B5
Belcaire F 36 B2
Belecke D 7 A4
Bélesta F 36 B2
Belfort F 20 B1
Belgentier F 32 B1
Belgodère F 38 A2
Belhade F 28 B2
Belin-Bèliet F 28 B2
Bellac F 23 B5
Belleau F 10 B3
Bellegarde
Gard F 31 B3
Loiret F 17 B4
Bellegarde-en-Diois F 32 A1
Bellegarde-en-Marche F 24 B2
Bellegarde-sur-Valserine F 26 A2
Belle-Isle-en-Terre F 14 A2
Bellême F 9 B4
Bellenaves F 24 A3
Bellentre F 26 B3
Bellevaux F 26 A3
Bellevesvre F 19 C4
Belleville F 25 A4
Belleville-sur-Vie F 22 B2
Bellevue-la-Montagne F 25 B3
Belley F 26 B2
Bellheim D 13 B4
Bellpuig d'Urgell E 37 C2
Belltall E 37 C2
Bellver de Cerdanya E 36 B2
Bellvis E 37 C1
Belmont-de-la-Loire F 25 A4
Belmont-sur-Rance F 30 B1
Beloeil B 5 B3
Belp CH 20 C2
Belpech F 36 A2
Belvès F 29 B3
Belvezet F 30 A2
Belz F 14 B2
Bemmel NL 6 A1
Benabarre E 35 B4
Benasque E 35 B4
Bendorf D 7 B3
Bénestroff F 12 C2
Benet F 22 B3
Bene Vagienna I 33 A3
Bénévent-l'Abbaye F 24 A1
Benfeld F 13 C3
Bénodet F 14 B1
Bensheim D 13 B4
Bérat F 36 A2
Berbegal E 35 C3
Bercenay-le-Hayer F 11 C3
Berchem B 5 B3
Berck F 4 B1
Berclaire d'Urgell E 37 C1
Berdún E 34 B3
Berga E 37 B2
Berge D 3 B4
Bergen NL 2 B1
Bergen op Zoom NL 5 A4
Bergerac F 29 B3
Bergères-lés-Vertus F 11 C4
Bergeyk NL 5 A5
Berghausen D 13 C4
Bergheim D 6 B2
Bergisch Gladbach D 6 B3
Bergkamen D 7 A3
Bergneustadt D 7 A3
Bergues F 4 B2
Bergum NL 2 A2
Bergün Bravuogn CH 21 C4
Beringen B 5 A5
Berkheim D 21 A5
Berlikum NL 2 A2
Bern CH 20 C2
Bernau D 20 B3
Bernaville F 10 A2
Bernay F 9 A4
Bernkastel-Kues D 12 B3
Bernués E 35 B3
Beromünster CH 20 B3
Berre-l'Etang F 31 B4
Bersenbrück D 3 B4
Berthelming F 12 C2
Bertincourt F 10 A2
Bertogne B 12 A1
Bertrix B 11 B5
Berville-sur-Mer F 9 A4
Besalú E 37 B3
Besançon F 19 B5
Besenfeld D 13 C4
Besigheim D 13 C5
Besle F 15 B4
Bessais-le-Fromental F 17 C4
Bessan F 30 B2
Besse-en-Chandesse F 24 B2
Bessèges F 31 A3
Bessé-sur-Braye F 16 B2
Bessines-sur-Gartempe F 23 B5
Best NL 5 A5
Betelu E 34 A2
Béthenville F 11 B4
Béthune F 4 B2
Beton-Bazoches F 10 C3
Bettembourg L 12 B2
Betterdorf L 12 B2
Betz F 10 B2
Betzdorf D 7 B3
Beuil F 32 A2
Beuzeville F 9 A4
Beveren B 5 A4
Bevern D 7 A5
Beverungen D 7 A5
Beverwijk NL 2 B1
Bex CH 27 A4
Beychevelle F 28 A2
Beynat F 29 A4
Bezau A 21 B4
Bèze F 19 B4
Bezenet F 24 A2
Béziers F 30 B2
Biandrate I 27 B5
Biarritz F 34 A2
Bias F 28 B1
Biberach
Baden-Württemberg D 13 C4
Baden-Württemberg D 21 A4
Biblis D 13 B4
Bidache F 28 C1
Bidart F 34 A2
Biddinghuizen NL 2 B2
Bieber D 7 B5
Biedenkopf D 7 B4
Biel E 34 B3
Biel / Bienne CH 20 B2
Biella I 27 B5
Bielsa E 35 B4
Bierné F 16 B1
Bierwart B 5 B5
Biescas E 35 B3
Bietigheim-Bissingen D 13 C5
Bièvre B 11 B5
Biganos F 28 B2
Bignasco CH 27 A5
Biguglia F 38 A2
Billerbeck D 3 C4
Billom F 24 B3
Bilstein D 7 A4
Bilthoven NL 2 B2
Bilzen B 6 B1
Binaced E 35 C4
Binche B 5 B4
Binefar E 35 C4
Bingen D 13 B3
Binic F 14 A3
Bionaz I 27 B4
Birkenfeld
Baden-Württemberg D 13 C4
Rheinland-Pfalz D 12 B3
Birresborn D 6 B2
Birstein D 7 B5
Biscarosse F 28 B1
Biscarosse Plage F 28 B1
Biscarrués E 34 B3
Bischheim F 13 C3
Bischofszell CH 21 B4
Bischwiller F 13 C3
Bisingen D 13 C4
Bissen L 12 B2
Bissendorf D 3 B5
Bistango I 27 C5
Bitburg D 12 B2
Bitche F 13 B3
Bitschwiller F 20 B2
Biville-sur-Mer F 9 A5
Biwer L 12 B2
Blacy F 11 C4
Blagnac F 29 C4
Blaichach D 21 B5
Blain F 15 B4
Blainville-sur-l'Eau F 12 C2
Blajan F 35 A4
Blâmont F 12 C2
Blanes E 37 C3
Blangy-sur-Bresle F 10 B1
Blankenberge B 4 A3
Blankenheim D 6 B2
Blanquefort F 28 B2
Blanzac F 23 C4
Blanzy F 18 C3
Blaricum NL 2 B2
Blatten CH 27 A4
Blatzheim D 6 B2
Blaye F 28 A2
Blaye-les-Mines F 30 A1
Blecua E 35 B3
Bleichenbach D 7 B5
Bléneau F 18 B1
Blérancourt F 10 B3
Bléré F 16 B2
Blesle F 24 B3
Blet F 17 C4
Bletterans F 19 C4
Blieskastel D 12 B3
Bligny-sur-Ouche F 18 B3
Blois F 17 B3
Blokzijl NL 2 B2
Blonville-sur-Mer F 9 A4
Bludenz A 21 B4
Blumberg D 21 B3
Bòbbio Pellice I 27 C4
Bobigny F 10 C2
Böblingen D 13 C5
Bocholt
B 6 A1
D 6 A2
Bochum D 6 A3
Bockhorn D 3 A5
Bocognano F 38 A2
Bödefeld-Freiheit D 7 A4
Boëge F 26 A3
Boën F 25 B3
Bognanco Fonti I 27 A5
Bohain-en-Vermandois F 11 B3
Bohmte D 3 B5
Bois-d'Amont F 19 C5
Boisseron F 31 B3
Boixols E 37 B2
Bolbec F 9 A4
Bolea E 35 B3
Bollène F 31 A3
Bologne F 19 A4
Bolsward NL 2 A2
Boltaña E 35 B4
Boltigen CH 20 C2
Bolzaneto I 33 A4
Bona F 18 B2
Bonaduz CH 21 C4
Bondorf D 13 C4
Bon-Encontre F 29 B3
Bonifacio F 38 B2
Bonigen CH 20 C2
Bonn D 6 B3
Bonnat F 24 A1
Bonndorf D 20 B3
Bonnétable F 16 A2
Bonnétage F 20 B1
Bonneuil-les-Eaux F 10 B2
Bonneuil-Matours F 23 B4
Bonneval F 17 A3
Bonneval-sur-Arc F 27 B4
Bonneville F 26 A3
Bonnières-sur-Seine F 10 B1
Bonnieux F 31 B4
Bönnigheim D 13 B5
Bonny-sur-Loire F 17 B4
Bono E 35 B4
Boom B 5 A4
Boos F 9 A5
Boppard D 7 B3
Boran-sur-Oise F 10 B2
Borculo NL 3 B3
Bordeaux F 28 B2
Bordighera I 33 B3
Borgentreich D 7 A5
Börger D 3 B4
Borger NL 3 B3
Borghetto d'Arróscia I 33 A3
Borghetto Santo Spirito I 33 A4
Borghorst D 3 B4
Borgloon B 5 B5
Borgo F 38 A2
Borgofranco d'Ivrea I 27 B4
Borgomanero I 27 B5
Borgomasino I 27 B4
Borgo San Dalmazzo I 33 A3
Borgosésia I 27 B5
Borgo Vercelli I 27 B5
Borja E 34 C2
Bork D 6 A3
Borken D 6 A2
Borkum D 3 A3
Bormes-les-Mimosas F 32 B2
Bórmio I 21 C5
Borne NL 3 B3
Bornheim D 6 B2
Borredá E 37 B2
Bort-les-Orgues F 24 B2
Bösel D 3 A4
Boskoop NL 2 B1
Bossast E 35 B4
Bossolasco I 33 A4
Bottendorf D 7 A4
Bottrop D 6 A2
Bötzingen D 20 A2
Bouaye F 15 B4
Boucau F 28 C1
Bouchain F 4 B3
Bouchoir F 10 B2
Boudreville F 19 B3
Boudry CH 20 C1
Bouesse F 17 C3
Bouguenais F 15 B4
Bouhy F 18 B2
Bouillargues F 31 B3
Bouillon B 11 B5
Bouilly F 18 A2
Bouin F 22 B2
Boulay-Moselle F 12 B2
Boulazac F 29 A3
Boule-d'Amont F 36 B3
Bouligny F 12 B1
Boulogne-sur-Gesse F 35 A4
Boulogne-sur-Mer F 4 B1
Bouloire F 16 B2
Bouquemaison F 4 B2
Bourbon-Lancy F 18 C2
Bourbon-l'Archambault F 18 C2
Bourbonne-les-Bains F 19 B4
Bourbourg F 4 B2
Bourbriac F 14 A2
Bourcefranc-le-Chapus F 22 C2
Bourdeaux F 31 A4
Bouresse F 23 B4
Bourg F 28 A2
Bourg-Achard F 9 A4
Bourganeuf F 24 B1
Bourg-Argental F 25 B4
Bourg-de-Péage F 25 B5
Bourg-de-Thizy F 25 A4
Bourg-de-Visa F 29 B3
Bourg-en-Bresse F 26 A2
Bourges F 17 B4
Bourg-et-Comin F 11 B3
Bourg-Lastic F 24 B2
Bourg-Madame F 36 B2
Bourgneuf-en-Retz F 22 A2
Bourgogne F 11 B4
Bourgoin-Jallieu F 26 B2
Bourg-St Andéol F 31 A3
Bourg-St Maurice F 27 B3
Bourgtheroulde F 9 A4
Bourgueil F 16 B2
Bourmont F 19 A4
Bourneville F 9 A4
Bournezeau F 22 B2
Bourran F 29 B3
Bourret F 29 C4
Bourron-Marlotte F 10 C2
Boussac F 24 A2
Boussens F 35 A4
Boutersem B 5 B4
Bouttencourt F 10 B1
Bouvières F 31 A4
Bouvron F 15 B4
Bouxwiller F 13 C3
Bouzonville F 12 B2
Boves F 10 B2
Bóves I 33 A3
Boxmeer NL 6 A1
Boxtel NL 5 A5
Bozouls F 30 A1
Bra I 27 C4
Bracieux F 17 B3
Brackenheim D 13 B5
Braine F 11 B3
Braine-le-Comte B 5 B4
Braives B 5 B5
Brakel
B 5 B3
D 7 A5
Bram F 36 A3
Bramafan F 32 B2
Bramsche D 3 B4
Brand A 21 B4
Brando F 38 A2
Branne F 28 B2
Brantôme F 23 C4
Bras d'Asse F 32 B2
Brasparts F 14 A2
Brassac F 30 B1
Brassac-les-Mines F 24 B3
Brasschaat B 5 A4
Braubach D 7 B3
Braunfels D 7 B4
Bray Dunes F 4 A2
Bray-sur-Seine F 10 C3
Bray-sur-Somme F 10 B2
Brazey-en-Plaine F 19 B4
Brécey F 8 B2
Brechen D 7 B4
Brecht B 5 A4
Brecketfeld D 6 A3
Brécy F 17 B4
Breda
E 37 C3
NL 5 A4
Bredelar D 7 A4
Bree B 6 A1
Bregenz A 21 B4
Bréhal F 8 B2
Breidenbach F 13 B3
Breil-sur-Roya F 33 B3
Breisach D 20 A2
Breitenbach
CH 20 B2
D 7 B5
Bremgarten CH 20 B3
Brem-sur-Mer F 22 B2
Brénod F 26 A2
Brensbach D 13 B4
Breskens NL 5 A3
Bresles F 10 B2
Bressuire F 16 C1
Brest F 14 A1
Bretenoux F 29 B4
Breteuil
Eure F 9 B4
Oise F 10 B2
Brétigny-sur-Orge F 10 C2
Bretten D 13 B4
Bretteville-sur-Laize F 9 A3
Breuil-Cervínia I 27 B4
Breukelen NL 2 B2
Bréziers F 32 A2
Brezolles F 9 B5
Briançon F 26 C3
Brianconnet F 32 B2
Briare F 17 B4
Briatexte F 29 C4
Briaucourt F 19 A4
Bricquebec F 8 A2
Briec F 14 A1
Brie-Comte-Robert F 10 C2
Brienne-le-Château F 11 C4
Brienon-sur-Armançon F 18 B2
Brienz CH 20 C3
Briey F 12 B1
Brig CH 27 A5
Brignogan-Plage F 14 A1
Brignoles F 32 B2
Brillon-en-Barrois F 11 C5
Brilon D 7 A4
Brinon-sur-Beuvron F 18 B2
Brinon-sur-Sauldre F 17 B4
Brionne F 9 A4
Brioude F 25 B3
Brioux-sur-Boutonne F 23 B3
Briouze F 9 B3
Briscous F 34 A2
Brissac-Quincé F 16 B1
Brive-la-Gaillarde F 29 A4
Brocas F 28 B2
Brock D 3 B4
Broden-bach D 6 B3
Broglie F 9 B4
Bromont-Lamothe F 24 B2
Broons F 15 A3
Broquies F 30 A1
Brossac F 23 C3
Broto E 35 B3
Brou F 17 A3
Brouage F 22 C2
Broût-Vernet F 24 A3
Brouvelieures F 20 A1
Brouwershaven NL 5 A3
Bruay-la-Buissière F 4 B2
Bruchsal D 13 B4
Brue-Auriac F 32 B1
Bruen CH 21 C3
Bruère-Allichamps F 17 C4
Brugg CH 20 B3
Brugge B 4 A3
Brüggen D 6 A2
Brühl D 6 B2
Bruinisse NL 5 A4
Brûlon F 16 B1
Brumath F 13 C3
Brummen NL 2 B3
Brunehamel F 11 B4
Brünen D 6 A2
Brunnen CH 21 C3
Brunssum NL 6 B1
Brusasco I 27 B5
Brusque F 30 B1
Brussels = Bruxelles B 5 B4
Brusson I 27 B4
Bruxelles = Brussels B 5 B4
Bruyères F 20 A1
Bruz F 15 A4
Bubbio I 27 C5
Bubry F 14 B2
Buchboden A 21 B4
Buchenberg D 21 B5

Buchères F 18 A3
Buchs CH 21 B4
Buchy F 9 A5
Bucy-lés-Pierreport F 11 B3
Büdingen D 7 B5
Bugeat F 24 B1
Bühl
Baden-Württemberg D 13 C4
Bayern D 21 B5
Bühlertal D 13 C4
Buis-les-Baronnies F 31 A4
Buitenpost NL 2 A3
Bülach CH 21 B3
Bulgnéville F 19 A4
Bulle CH 20 C2
Büllingen B 6 B2
Bunde D 3 A4
Bunsbeek B 5 B4
Buñuel E 34 C2
Burbach D 7 B4
Burdons-sur-Rognon F 19 A4
Büren D 7 A4
Büren an der Aare CH 20 B2
Burgdorf CH 20 B2
Burgui E 34 B3
Burhave D 3 A5
Burie F 22 C3
Burlada E 34 B2
Burladingen D 21 A4
Burlage D 3 A4
Buronzo I 27 B5
Burret F 36 B2
Bürs A 21 B4
Bürstadt D 13 B4
Busano I 27 B4
Busca I 33 A3
Bussang F 20 B1
Bussière-Badil F 23 C4
Bussière-Poitevine F 23 B4
Bussoleno I 27 B4
Bussum NL 2 B2
Butgenbach B 6 B2
Bütschwil CH 21 B4
Butzbach D 7 B4
Buxières-les-Mines F 18 C1
Buxy F 18 C3
Buzançais F 17 C3
Buzancy F 11 B4
Buzy F 35 A3

C

Cabanac-et-Villagrains F 28 B2
Cabanelles E 37 B3
Cabanillas E 34 B2
Cabasse F 32 B2
Cabdella E 36 B2
Cabourg F 9 A3
Cadalen F 29 C5
Cadaqués E 37 B4
Cadéac F 35 B4
Cadenet F 31 B4
Cadeuil F 22 C3
Cadillac F 28 B2
Cadouin F 29 B3
Cadours F 29 C4
Caen F 9 A3
Cagnes-sur-Mer F 32 B3
Cahors F 29 B4
Cairo Montenotte I 33 A4
Cajarc F 29 B4
Calacuccia F 38 A2
Calaf E 37 C2
Calafell E 37 C2
Calahorra E 34 B2
Calais F 4 B1
Caldas de Boì E 35 B4
Caldas de Malavella E 37 C3
Caldearenas E 35 B3
Calders E 37 C2
Caldes de Montbui E 37 C3
Calella
Barcelona E 37 C3
Girona E 37 C4
Calenzana F 38 A1
Calizzano I 33 A4
Callac F 14 A2
Callas F 32 B2
Calliano I 27 B5
Callús E 37 C2
Calmbach D 13 C4
Calonge E 37 C4
Caluire-et-Cuire F 25 B4
Caluso I 27 B4
Calvi F 38 A1
Calvinet F 24 C2
Calvisson F 31 B3
Calw D 13 C4
Camarasa E 35 C4
Camarès F 30 B1
Camaret-sur-Aigues F 31 A3
Camaret-sur-Mer F 14 A1
Cambligeu F 4 B2
Cambo-les-Bains F 34 A2
Cambrai F 4 B3
Cambrils E 37 C2
Camors F 14 B3
Campan F 35 A4
Campo E 35 B4
Campo Ligure I 33 A4
Campo Molino I 33 A3
Campomono F 38 B1
Camporrells E 35 C4
Camprodón E 37 B3
Campsegret F 29 B3
Canale I 27 C4
Cancale F 8 B2
Cancon F 29 B3
Candanchu E 35 B3
Candé F 15 B4
Canelli I 27 C5
Canet F 30 B2
Canet de Mar E 37 C3
Canet-en-Roussillon F 36 B4
Canfranc E 35 B3
Canisy F 8 A2
Cannes F 32 B3
Cany-Barville F 9 A4
Canyet de Mar E 37 C3
Caparroso E 34 B2
Capbreton F 28 C1
Capdenac-Gare F 24 C2
Cap-de-Pin F 28 B2
Capellades E 37 C2
Capendu F 36 A3
Capestang F 30 B2
Cap Ferret F 28 B1
Cappeln D 3 B5
Captieux F 28 B2
Capvern F 35 A4
Caráglio I 33 A3
Caraman F 36 A2
Carantec F 14 A2
Carbon-Blanc F 28 B2
Carbonne F 36 A2
Carcans F 28 A1
Carcans-Plage F 28 A1
Carcar E 34 B2
Cárcare I 33 A4
Carcassonne F 36 A3
Carcastillo E 34 B2
Carcès F 32 B2
Cardedeu E 37 C3
Cardona E 37 C2
Carentan F 8 A2
Carentoir F 15 B3
Cargèse F 38 A1
Carhaix-Plouguer F 14 A2
Carignan F 11 B5
Carignano I 27 C4
Carlepont F 10 B3
Carmagnola I 27 C4
Carmaux F 30 A1
Carmine I 33 A3
Carnac F 14 B2
Carnon Plage F 31 B2
Carolinensiel D 3 A4
Carolles F 8 B2
Carpentras F 31 A4
Carpignano Sésia I 27 B5
Carquefou F 15 B4
Carqueiranne F 32 B2
Carro F 31 B4
Carros F 33 B3
Carrouge CH 20 C1
Carrouges F 9 B3
Carrù I 33 A3
Carry-le-Rouet F 31 B4
Carteret F 8 A2
Carvin F 4 B2
Casalborgone I 27 B4
Casale Monferrato I 27 B5
Casamozza F 38 A2
Cascante E 34 C2
Cáseda E 34 B2
Caselle Torinese I 27 B4
Cassàde la Selva E 37 C3
Cassagnas F 30 A2
Cassagnes-Bégonhès F 30 A1
Cassel F 4 B2
Cassine I 27 C5
Cassis F 32 B1
Cassuéjouls F 24 C2
Castejón E 34 B2
Castejón de Sos E 35 B4
Castejón de Valdejasa E 34 C3
Casteldelfino I 32 A3
Casteljaloux F 28 B3
Castellamonte I 27 B4
Castellane F 32 B2
Castellar de la Ribera E 37 B2
Castellar del Vallés E 37 C3
Castellbell i Villar E 37 C2
Castelldefels E 37 C2
Castellet E 37 C2
Castellfollit de la Roca E 37 B3
Castellfollit de Riubregos E 37 C2
Castellóde Farfaña E 35 C4
Castello d'Empùries E 37 B4
Castelloli E 37 C2
Castellterçol E 37 C3
Castelmoron-sur-Lot F 29 B3
Castelnaudary F 36 A2
Castelnau-de-Médoc F 28 A2
Castelnau-de-Montmirail F 29 C4
Castelnau-Magnoac F 35 A4
Castelnau-Montratier F 29 B4
Castelnuovo Don Bosco I 27 B4
Castelsarrasin F 29 B4
Castets F 28 C1
Castilfrio de la Sierra E 34 C1
Castilgaleu E 35 B4
Castilisar E 34 B2
Castillonès F 29 B3
Castillon-la-Bataille F 28 B2
Castillon-Len-Couserans F 36 B2
Castillonroy E 35 C4
Castilruiz E 34 C1
Castirla F 38 A2
Castres F 30 B1
Castricum NL 2 B1
Castries F 31 B2
Catillon F 11 A3
Caudebec-en-Caux F 9 A4
Caudiès-de-Fenouillèdes F 36 B3
Caudry F 11 A3
Caulnes F 15 A3
Caumont-l'Evente F 8 A3
Caunes-Minervois F 36 A3
Cauro F 38 B1
Caussade F 29 B4
Causse-de-la-Selle F 30 B2
Cauterets F 35 B3
Cavaglia I 27 B5
Cavaillon F 31 B4
Cavalaire-sur-Mer F 32 B2
Cavallermaggiore I 27 C4
Cavignac F 28 A2
Cavour I 27 C4
Cayeux-sur-Mer F 4 B1
Caylus F 29 B4
Cayres F 25 C3
Cazals F 29 B4
Cazaubon F 28 C2
Cazaux F 28 B1
Cazavet F 36 A2
Cazères F 36 A2
Cazis CH 21 C4
Cazouls-lès-Béziers F 30 B2
Ceauce F 8 B3
Ceilhes-et-Rocozels F 30 B2
Celle Ligure I 33 A4
Celles B 5 B4
Celles-sur-Belle F 23 B3
Censeau F 19 C5
Centallo I 33 A3
Centelles E 37 C3
Cépet F 29 C4
Cérans Foulletourte F 16 B2
Cerbère F 36 B4
Cercs E 37 B2
Cercy-la-Tour F 18 C2
Cerdon F 17 B4
Ceres I 27 B4
Ceresole-Reale I 27 B4
Cereste F 32 B1
Céret F 36 B3
Cerfontaine B 5 B4
Cergy F 10 B2
Cérilly F 17 C4
Cerisiers F 18 A2
Cerizay F 22 B3
Cernay F 20 B2
Cérons F 28 B2
Certosa di Pésio I 33 A3
Cervera E 37 C2
Cervera del Río Alhama E 34 B2
Cerviáde les Garriques E 37 C1
Cervione F 38 A2
Cervon F 18 B2
Cesana Torinese I 27 C3
Cessenon F 30 B2
Cesson-Sévigné F 15 A4
Cestas F 28 B2
Ceva I 33 A4
Cevins F 26 B3
Cévio CH 27 A5
Ceyrat F 24 B3
Ceyzériat F 26 A2
Chaam NL 5 A4
Chabanais F 23 C4
Chabeuil F 25 C5
Chablis F 18 B2
Châbons F 26 B2
Chabreloche F 25 B3
Chabris F 17 B3
Chagny F 19 C3
Chailland F 8 B3
Chaillé-les-Marais F 22 B2
Chailles F 17 B3
Chailley F 18 A2
Chalabre F 36 B3
Chalais F 28 A3
Chalamont F 26 B2
Châlette-sur-Loing F 17 A4
Chalindrey F 19 B4
Challans F 22 B2
Challes-les-Eaux F 26 B2
Chalmazel F 25 B3
Chalmoux F 18 C2
Chalonnes-sur-Loire F 16 B1
Châlons-en-Champagne F 11 C4
Chalon-sur-Saône F 19 C3
Châlus F 23 C4
Cham CH 20 B3
Chamberet F 24 B1
Chambéry F 26 B2
Chambilly F 25 A4
Chambley F 12 B1
Chambly F 10 B2
Chambois F 9 B4
Chambon-sur-Lac F 24 B2
Chambon-sur-Voueize F 24 A2
Chambord F 17 B3
Chamborigaud F 31 A2
Chamboulive F 24 B1
Chamonix-Mont Blanc F 27 B3
Chamoux-sur-Gelon F 26 B3
Champagnac-le-Vieux F 25 B3
Champagney F 20 B1
Champagnole F 19 C4
Champagny-Mouton F 23 B4
Champaubert F 11 C3
Champdeniers-St Denis F 22 B3
Champdieu F 25 B4
Champdôtre F 19 B4
Champeix F 24 B3
Champéry CH 27 A3
Champigne F 16 B1
Champignelles F 18 B2
Champigny-sur-Veude F 16 B2
Champlitte-et-le-Prelot F 19 B4
Champoluc I 27 B4
Champoly F 25 B3
Champorcher I 27 B4
Champrond-en-Gâtine F 9 B5
Champs-sur-Tarentaine F 24 B2
Champs-sur-Yonne F 18 B2
Champtoceaux F 15 B4
Chamrousse F 26 B2
Chanac F 30 A2
Chanaleilles F 25 C3
Changy F 25 A3
Channes F 18 B3
Chantelle F 24 A3
Chantenay-St Imbert F 18 C2
Chanteuges F 25 B3
Chantilly F 10 B2
Chantonnay F 22 B2
Chaource F 18 A3
Chapareillan F 26 B2
Chapelle Royale F 17 A3
Chapelle-St Laurent F 16 C1
Charbonnat F 18 C3
Charenton-du-Cher F 17 C4
Charleroi B 5 B4
Charleville-Mézières F 11 B4
Charlieu F 25 A4
Charly F 10 C3
Charmes F 12 C2
Charmes-sur-Rhône F 25 C4
Charmey CH 20 C2
Charmont-en-Beauce F 17 A4
Charny F 18 B2
Charolles F 25 A4
Chârost F 17 C4
Charquemont F 20 B1
Charrin F 18 C2
Charroux F 23 B4
Chartres F 10 C1
Chasseneuil-sur-Bonnieure F 23 C4
Chassigny F 19 B4
Château-Arnoux F 32 A2
Châteaubernard F 23 C3
Châteaubourg F 15 A4
Châteaubriant F 15 B4
Château-Chinon F 18 B2
Château-d'Oex CH 20 C2
Château-d'Olonne F 22 B2
Château-du-Loir F 16 B2
Châteaudun F 17 A3
Châteaugiron F 15 A4
Château-Gontier F 16 B1
Château-Landon F 17 A4
Château-la-Vallière F 16 B2
Château-l'Evêque F 29 A3
Châteaulin F 14 A1
Châteaumeillant F 17 C4
Châteauneuf
Nièvre F 18 B2
Saône-et-Loire F 25 A4
Châteauneuf-de-Randon F 25 C3
Châteauneuf-d'Ille-et-Vilaine F 8 B2
Châteauneuf-du-Faou F 14 A2
Châteauneuf-du-Pape F 31 A3
Châteauneuf-en-Thymerais F 9 B5
Châteauneuf la-Forêt F 24 B1
Châteauneuf-le-Rouge F 32 B1
Châteauneuf-sur-Charente F 23 C3
Châteauneuf-sur-Cher F 17 C4
Châteauneuf-sur-Loire F 17 B4
Châteauneuf-sur-Sarthe F 16 B1
Châteauponsac F 23 B5
Château-Porcien F 11 B4
Châteauredon F 32 A2
Châteaurenard
Bouches du Rhône F 31 B3
Loiret F 18 B1
Château-Renault F 16 B2
Châteauroux F 17 C3
Châteauroux-les-Alpes F 26 C3
Château-Salins F 12 C2
Château-Thierry F 11 B3
Châteauvillain F 19 A3
Châtel F 27 A3
Châtelaillon-Plage F 22 B2
Châtelaudren F 14 A3
Châtel-Censoir F 18 B2
Châtel-de-Neuvre F 24 A3
Châtelet B 5 B4
Châtel-Guyon F 24 B3
Châtellerault F 23 B4
Châtel-Montagne F 25 A3
Châtel-St Denis CH 20 C1
Châtel-sur-Moselle F 12 C2
Châtelus-Malvaleix F 24 A2
Châtenois F 19 A4
Châtenois-les-Forges F 20 B1
Châtillon I 27 B4
Châtillon-Coligny F 17 B4
Châtillon-en-Bazois F 18 B2
Châtillon-en-Diois F 26 C2
Châtillon-sur Chalaronne F 25 A4
Châtillon-sur-Indre F 17 C3
Châtillon-sur-Loire F 17 B4
Châtillon-sur-Marne F 11 B3
Châtillon-sur-Seine F 18 B3
Châtres F 11 C3
Chaudes-Aigues F 24 C3
Chaudrey F 11 C4
Chauffailles F 25 A4
Chaulnes F 10 B2
Chaument Gistoux B 5 B4
Chaumergy F 19 C4
Chaumont F 19 A4
Chaumont-en-Vexin F 10 B1
Chaumont-Porcien F 11 B4
Chaumont-sur-Aire F 11 C5
Chaumont-sur-Loire F 17 B3
Chaunay F 23 B4
Chauny F 10 B3
Chaussin F 19 C4
Chauvigny F 23 B4
Chavagnes-en-Paillers F 22 B2
Chavanges F 11 C4
Chavignon F 11 B3
Chazelles-sur-Lyon F 25 B4
Chazey-Bons F 26 B2
Chef-Boutonne F 23 B3
Chelles F 10 C2
Chémery F 17 B3
Chemery-sur-Bar F 11 B4
Chemillé F 16 B1
Chemin F 19 C4
Chénerailles F 24 A2
Cheniménil F 19 A5
Chenonceaux F 17 B3
Chenôve F 19 B3
Cherasco I 27 C4
Cherbonnières F 23 C3
Cherbourg F 8 A2
Chéroy F 18 A1
Chessy-lès-Pres F 18 A2
Chevagnes F 18 C2
Chevanceaux F 23 C3
Chevillon F 11 C5
Chevilly F 17 A3
Chézery-Forens F 26 A2
Chialamberto I 27 B4
Chianale I 27 C4
Chiché F 16 C1
Chieri I 27 B4
Chilleurs-aux-Bois F 17 A4
Chimay B 11 A4
Chinon F 16 B2
Chiomonte I 27 B3
Chirac F 30 A2
Chirens F 26 B2
Chissey-en-Morvan F 18 B3
Chiusa di Pésio I 33 A3
Chivasso I 27 B4
Cholet F 22 A3
Chomérac F 25 C4
Chorges F 32 A2
Chouilly F 11 B4
Chouzy-sur-Cisse F 17 B3
Chur CH 21 C4
Churwalden CH 21 C4
Cierp-Gaud F 35 B4
Cieutat F 35 A4
Cigliano I 27 B5
Cimalmotto CH 27 A5
Ciney B 5 B5
Cinq-Mars-la-Pile F 16 B2
Cintegabelle F 36 A2
Cintruénigo E 34 B2
Cirey-sur-Vezouze F 12 C2
Ciriè I 27 B4
Ciry-le-Noble F 18 C3
Cissac-Médoc F 28 A2
Ciutadilla E 37 C2
Civray F 23 B4
Cizur Mayor E 34 B2
Clairvaux-les-Lacs F 19 C4
Clamecy F 18 B2
Claye-Souilly F 10 C2
Cléder F 14 A1
Clefmont F 19 A4
Cléguérec F 14 A2
Clelles F 26 C2
Cléon-d'Andran F 25 C4
Cléré-les-Pins F 16 B2
Clères F 9 A5
Clermont F 10 B2
Clermont-en-Argonne F 11 B5
Clermont-Ferrand F 24 B3
Clermont-l'Hérault F 30 B2
Clerval F 19 B5
Clervaux L 12 A2
Cléry-St André F 17 B3
Clisson F 15 B4
Clohars-Carnoët F 14 B2
Cloppenburg D 3 B5
Cloyes-sur-le-Loir F 17 B3
Cluis F 17 C3
Cluny F 25 A4
Cluses F 26 A3
Cochem D 6 B3
Coesfeld D 3 C4
Coevorden NL 3 B3
Cognac F 23 C3
Cogne I 27 B4
Cognin F 26 B2
Cogolin F 32 B2
Cölbe D 7 B4
Colera E 36 B4
Coligny F 26 A2
Collat F 25 B3
Coll de Nargó E 37 B2
Collinée F 15 A3
Collinghorst D 3 A4
Collobrières F 32 B2
Colmar F 20 A2
Colmars F 32 A2
Cologne F 29 C3
Cologne = Köln D 6 B2
Colombey-les-Belles F 12 C1
Colombey-les-deux-Églises F 19 A3
Colomers E 37 B3
Colomiers F 29 C4
Coma-ruga E 37 C2
Combeaufontaine F 19 B4
Comblain-au-Pont B 6 B1
Combloux F 26 B3
Combourg F 8 B2
Combronde F 24 B3
Comines F 4 B3
Commensacq F 28 B2
Commentry F 24 A2
Commercy F 12 C1
Compiègne F 10 B2
Comps-sur-Artuby F 32 B2
Concarneau F 14 B2
Conches-en-Ouche F 9 B4
Concots F 29 B4
Condat F 24 B2
Condé-en-Brie F 11 C3
Condé-sur-l'Escaut F 5 B3
Conde-sur-Marne F 11 B4
Condé-sur-Noireau F 8 B3
Condom F 29 C3
Condove I 27 B4
Condrieu F 25 B4
Conflans-sur-Lanterne F 19 B5
Confolens F 23 B4
Conlie F 16 A1
Conliège F 19 C4
Connantre F 11 C3
Connaux F 31 A3
Connerré F 16 A2
Conques F 24 C2
Conques-sur-Orbiel F 36 A3
Consenvoye F 11 B5
Constanti E 37 C2
Contay F 10 B2
Conthey CH 27 A4
Contis-Plage F 28 B1
Contres F 17 B3
Contrexéville F 19 A4
Conty F 10 B2
Coole F 11 C4
Coray F 14 A2
Corbeil-Essonnes F 10 C2
Corbeny F 11 B3
Corbie F 10 B2

Corbigny F 18 B2
Corbion B 11 B4
Cordes-sur-Ciel F 29 B4
Corella E 34 B2
Cório I 27 B4
Corlay F 14 A2
Cormainville F 17 A3
Cormatin F 18 C3
Cormeilles F 9 A4
Cormery F 16 B2
Cormoz F 26 A2
Cornago E 34 B1
Cornimont F 20 B1
Cornudella de Montsant E 37 C1
Cornus F 30 B2
Corps F 26 C2
Corps Nuds F 15 B4
Corrèze F 24 B1
Corte F 38 A2
Cortemilia I 33 A4
Cortes E 34 C2
Cosne-Cours-sur-Loire F 18 B1
Cosne d'Allier F 17 C4
Cossato I 27 B5
Cossaye F 18 C2
Cossé-le-Vivien F 15 B5
Cossonay CH 19 C5
Costaros F 25 C3
Costigliole d'Asti I 27 C5
Costigliole Saluzzo I 33 A3
Coublanc F 19 B4
Couches F 18 C3
Coucouron F 25 C3
Coucy-le-Château-Auffrique F 10 B3
Couëron F 15 B4
Couflens F 36 B2
Couhé F 23 B4
Couiza F 36 B3
Coulanges F 18 C2
Coulanges-la-Vineuse F 18 B2
Coulanges-sur-Yonne F 18 B2
Couleuvre F 18 C1
Coulmier-le-Sec F 18 B3
Coulommiers F 10 C3
Coulonges-sur-l'Autize F 22 B3
Coulounieix-Chamiers F 29 A3
Coupéville F 11 C4
Couptrain F 9 B3
Courcelles B 5 B4
Courcelles-Chaussy F 12 B2
Courchevel F 26 B3
Cour-Cheverny F 17 B3
Courcôme F 23 C4
Courçon F 22 B3
Cour-et-Buis F 25 B4
Courgenay CH 20 B2
Courmayeur I 27 B3
Courniou F 30 B1
Cournon-d'Auvergne F 24 B3
Cournonterral F 30 B2
Courpière F 25 B3
Coursan F 30 B2
Courseulles-sur-Mer F 9 A3
Cours-la-Ville F 25 A4
Courson-les-Carrières F 18 B2
Courtalain F 17 A3
Courtenay F 18 A2
Courtomer F 9 B4
Courville
Eure-et-Loire F 9 B5
Marne F 11 B3
Coussac-Bonneval F 23 C5
Coutances F 8 A2
Couterne F 9 B3
Coutras F 28 A2
Couvet CH 20 C1
Couvin B 11 A4
Couzon F 18 C2
Cox F 29 C4
Cozes F 22 C3
Cozzano F 38 B2
Craon F 15 B5
Craonne F 11 B3
Craponne F 25 B4
Craponne-sur-Arzon F 25 B3
Crèches-sur-Saône F 25 A4
Crécy-en-Ponthieu F 4 B1
Crécy-la-Chapelle F 10 C2
Crécy-sur-Serre F 11 B3
Creil F 10 B2
Creissels F 30 A2
Cremeaux F 25 B3
Crémieu F 26 B2
Creney F 11 C4
Créon F 28 B2
Crépey F 12 C1
Crépy F 11 B3
Crépy-en-Valois F 10 B2
Crescentino I 27 B5
Cressensac F 29 A4
Cressia F 19 C4
Crest F 25 C5
Cresta CH 21 C4
Créteil F 10 C2
Creully F 8 A3
Creutzwald F 12 B2
Crèvecoeur-le-Grand F 10 B2
Crévola d'Ossola I 27 A5
Criel-sur-Mer F 10 A1
Crillon F 10 B1
Criquetot-l'Esneval F 9 A4
Crissolo I 27 C4
Crocq F 24 B2
Crodo I 27 A5
Cronat F 18 C2
Crouy F 10 B3
Crozon F 14 A1
Cruas F 25 C4
Cruis F 32 A1
Cruseilles F 26 A3
Cubelles E 37 C2
Cubjac F 29 A3
Cucuron F 31 B4
Cuers F 32 B2
Cueva de Agreda E 34 C2
Cuges-les-Pins F 32 B1
Cugnaux F 29 C4
Cuijk NL 6 A1
Cuinzier F 25 A4
Cuiseaux F 19 C4
Cuisery F 19 C4
Culan F 17 C4
Culemborg NL 5 A5
Cully CH 20 C1
Culoz F 26 B2
Cumiana I 27 C4
Cúneo I 33 A3
Cunlhat F 25 B3
Cuorgnè I 27 B4
Cusset F 25 A3
Cussy-les-Forges F 18 B3
Custines F 12 C2
Cuts F 10 B3
Cuvilly F 10 B2

D

Daaden D 7 B3
Dabo F 12 C3
Dagmersellen CH 20 B2
Dahn D 13 B3
Dalaas A 21 B5
Dalheim L 12 B2
Daluis F 32 A2
Dalum D 3 B4
Damazan F 29 B3
Damgan F 15 B3
Dammarie-les-Lys F 10 C2
Dammartin-en-Goële F 10 B2
Damme D 3 B5
Dampierre F 19 B4
Dampierre-sur-Salon F 19 B4
Damüls A 21 B4
Damville F 9 B5
Damvillers F 12 B1
Damwoude NL 2 A2
Dangers F 9 B5
Dangé-St Romain F 16 C2
Dangeul F 9 B4
Danjoutin F 20 B1
Dannemarie F 20 B2
Daoulas F 14 A1
Darfeld D 3 B4
Darmstadt D 13 B4
Darney F 19 A5
Datteln D 6 A3
Dattenfeld D 7 B3
Daumeray F 16 B1
Daun D 6 B2
Davos CH 21 C4
Dax F 28 C1
Deauville F 9 A4
Decazeville F 30 A1
Decize F 18 C2
De Cocksdorp NL 2 A1
Dedemsvaart NL 3 B3
Dego I 33 A4
De Haan B 4 A3
Deinze B 5 B3
De Koog NL 2 A1
Delbrück D 7 A4
Delden NL 3 B3
Delémont CH 20 B2
Delft NL 2 B1
Delfzijl NL 3 A3
Delle F 20 B2
Delme F 12 C2
Demigny F 19 C3
Demonte I 33 A3
Denain F 4 B3
Den Burg NL 2 A1
Dender-monde B 5 A4
Denekamp NL 3 B4
Den Ham NL 3 B3
Den Helder NL 2 B1
Denklingen D 7 B3
Den Oever NL 2 B2
Déols F 17 C3
De Panne B 4 A2
Derval F 15 B4
Desana I 27 B5
Descartes F 16 C2
Desvres F 4 B1
Dettingen D 21 B4
Dettwiller F 13 C3
Deurne NL 6 A1
Deventer NL 2 B3
De Wijk NL 3 B3
Diano d'Alba I 27 C5
Diano Marina I 33 B4
Die F 26 C2
Diebling F 12 B2
Dieburg D 13 B4
Diekirch L 12 B2
Diélette F 8 A2
Diemelstadt D 7 A5
Diémoz F 26 B2
Diepenbeck B 5 B5
Diepholz D 3 B5
Dieppe F 9 A5
Dierdorf D 7 B3
Dieren NL 2 B3
Diest B 5 B5
Dietikon CH 20 B3
Dietzenbach D 13 A4
Dieue-sur-Meuse F 12 B1
Dieulefit F 31 A4
Dieulouard F 12 C2
Dieuze F 12 C2
Diever NL 3 B3
Diez D 7 B4
Differdange L 12 B1
Dignac F 23 C4
Digne-les-Bains F 32 A2
Digny F 9 B5
Digoin F 18 C2
Dijon F 19 B4
Diksmuide B 4 A2
Dillenburg D 7 B4
Dillingen D 12 B2
Dilsen B 6 A1
Dinan F 15 A3
Dinant B 5 B4
Dinard F 15 A3
Dingden D 6 A2
Dinklage D 3 B5
Dinslaken D 6 A2
Dinxperlo NL 6 A2
Diou F 18 C2
Dirksland NL 5 A4
Disentis CH 21 C3
Dissen D 3 B5
Ditzingen D 13 C5
Ditzum D 3 A4
Dives-sur-Mer F 9 A3
Divion F 4 B2
Divonne les Bains F 26 A3
Dixmont F 18 A2
Dizy-le-Gros F 11 B4
Dochamps B 6 B1
Doesburg NL 2 B3
Doetinchem NL 3 C3
Dogliani I 33 A3
Doische B 11 A4
Dokkum NL 2 A2
Dolancourt F 18 A3
Dolceácqua I 33 B3
Dol-de-Bretagne F 8 B2
Dole F 19 B4
Dollot F 18 A2
Domat-Ems CH 21 C4
Dombasle-sur-Meurthe F 12 C2
Domène F 26 B2
Domérat F 24 A2
Domfessel F 12 C3
Domfront F 8 B3
Domfront-en-Champagne F 16 A2
Dommartin F 11 C4
Dommartin-le-Franc F 11 C4
Domme F 29 B4
Domodóssola I 27 A5
Dompaire F 19 A5
Dompierre-du-Chemin F 8 B2
Dompierre-sur-Besbre F 18 C2
Dompierre-sur-Mer F 22 B2
Domrémy-la-Pucelle F 12 C1
Domsure F 26 A2
Donaueschingen D 20 B3
Donestebe-Santesteban E 34 A2
Donges F 15 B3
Donnemarie-Dontilly F 10 C3
Donostia-San Sebastián E 34 A2
Donzenac F 29 A4
Donzère F 31 A3
Donzy F 18 B2
Doorn NL 2 B2
Dordrecht NL 5 A4
Dörenthe D 3 B4
Dormagen D 6 A2
Dormans F 11 B3
Dornbirn A 21 B4
Dornecy F 18 B2
Dornes F 18 C2
Dornhan D 13 C4
Dornum D 3 A4
Dörpen D 3 B4
Dorsten D 6 A2
Dortan F 26 A2
Dortmund D 6 A3
Dottignies B 4 B3
Döttingen CH 20 B3
Douai F 4 B3
Douarnenez F 14 A1
Douchy F 18 B2
Douchy-les-Mines F 4 B3
Doucier F 19 C4
Doudeville F 9 A4
Doué-la-Fontaine F 16 B1
Doulaincourt-Saucourt F 11 C5
Doulevant-le-Château F 11 C4
Doullens F 10 A2
Dour B 5 B3
Dourdan F 10 C2
Dourgne F 36 A3
Dournazac F 23 C4
Douvaine F 26 A3
Douvres-la-Délivrande F 9 A3
Douzy F 11 B5
Doyet F 24 A2
Dozule F 9 A3
Drachten NL 2 A3
Draguignan F 32 B2
Dreieich D 13 A4
Dreisen D 13 B4
Drensteinfurt D 7 A3
Dreux F 9 B5
Dringenberg D 7 A5
Dronero I 33 A3
Dronrijp NL 2 A2
Dronten NL 2 B2
Droué F 17 A3
Drulingen F 12 C3
Drunen NL 5 A5
Druten NL 6 A1
Dübendorf CH 21 B3
Ducey F 8 B2
Duclair F 9 A4
Duffel B 5 A4
Dugny-sur-Meuse F 12 B1
Duisburg D 6 A2
Dülken D 6 A2
Dülmen D 6 A3
Dümpelfeld D 6 B2
Dunkerque = Dunkirk F 4 A2
Dunkirk = Dunkerque F 4 A2
Dun-le-Palestel F 24 A1
Dun-les-Places F 18 B3
Dunningen D 21 A3
Dun-sur-Auron F 17 C4
Dun-sur-Meuse F 11 B5
Durach D 21 B5
Durance F 28 B3
Duras F 28 B3
Durban-Corbières F 36 B3
Dürbheim D 21 A3
Durbuy B 5 B5
Düren D 6 B2
Durlach D 13 C4
Dürrboden CH 21 C4
Dürrenboden CH 21 C3
Durtal F 16 B1
Düsseldorf D 6 A2
Dusslingen D 13 C5

E

Eaux-Bonnes F 35 B3
Eauze F 28 C3
Eberbach D 13 B4
Ebnat-Kappel CH 21 B4
Ebreuil F 24 A3
Echallens CH 20 C1
Echauri E 34 B2
Echiré F 22 B3
Échirolles F 26 B2
Echourgnac F 28 A3
Echt NL 6 A1
Echternach L 12 B2
Eckelshausen D 7 B4
Éclaron F 11 C4
Écommoy F 16 B2
Écouché F 9 B3
Ecouis F 10 B1
Écueillé F 17 B3
Edam NL 2 B2
Ede NL 2 B2
Edenkoben D 13 B4
Edesheim D 13 B4
Edewecht D 3 A4
Eekloo B 5 A3
Eemshaven NL 3 A3
Eerbeek NL 2 B3
Eersel NL 5 A5
Effiat F 24 A3
Egg
A 21 B4
D 21 A5
Éghezée B 5 B4
Égletons F 24 B2
Eglisau CH 21 B3
Égliseneuve-d'Entraigues F 24 B2
Eglofs D 21 B4
Egmond aan Zee NL 2 B1
Eguilles F 31 B4
Eguilly-sous-Bois F 18 A3
Éguzon-Chantôme F 17 C3
Ehrang D 12 B2
Ehringshausen D 7 B4
Eibergen NL 3 B3
Eickelborn D 7 A4
Eindhoven NL 5 A5
Einsiedeln CH 21 B3
Einville-au-Jard F 12 C2
Eisenberg D 13 B4
Eitorf D 6 B3
Ejea de los Caballeros E 34 B2
Eke B 5 B3
Élancourt F 10 C1
Elbeuf F 9 A4
Elburg NL 2 B2
El Buste E 34 C2
El Frago E 34 B3
El Grado E 35 B4
Elizondo E 34 A2
Ellezelles B 5 B3
Elm CH 21 C4
El Masnou E 37 C3
El Morell E 37 C2
Elmstein D 13 B3
Elne F 36 B3
Éloyes F 19 A5
El Pla de Santa Maria E 37 C2
El Pont d'Armentera E 37 C2
El Port de la Selva E 37 B4
El Port de Llançà E 36 B4
El Prat de Llobregat E 37 C3
Els Castells E 37 B2
Elsdorf D 6 B2
Elsenfeld D 13 B5
El Serrat AND 36 B2
Elspeet NL 2 B2
Elst NL 2 C2
El Temple E 34 C3
El Tormillo E 35 C3
Eltville D 13 A4
Elven F 15 B3
El Vendrell E 37 C2
El Villar de Arnedo E 34 B1
Elzach D 20 A3
Embrun F 32 A2
Embún E 34 B3
Emden D 3 A4
Emlichheim D 3 B3
Emmeloord NL 2 B2
Emmen
CH 20 B3
NL 3 B3
Emmendingen D 20 A2
Emmer-Compascuum NL 3 B4
Emmerich D 6 A2
Emsbüren D 3 B4
Emsdetten D 3 B4
Emstek D 3 B5
Encamp AND 36 B2
Enciso E 34 B1
Endingen D 20 A2
Engelberg CH 20 C3
Engelskirchen D 6 B3
Engen D 21 B3
Enghien B 5 B4
Engter D 3 B5
Enkenbach D 13 B3
Enkhuizen NL 2 B2
Ennezat F 24 B3
Ennigerloh D 7 A4
Ens NL 2 B2
Enschede NL 3 B3
Ensisheim F 20 B2
Entlebuch CH 20 B3
Entrácque I 33 A3
Entrains-sur-Nohain F 18 B2
Entraygues-sur-Truyère F 24 C2
Entrevaux F 32 B2
Entzheim F 13 C3
Envermeu F 9 A5
Enzklösterle D 13 C4
Épagny F 10 B3
Epalinges CH 20 C1
Epannes F 22 B3
Epe
D 3 B4
NL 2 B2
Épernay F 11 B3
Épernon F 10 C1
Epfig F 13 C3
Epierre F 26 B3
Épinac F 18 C3
Épinal F 19 A5
Epoisses F 18 B3
Eppenbrunn D 13 B3
Eppingen D 13 B4
Erbach D 13 B4
Erbalunga F 38 A2
Erfstadt D 6 B2
Eriswil CH 20 B2
Erkelenz D 6 A2
Erkrath D 6 A2
Erla E 34 B3
Erli I 33 A4
Ermelo NL 2 B2
Ermenonville F 10 B2
Erndtebrück D 7 B4
Ernée F 8 B3
Erolzheim D 21 A5
Erquelinnes B 5 B4
Erquy F 15 A3
Erratzu E 34 A2
Erro E 34 B2
Ersa F 38 A2
Erstein F 13 C3
Erstfeld CH 21 C3
Ertingen D 21 A4
Ervy-le-Châtel F 18 A2
Erwitte D 7 A4
Esbly F 10 C2
Eschach D 21 B4
Eschenz CH 21 B3
Esch-sur-Alzette L 12 B1
Esch-sur-Sûre L 12 B1
Eschweiler D 6 B2
Escoeuilles F 4 B1
Escos F 34 A2
Escource F 28 B1
Escragnolles F 32 B2
Esens D 3 A4
Eslava E 34 B2
Eslohe D 7 A4
Espalion F 30 A1
Esparreguera E 37 C2
Esparron F 32 B1
Espeluche F 31 A3
Espéraza F 36 B3
Espinasses F 32 A2
Espinelves E 37 C3
Espluga de Francolí E 37 C2
Esplús E 35 C4
Espolla E 36 B3
Espot E 36 B2
Esquedas E 35 B3
Essay F 9 B4
Essen
B 5 A4
Niedersachsen D 3 B4
Nordrhein-Westfalen D 6 A3
Essertaux F 10 B2
Essoyes F 18 A3
Estadilla E 35 B4
Estagel F 36 B3
Estaires F 4 B2
Estang F 28 C2
Estartit E 37 B4
Estavayer-le-Lac CH 20 C1
Estella E 34 B1
Esternay F 11 C3
Esterri d'Aneu E 36 B2
Esterwegen D 3 B4
Estissac F 18 A2
Estivareilles F 24 A2
Estopiñán E 35 C4
Estoublon F 32 B2
Estrée-Blanche F 4 B2
Estrées-St Denis F 10 B2
Esyres F 16 B2
Etables-sur-Mer F 14 A3
Étain F 12 B1
Étalans F 19 B5
Etalle B 12 B1
Étampes F 10 C2
Etang-sur-Arroux F 18 C3
Étaples F 4 B1
Etauliers F 28 A2
Etoges F 11 C3
Etréaupont F 11 B3
Étréchy F 10 C2
Étrépagny F 10 B1
Étretat F 9 A4
Étroeungt F 11 A3
Étroubles I 27 B4
Ettelbruck L 12 B2
Etten NL 5 A4
Ettenheim D 20 A2
Ettlingen D 13 C4
Etuz F 19 B4
Etxarri-Aranatz E 34 B1
Eu F 10 A1
Eulate E 34 B1
Eupen B 6 B2
Europoort NL 5 A4
Euskirchen D 6 B2
Évaux-les-Bains F 24 A2
Evergem B 5 A3
Eversberg D 7 A4
Everswinkel D 3 C4
Évian-les-Bains F 26 A3
Evisa F 38 A1
Evolène CH 27 A4
Evran F 15 A4
Evrecy F 9 A3
Évreux F 9 A5
Évron F 16 A1
Évry F 10 C2
Ewersbach D 7 B4
Excideuil F 23 C5
Exmes F 9 B4
Eyguians F 32 A1
Eyguières F 31 B4
Eygurande F 24 B2
Eylie F 35 B4
Eymet F 29 B3
Eymoutiers F 24 B1
Ezcároz E 34 B2

F

Fabrègues F 30 B2
Fagnières F 11 C4
Faido CH 21 C3
Fains-Véel F 11 C5
Falaise F 9 B3
Falces E 34 B2
Falset E 37 C1
Fanjeaux F 36 A3
Fara Novarese I 27 B5
Farasdues E 34 B2
Faucogney-et-la-Mer F 19 B5
Fauguerolles F 28 B3
Faulquemont F 12 B2
Fauquembergues F 4 B2
Fauville-en-Caux F 9 A4
Fauvillers B 12 B1
Faverges F 26 B3
Faverney F 19 B5
Fay-aux-Loges F 17 B4
Fayence F 32 B2
Fayet F 30 B1
Fayl-Billot F 19 B4
Fécamp F 9 A4
Feldkirch A 21 B4
Felizzano I 27 C5
Felletin F 24 B2
Felsberg D 7 A5
Fenestrelle I 27 B4
Fénétrange F 12 C3
Feneu F 16 B1
Fère-Champenoise F 11 C3
Fère-en-Tardenois F 11 B3
Fernay-Voltaire F 26 A3
Ferpècle CH 27 A4
Ferrals-les-Corbières F 36 A3
Ferret CH 27 B4
Ferrette F 20 B2
Ferrière-la-Grande F 5 B3
Ferrières
Hautes-Pyrénées F 35 A3
Loiret F 17 A4
Oise F 10 B2
Ferrières-sur-Sichon F 25 A3
Ferwerd NL 2 A2
Festieux F 11 B3
Feudingen D 7 B4
Feuges F 11 C4
Feuquières F 10 B1
Feurs F 25 B4

Fiano I 27 B4
Fiesch CH 27 A5
Figari F 38 B2
Figeac F 24 C2
Figols E 35 B4
Figueres E 37 B3
Filisur CH 21 C4
Finale Lígure I 33 A4
Finsterwolde NL 3 A4
Firmi F 30 A1
Firminy F 25 B4
Fischbach D 13 B3
Fischen D 21 B5
Fismes F 11 B3
Fitero E 34 B2
Flaça E 37 B3
Flace F 25 A4
Flaine F 26 A3
Flamatt CH 20 C2
Flammersfeld D 7 B3
Flassans-sur-Issole F 32 B2
Flavigny-sur-Moselle F 12 C2
Flavy-le-Martel F 10 B3
Flawil CH 21 B4
Flayosc F 32 B2
Flehingen D 13 B4
Flers F 8 B3
Fleurance F 29 C3
Fleuré F 23 B4
Fleurier CH 19 C5
Fleurus B 5 B4
Fleury
Hérault F 30 B2
Yonne F 18 B2
Fleury-les-Aubrais F 17 B3
Fleury-sur-Andelle F 9 A5
Fleury-sur-Orne F 9 A3
Flieden D 7 B5
Flims CH 21 C4
Flines-lèz-Raches F 4 B3
Flirey F 12 C1
Flixecourt F 10 A2
Flize F 11 B4
Flobecq B 5 B3
Flogny-la-Chapelle F 18 B2
Flonheim D 13 B4
Florac F 30 A2
Floreffe B 5 B4
Florennes B 5 B4
Florensac F 30 B2
Florentin F 29 C5
Florenville B 11 B5
Flörsheim D 13 A4
Flühli CH 20 C3
Flumet F 26 B3
Flums CH 21 B4
Foix F 36 B2
Folelli F 38 A2
Foncine-le-Bas F 19 C5
Fontaine F 11 C4
Fontainebleau F 10 C2
Fontaine de Vaucluse F 31 B4
Fontaine-Française F 19 B4
Fontaine-le-Dun F 9 A4
Fontan F 33 A3
Fontane I 33 A3
Fontanières F 24 A2
Fontenay-le-Comte F 22 B3
Fontenay-Trésigny F 10 C2
Fontevrault-l'Abbaye F 16 B2
Fontoy F 12 B1
Fontpédrouse F 36 B3
Font-Romeu F 36 B3
Fonz E 35 B4
Forbach
D 13 C4
F 12 B2
Forcalquier F 32 B1
Forges-les-Eaux F 10 B1
Formazza I 27 A5
Formerie F 10 B1
Formigliana I 27 B5
Formiguères F 36 B3
Forno
Piemonte I 27 B4
Piemonte I 27 B5
Forno Alpi-Gráie I 27 B4
Fort-Mahon-Plage F 4 B1
Fos F 35 B4
Fossano I 33 A3
Fosse-la-Ville B 5 B4
Fos-sur-Mer F 31 B3
Fouchères F 18 A3
Fouesnant F 14 B1
Foug F 12 C1
Fougères F 8 B2
Fougerolles F 19 B5
Foulain F 19 A4
Fouras F 22 C2
Fourchambault F 18 B2
Fourmies F 11 A4
Fournels F 24 C3
Fournols F 25 B3
Fourques F 36 B3
Fourquevaux F 36 A2
Fours F 18 C2
Frabosa Soprana I 33 A3
Fraire B 5 B4
Fraize F 20 A1
Francaltroff F 12 C2
Francescas F 29 B3
Franeker NL 2 A2
Frangy F 26 A2
Frankenau D 7 A4
Frankenberg D 7 A4
Frankenthal D 13 B4
Frankfurt D 7 B4
Frasne F 19 C5
Frasnes-lez-Anvaing B 5 B3
Frasseto F 38 B2
Frastanz A 21 B4
Frauenfeld CH 21 B3
Frayssinet F 29 B4
Frayssinet-le-Gélat F 29 B4
Frechen D 6 B2
Freckenhorst D 3 C4
Fredeburg D 7 A4
Freiburg D 20 B2
Freienhagen D 7 A5
Freiensteinau D 7 B5
Freisen D 12 B3
Fréjus F 32 B2
Freren D 3 B4
Fresnay-sur-Sarthe F 9 B4
Fresnes-en-Woevre F 12 B1
Fresne-St Mamès F 19 B4
Fresnoy-Folny F 10 B1
Fresnoy-le-Grand F 11 B3
Fressenville F 10 A1
Fréteval F 17 B3
Fretigney F 19 B4
Freudenberg D 7 B3
Freudenstadt D 13 C4
Freux B 12 B1
Frévent F 4 B2
Freyming-Merlebach F 12 B2
Fribourg CH 20 C2
Frick CH 20 B3
Friedberg D 7 B4
Friedeburg D 3 A4
Friedrichsdorf D 7 B4
Friedrichshafen D 21 B4
Friesenheim D 13 C3
Friesoythe D 3 A4
Fritzlar D 7 A5
Froges F 26 B2
Frohnhausen D 7 B4
Froissy F 10 B2
Fröndenberg D 7 A3
Fronsac F 28 B2
Front I 27 B4
Frontenay-Rohan-Rohan F 22 B3
Frontignan F 30 B2
Fronton F 29 C4
Frouard F 12 C2
Fruges F 4 B2
Frutigen CH 20 C2
Fuendejalón E 34 C2
Fully CH 27 A4
Fumay F 11 B4
Fumel F 29 B3
Fürstenau D 3 B4
Furstenau D 7 A5
Fürth D 13 B4
Furtwangen D 20 A3
Fusio CH 21 C3
Fustiñana E 34 B2

G

Gabarret F 28 C2
Gabriac F 30 A1
Gaby I 27 B4
Gacé F 9 B4
Gadmen CH 20 C3
Gael F 15 A3
Gaggenau D 13 C4
Gaillac F 29 C4
Gaillefontaine F 10 B1
Gaillon F 9 A5
Gaja-la-Selve F 36 A2
Galan F 35 A4
Galéria F 38 A1
Galgon F 28 B2
Gallardon F 10 C1
Gallur E 34 C2
Galtür A 21 C5
Gamaches F 10 B1
Gammertingen D 21 A4
Gams CH 21 B4
Gan F 35 A3
Ganges F 30 B2
Gannat F 24 A3
Gannay-sur-Loire F 18 C2
Gap F 32 A2
Gardanne F 31 B4
Gardouch F 36 A2
Garein F 28 B2
Garéoult F 32 B2
Garéssio I 33 A4
Gargellen A 21 C4
Gargilesse-Dampierre F 17 C3
Garlin F 28 C2
Garnat-sur-Engièvre F 18 C2
Garrel D 3 B5
Garriguella E 36 B4
Gaschurn A 21 C5
Gasny F 10 B1
Gastes F 28 B1
Gattinara I 27 B5
Gava E 37 C3
Gavarnie F 35 B3
Gavray F 8 B2
Géaudot F 11 C4
Geaune F 28 C2
Gedern D 7 B5
Gedinne B 11 B4
Gèdre F 35 B4
Geel B 5 A4
Geetbets B 5 B5
Geilenkirchen D 6 B2
Geinsheim D 13 B4
Geisenheim D 13 B4
Geisingen D 21 B3
Geldermalsen NL 5 A5
Geldern D 6 A2
Geldrop NL 6 A1
Geleen NL 6 B1
Gelida E 37 C2
Gelnhausen D 7 B5
Gelsenkirchen D 6 A3
Gelterkinden CH 20 B2
Gembloux B 5 B4
Gemeaux F 19 B4
Gémenos F 32 B1
Gemert NL 6 A1
Gemmenich B 6 B1
Gémozac F 22 C3
Gemund D 6 B2
Gemünden
Hessen D 7 B4
Rheinland-Pfalz D 13 B3
Genappe B 5 B4
Gençay F 23 B4
Gendringen NL 6 A2
Genelard F 18 C3
Genemuiden NL 2 B3
Geneva = Genève CH 26 A3
Genève = Geneva CH 26 A3
Genevriéres F 19 B4
Gengenbach D 13 C4
Genillé F 17 B3
Genk B 6 B1
Genlis F 19 B4
Gennep NL 6 A1
Gennes F 16 B1
Genola I 33 A3
Gensingen D 13 B3
Gent = Ghent B 5 A3
Gentioux F 24 B1
Georgsmarienhütte D 3 B5
Geraards-bergen B 5 B3
Gérardmer F 20 A1
Gerbéviller F 12 C2
Gergy F 19 C3
Germay F 12 C1
Germersheim D 13 B4
Gernsbach D 13 C4
Gernsheim D 13 B4
Gerolstein D 6 B2
Gerpinnes B 5 B4
Gerri de la Sal E 37 B2
Gerzat F 24 B3
Gescher D 3 C4
Geseke D 7 A4
Gespunsart F 11 B4
Gesté F 15 B4
Gevrey-Chambertin F 19 B3
Gex F 26 A3
Gey D 6 B2
Ghent = Gent B 5 A3
Ghigo I 27 C4
Ghisonaccia F 38 A2
Ghisoni F 38 A2
Giat F 24 B2
Giaveno I 27 B4
Gien F 17 B4
Giens F 32 B2
Gieselwerder D 7 A5
Giessen D 7 B4
Gieten NL 3 A3
Giethoorn NL 2 B3
Giffaumont-Champaubert F 11 C4
Gignac F 30 B2
Gilley F 19 B5
Gilley-sur-Loire F 18 C2
Gilocourt F 10 B2
Gilserberg D 7 B5
Gilze NL 5 A4
Gimont F 29 C3
Ginasservis F 32 B1
Gingelom B 5 B5
Giromagny F 20 B1
Girona E 37 C3
Gironcourt-sur-Vraine F 12 C1
Gironella E 37 B2
Gironville-sous-les-Côtes F 12 C1
Gisors F 10 B1
Gistel B 4 A2
Giswil CH 20 C3
Givet F 11 A4
Givors F 25 B4
Givry
B 5 B4
F 18 C3
Givry-en-Argonne F 11 C4
Gizeux F 16 B2
Gladbeck D 6 A2
Gladenbach D 7 B4
Gland CH 19 C5
Glandorf D 3 B4
Glarus CH 21 B4
Gletsch CH 20 C3
Glomel F 14 A2
Goch D 6 A2
Goddelsheim D 7 A4
Godelheim D 7 A5
Goderville F 9 A4
Goes NL 5 A3
Goetzenbrück F 13 C3
Góglio I 27 A5
Goirle NL 5 A5
Goizueta E 34 A2
Goldach CH 21 B4
Goldbach D 13 A5
Gomaringen D 13 C5
Goncelin F 26 B2
Gondrecourt-le-Château F 12 C1
Gondrin F 28 C3
Gonfaron F 32 B2
Goñi E 34 B2
Gooik B 5 B4
Goor NL 3 B3
Goppenstein CH 27 A4
Gorey UK 8 A1
Gorinchem NL 5 A4
Gorredijk NL 2 A3
Gorron F 8 B3
Gossau CH 21 B4
Götzis A 21 B4
Gouarec F 14 A2
Gouda NL 2 B1
Gourdon F 29 B4
Gourgançon F 11 C4
Gourin F 14 A2
Gournay-en-Bray F 10 B1
Gouvy B 6 B1
Gouzeacourt F 10 A3
Gouzon F 24 A2
Gozee B 5 B4
Grabs CH 21 B4
Graçay F 17 B3
Gramat F 29 B4
Grancey-le-Château F 19 B4
Grandcamp-Maisy F 8 A2
Grand-Champ F 14 B3
Grand Couronne F 9 A5
Grand-Fougeray F 15 B4
Grandpré F 11 B4
Grandrieu
B 5 B4
F 25 C3
Grandson CH 20 C1
Grandvillars F 20 B1
Grandvilliers F 10 B1
Grañén E 35 C3
Granges-de Crouhens F 35 B4
Granges-sur-Vologne F 20 A1
Granollers E 37 C3
Granville F 8 B2
Grasse F 32 B2
Graulhet F 29 C4
Graus E 35 B4
Grávalos E 34 B2
Grave NL 6 A1
Gravelines F 4 A2
Gravellona Toce I 27 B5
Graveson F 31 B3
Gray F 19 B4
Grebenstein D 7 A5
Grefrath D 6 A2
Grenade F 29 C4
Grenade-sur-l'Adour F 28 C2
Grenchen CH 20 B2
Grenoble F 26 B2
Gréoux-les-Bains F 32 B1
Gressoney-la-Trinité I 27 B4
Gressoney-St-Jean I 27 B4
Greven D 3 B4
Grevenbroich D 6 A2
Grevenbrück D 7 A4
Grevenmacher L 12 B2
Grez-Doiceau B 5 B4
Grèzec F 29 B4
Grez-en-Bouère F 16 B1
Griesheim D 13 B4
Grignan F 31 A3
Grignols F 28 B2
Grignon F 26 B3
Grijpskerk NL 3 A3
Grimaud F 32 B2
Grimbergen B 5 B4
Grimmialp CH 20 C2
Grindelwald CH 20 C3
Grisolles F 29 C4
Groenlo NL 3 B3
Groesbeek NL 6 A1
Groix F 14 B2
Gronau D 3 B4
Grönenbach D 21 B5
Groningen NL 3 A3
Grootegast NL 3 A3
Grossenkneten D 3 B5
Grossenlüder D 7 B5
Gross-Gerau D 13 B4
Grosshöchstetten CH 20 C2
Grossostheim D 13 B5
Gross Reken D 6 A3
Gross Umstadt D 13 B4
Grostenquin F 12 C2
Grouw NL 2 A2
Gruissan F 30 B2
Grünberg D 7 B4
Gründau D 7 B5
Grünstadt D 13 B4
Gruyères CH 20 C2
Gstaad CH 20 C2
Gsteig CH 27 A4
Guagno F 38 A1
Guardiola de Bergueda E 37 B2
Guebwiller F 20 B2
Guémené-Penfao F 15 B4
Guémené-sur-Scorff F 14 A2
Guer F 15 B3
Guérande F 15 B3
Guéret F 24 A1
Guérigny F 18 B2
Guesa E 34 B2
Gueugnon F 18 C3
Guichen F 15 B4
Guignes F 10 C2
Guillaumes F 32 A2
Guillestre F 26 C3
Guillos F 28 B2
Guilvinec F 14 B1
Guînes F 4 B1
Guingamp F 14 A2
Guipavas F 14 A1
Guiscard F 10 B3
Guiscriff F 14 A2
Guise F 11 B3
Guisona E 37 C2
Guîtres F 28 A2
Gujan-Mestras F 28 B1
Gummersbach D 7 A3
Gundel-fingen D 20 A2
Gundelsheim D 13 B5
Gunderschoffen F 13 C3
Guntersblum D 13 B4
Gurrea de Gállego E 34 B3
Gütersloh D 7 A4
Guttannen CH 20 C3
Güttingen CH 21 B4
Gy F 19 B4
Gyé-sur-Seine F 18 A3
Gypsera CH 20 C2

H

Haacht B 5 B4
Haaksbergen NL 3 B3
Haamstede NL 5 A3
Haan D 6 A3
Haarlem NL 2 B1
Habas F 28 C2
Habay B 12 B1
Habsheim F 20 B2
Hachenburg D 7 B3
Hadamar D 7 B4
Hage D 3 A4
Hagen D 6 A3
Hagenbach D 13 B4
Hagetmau F 28 C2
Hagondange F 12 B2
Haguenau F 13 C3
Hahnslätten D 7 B4
Haiger D 7 B4
Haigerloch D 13 C4
Haldem D 3 B5
Halle B 5 B4
Hallenberg D 7 A4
Halluin F 4 B3
Haltern D 6 A3
Halver D 6 A3
Ham F 10 B3
Hambach F 12 B3
Hamm D 7 A3
Hamme B 5 A4
Hamminkeln D 6 A2
Hamoir B 6 B1
Hamont B 6 A1
Hanau D 7 B4
Hannut B 5 B5
Hardegarijp NL 2 A2
Hardelot Plage F 4 B1
Hardenberg NL 3 B3
Harderwijk NL 2 B2
Hardt D 20 A3
Haren
D 3 B4
NL 3 A3
Harfleur F 9 A4
Hargicourt F 10 B3
Hargnies F 11 A4
Harkebrügge D 3 A4
Harlingen NL 2 A2
Haroué F 12 C2
Harsewinkel D 3 C5
Hartennes F 10 B3
Haselünne D 3 B4
Haslach D 20 A3
Hasparren F 34 A2
Hasselt
B 5 B5
NL 2 B3
Hassloch D 13 B4
Hastière-Lavaux B 5 B4
Hattem NL 2 B3
Hatten
D 3 A5
F 13 C3
Hattingen D 6 A3
Hattstadt F 20 A2
Hau D 6 A2
Haudainville F 12 B1
Haulerwijk NL 3 A3
Hausach D 20 A3
Hautefort F 29 A4
Hauterives F 25 B5
Hauteville-Lompnès F 26 B2
Haut-Fays B 11 A5
Hautmont F 5 B3
Hautrage B 5 B3
Havelange B 5 B5
Havelte NL 2 B3
Havixbeck D 3 C4
Hayange F 12 B2
Hazebrouck F 4 B2
Héas F 35 B4
Hechingen D 13 C4
Hecho E 34 B3
Hechtel B 5 A5
Hédé F 15 A4
Heede D 3 B4
Heek D 3 B4
Heemstede NL 2 B1
Heerde NL 2 B3
Heerenveen NL 2 B2
Heerhugowaard NL 2 B1
Heerlen NL 6 B1
Heeze NL 6 A1
Heidelberg D 13 B4
Heiden D 6 A2
Heilbronn D 13 B5
Heiligenhaus D 6 A2
Heiloo NL 2 B1
Heinerscheid L 12 A2
Heinsberg D 6 A2
Heist-op-den-Berg B 5 A4
Helchteren B 5 A5
Hellendoorn NL 3 B3
Hellenthal D 6 B2
Hellevoetsluis NL 5 A4
Helmond NL 6 A1
Hemer D 7 A3
Héming F 12 C2
Hendaye F 34 A2
Hengelo
Gelderland NL 3 B3
Overijssel NL 3 B3
Hénin-Beaumont F 4 B2
Hennebont F 14 B2
Henrichemont F 17 B4
Heppenheim D 13 B4
Herbault F 17 B3
Herbern D 7 A3
Herbeumont B 11 B5
Herbignac F 15 B3
Herbisse F 11 C4
Herbitzheim F 12 B3
Herbolzheim D 20 A2
Herborn D 7 B4
Herchen D 6 B3
Herent B 5 B4
Herentals B 5 A4
Hérépian F 30 B2
Héric F 15 B4
Héricourt F 20 B1
Héricourt-en-Caux F 9 A4
Hérimoncourt F 20 B1
Herisau CH 21 B4
Hérisson F 17 C4
Herk-de-Stad B 5 B5
Herment F 24 B2
Hermeskeil D 12 B2
Hermonville F 11 B3
Hernani E 34 A2
Herne D 6 A3
Herrenberg D 13 C4
Herrlisheim F 13 C3
Herscheid D 7 A3
Herselt B 5 A4
Herstal B 6 B1
Herten D 6 A3
Herxheim D 13 B4
Herzebrock D 7 A4
Herzlake D 3 B4
Herzogenbuchsee CH 20 B2
Hesdin F 4 B2
Hesel D 3 A4
Hettange-Grande F 12 B2
Heuchin F 4 B2
Heudicourt-sous-les-Côtes F 12 C1
Heunezel F 19 A5
Heuqueville F 9 A4
Hiersac F 23 C4
Hilchenbach D 7 A4
Hilden D 6 A2
Hillegom NL 2 B1
Hillesheim D 6 B2
Hilvarenbeek NL 5 A5
Hilversum NL 2 B2
Hindelbank CH 20 B2
Hinterweidenthal D 13 B3
Hinwil CH 21 B3
Hippolytushoef NL 2 B1
Hirschhorn D 13 B4
Hirsingue F 20 B2
Hirson F 11 B4
Hirzenhain D 7 B5
Hittisau A 21 B4
Hobscheid L 12 B1
Hochdorf CH 20 B3
Hochfelden F 13 C3
Hochspeyer D 13 B3
Hochstenbach D 7 B3
Höchst im Odenwald D 13 B5
Hockenheim D 13 B4
Hoedekenskerke NL 5 A3
Hoegaarden B 5 B4
Hoek van Holland NL 5 A4
Hoenderlo NL 2 B2
Hofgeismar D 7 A5
Hofheim D 13 A4
Hohenems A 21 B4
Hohenkirchen D 3 A4
Hohentengen D 20 B3
Hohenwepel D 7 A5
Holdorf D 3 B5
Hollum NL 2 A2
Holten NL 3 B3
Holtwick D 3 B4
Holwerd NL 2 A2
Holzminden D 7 A5
Homberg
Hessen D 7 A5
Hessen D 7 B5
Homburg D 13 B3
Hondarribia E 34 A2
Hondschoote F 4 B2
Honfleur F 9 A4
Hönningen D 6 B2
Hontheim D 12 A2
Hoofddorp NL 2 B1
Hoogerheide NL 5 A4
Hoogeveen NL 3 B3
Hoogezand-Sappemeer NL 3 A3
Hoogkarspel NL 2 B2
Hoogkerk NL 3 A3
Hoogstede D 3 B3
Hoogstraten B 5 A4
Hooksiel D 3 A5
Hoorn NL 2 B2
Hopsten D 3 B4
Horb am Neckar D 13 C4
Horgen CH 21 B3
Horn D 7 A4
Hornberg D 20 A3

Hornoy-le-Bourg F 10 B1
Horst NL 6 A2
Horstel D 3 B4
Horsten D 3 A4
Horstmar D 3 B4
Hösbach D 13 A5
Hosenfeld D 7 B5
Hosingen L 12 A2
Hospental CH 21 C3
Hossegor F 28 C1
Hostal de Ipiés E 35 B3
Hostalric E 37 C3
Hostens F 28 B2
Hotton B 5 B5
Houdain F 4 B2
Houdan F 10 C1
Houdelaincourt F 12 C1
Houeillès F 28 B3
Houffalize B 12 A1
Houlgate F 9 A3
Hourtin F 28 A1
Hourtin-Plage F 28 A1
Houthalen B 5 A5
Houyet B 5 B4
Hovelhof D 7 A4
Höxter D 7 A5
Hückel-hoven D 6 A2
Hückeswagen D 6 A3
Hucqueliers F 4 B1
Huelgoat F 14 A2
Huesca E 35 B3
Hüfingen D 20 B3
Huissen NL 2 C2
Huizen NL 2 B2
Hüls D 6 A2
Hulst NL 5 A4
Hungen D 7 B4
Hünxe D 6 A2
Hürbel D 21 A4
Hürth D 6 B2
Hüsten D 7 A3
Huttwil CH 20 B2
Huy B 5 B5
Hyères F 32 B2
Hyéres Plage F 32 B2

I

Ibbenbüren D 3 B4
Ichtegem B 4 A3
Idar-Oberstein D 13 B3
Idiazábal E 34 B1
Idstein D 7 B4
Ieper = Ypres B 4 B2
Igea E 34 B1
Igny-Comblizy F 11 B3
Igries E 35 B3
Igualada E 37 C2
Iguerande F 25 A4
Ihringen D 20 A2
IJmuiden NL 2 B1
IJsselmuiden NL 2 B2
IJzendijke NL 5 A3
Ilanz CH 21 C4
Ilche E 35 C4
Illats F 28 B2
Ille-sur-Têt F 36 B3
Illfurth F 20 B2
Illiers-Combray F 9 B5
Illkirch-Graffenstaden F 13 C3
Immenhausen D 7 A5
Immenstadt D 21 B5
Impéria I 33 B4
Imphy F 18 C2
Inerthal CH 21 B3
Ingelheim D 13 B4
Ingelmunster B 4 B3
Ingrandes
Maine-et-Loire F 15 B5
Vienne F 16 C2
Ingwiller F 13 C3
Innertkirchen CH 20 C3
Ins CH 20 B2
Interlaken CH 20 C2
Irrel D 12 B2
Irún E 34 A2
Irurita E 34 A2
Irurzun E 34 B2
Isaba E 34 B3
Ischgl A 21 B5
Isdes F 17 B4
Iselle I 27 A5
Iseltwald CH 20 C2
Iserlohn D 7 A3
Isigny-sur-Mer F 8 A2
Isny D 21 B5
Isola F 32 A3
Isola d'Asti I 27 C5
Isona E 37 B2
Ispagnac F 30 A2
Isselburg D 6 A2
Issigeac F 29 B3
Issogne I 27 B4
Issoire F 24 B3
Issoncourt F 11 C5
Issoudun F 17 C4
Issum D 6 A2
Is-sur-Tille F 19 B4
Issy-l'Evêque F 18 C2
Istres F 31 B3
Itoiz E 34 B2
Ivoz Ramet B 5 B5
Ivrea I 27 B4
Ivry-en-Montagne F 18 B3
Ivry-la-Bataille F 10 C1
Iwuy F 4 B3
Izegem B 4 B3
Izernore F 26 A2

J

Jaca E 35 B3
Jade D 3 A5
Jalhay B 6 B1
Jaligny-sur-Besbre F 25 A3
Jallais F 16 B1
Jâlons F 11 C4
Jamoigne B 12 B1
Janville F 17 A3
Janzé F 15 B4
Jard-sur-Mer F 22 B2
Jargeau F 17 B4
Jarnac F 23 C3
Jarny F 12 B1
Jarzé F 16 B1
Jasseron F 26 A2
Jaun CH 20 C2
Jausiers F 32 A2
Javerlhac F 23 C4
Javier E 34 B2
Javron F 9 B3
Jegun F 29 C3
Jemgum D 3 A4
Jenaz CH 21 C4
Jesberg D 7 B5
Jeumont F 5 B4
Jever D 3 A4
Jodoigne B 5 B4
Joeuf F 12 B1
Joigny F 18 B2
Joinville F 11 C5
Jonchery-sur-Vesle F 11 B3
Jonzac F 22 C3
Jorba E 37 C2
Josselin F 15 B3
Jouarre F 10 C3
Joué-lès-Tours F 16 B2
Joué-sur-Erdre F 15 B4
Joure NL 2 B2
Joux-la-Ville F 18 B2
Jouy F 10 C1
Jouy-le-Châtel F 10 C3
Jouy-le-Potier F 17 B3
Joyeuse F 31 A3
Joze F 24 B3
Juan-les-Pins F 32 B3
Jubera E 34 B1
Jugon-les-Lacs F 15 A3
Juillac F 29 A4
Juillan F 35 A4
Juist D 3 A4
Julianadorp NL 2 B1
Jülich D 6 B2
Jullouville F 8 B2
Jumeaux F 25 B3
Jumièges F 9 A4
Jumilhac-le-Grand F 23 C5
Juneda E 37 C1
Jungingen D 13 C5
Junglingster L 12 B2
Juniville F 11 B4
Juprelle B 6 B1
Jussac F 24 C2
Jussey F 19 B4
Jussy F 10 B3
Juvigny-le-Terte F 8 B2
Juvigny-sous-Andaine F 9 B3
Juzennecourt F 19 A3

K

Kaatscheuvel NL 5 A5
Kahl D 13 A5
Kaisersesch D 6 B3
Kaiserslautern D 13 B3
Kalkar D 6 A2
Kall D 6 B2
Kalmthout B 5 A4
Kaltbrunn CH 21 B4
Kamen D 7 A3
Kampen NL 2 B2
Kamp-Lintfort D 6 A2
Kandel D 13 B4
Kandern D 20 B2
Kandersteg CH 20 C2
Kapellen B 5 A4
Kappel D 13 C3
Kappl A 21 B5
Karlsruhe D 13 B4
Kassel D 7 A5
Kastellaun D 13 A3
Kasterlee B 5 A4
Katwijk NL 2 B1
Katzenelnbogen D 7 B3
Kaub D 13 A3
Kaysersberg F 20 A2
Keerbergen B 5 A4
Kehl D 13 C3
Kelberg D 6 B2
Kell D 12 B2
Kelmis B 6 B2
Kelsterbach D 13 A4
Kempen D 6 A2
Kempten D 21 B5
Kemptthal CH 21 B3
Kenzingen D 20 A2
Kérien F 14 A2
Kerken D 6 A2
Kerkrade NL 6 B2
Kerlouan F 14 A1
Kernascléden F 14 A2
Kerns CH 20 C3
Kerpen D 6 B2
Kerzers CH 20 C2
Kevelaer D 6 A2
Kierspe D 7 A3
Kimratshofen D 21 B5
Kinrooi B 6 A1
Kirberg D 7 B4
Kirchberg
CH 20 B2
Rheinland-Pfalz D 13 B3
Kirchhain D 7 B4
Kirchheim D 7 B5
Kirchheimbolanden D 13 B4
Kirchhundem D 7 A4
Kirchzarten D 20 B2
Kirn D 13 B3
Kirtorf D 7 B5
Kisslegg D 21 B4
Klazienaveen NL 3 B3
Kleve D 6 A2
Klingenberg D 13 B5
Klingenmunster D 13 B4
Kloosterzande NL 5 A4
Klösterle A 21 B5
Klosters CH 21 C4
Kloten CH 21 B3
Kluisbergen B 5 B3
Klundert NL 5 A4
Knesselare B 4 A3
Knokke-Heist B 4 A3
Koblenz
CH 20 B3
D 7 B3
Koekelare B 4 A2
Koksijde B 4 A2
Kollum NL 2 A3
Köln = Cologne D 6 B2
Königstein D 7 B4
Königswinter D 6 B3
Köniz CH 20 C2
Konstanz D 21 B4
Kontich B 5 A4
Konz D 12 B2
Kopstal L 12 B2
Korbach D 7 A4
Körbecke D 7 A4
Kortrijk B 4 B3
Koudum NL 2 B2
Kranenburg D 6 A2
Krefeld D 6 A2
Kressbronn D 21 B4
Kreuzau D 6 B2
Kreuzlingen CH 21 B4
Kreuztal D 7 B3
Kriegsfeld D 13 B3
Kriens CH 20 B3
Krimpen aan de IJssel NL 5 A4
Krommenie NL 2 B1
Kruft D 6 B3
Kruishoutem B 5 B3
Küblis CH 21 C4
Kuinre NL 2 B2
Kuppenheim D 13 C4
Kürten D 6 A3
Kusel D 13 B3
Küsnacht CH 20 B3
Küttingen CH 20 B3
Kyllburg D 12 A2

L

La Balme-de-Sillingy F 26 B3
La Barre-de-Monts F 22 B1
La Barre-en-Ouche F 9 B4
La Barthe-de-Neste F 35 A4
La Bassée F 4 B2
La Bastide-de-Sèrou F 36 A2
La Bastide-des-Jourdans F 32 B1
Labastide-Murat F 29 B4
La Bastide-Puylaurent F 25 C3
Labastide-Rouairoux F 30 B1
Labastide-St Pierre F 29 C4
La Bathie F 26 B3
La Baule-Escoublac F 15 B3
La Bazoche-Gouet F 16 A2
La Bégude-de-Mazenc F 31 A3
Labenne F 28 C1
La Bernerie-en-Retz F 22 A1
La Bisbal d'Empordà E 37 C4
Lablachère F 31 A3
La Boissière F 9 A4
Labouheyre F 28 B2
La Bourboule F 24 B2
La Brède F 28 B2
La Bresse F 20 A1
La Bridoire F 26 B2
La Brillanne F 32 B1
Labrit F 28 B2
La Bruffière F 22 A2
Labruguière F 30 B1
L'Absie F 22 B3
La Bussière F 17 B4
La Caillère F 22 B3
La Calmette F 31 B3
Lacanau F 28 B1
Lacanau-Océan F 28 A1
Lacanche F 18 B3
La Canourgue F 30 A2
La Capelle F 11 B3
Lacapelle-Marival F 29 B4
Lacaune F 30 B1
La Cavalerie F 30 A2
La Celle-en-Moravan F 18 B3
La Celle-St Avant F 16 B2
La Chaise-Dieu F 25 B3
La Chaize-Giraud F 22 B2
La Chaize-le-Vicomte F 22 B2
La Chambre F 26 B3
La Chapelaude F 24 A2
La Chapelle-d'Angillon F 17 B4
La Chapelle-en-Aalgaudémar F 26 C3
La Chapelle-en-Vercors F 26 C2
La Chapelle-Glain F 15 B4
La Chapelle-la-Reine F 10 C2
La Chapelle-Laurent F 24 B3
La Chapelle-St Luc F 11 C4
La Chapelle-sur-Erdre F 15 B4
La Chapelle-Vicomtesse F 17 B3
La Charce F 32 A1
La Charité-sur-Loire F 18 B2
La Chartre-sur-le-Loir F 16 B2
La Châtaigneraie F 22 B3
La Châtre F 17 C3
La Chaussée-sur-Marne F 11 C4
La Chaux-de-Fonds CH 20 B1
Lachen CH 21 B3
La Cheppe F 11 B4
La Chèze F 15 A3
La Ciotat F 32 B1
La Clayette F 25 A4
La Clusaz F 26 B3
La Condamine-Châtelard F 32 A2
La Coquille F 23 C4
La Côte-St André F 26 B2
La Cotinière F 22 C2
La Courtine F 24 B2
Lacq F 35 A3
La Crau F 32 B2
La Crèche F 23 B3
La Croix F 16 B2
Lacroix-Barrez F 24 C2
Lacroix-St Ouen F 10 B2
Lacroix-sur-Meuse F 12 C1
La Croix-Valmer F 32 B2
Ladbergen D 3 B4
Ladignac-le-Long F 23 C5
Ladon F 17 B4
La Douze F 29 A3
Laer D 3 B4
La Farga de Moles E 36 B2
La Fère F 10 B3
La Ferrière
Indre-et-Loire F 16 B2
Vendée F 22 B2
La Ferrière-en-Parthenay F 23 B3
La-Ferté-Alais F 10 C2
La Ferté-Bernard F 16 A2
La Ferté-Frênel F 9 B4
La Ferté-Gaucher F 10 C3
La Ferté-Imbault F 17 B3
La Ferté-Macé F 9 B3
La Ferté-Milon F 10 B3
La Ferté-sous-Jouarre F 10 C3
La Ferté-St-Aubin F 17 B3
La Ferté-St-Cyr F 17 B3
La Ferté-Vidame F 9 B4
La Ferté Villeneuil F 17 B3
La Feuillie F 10 B1
La Flèche F 16 B1
La Flotte F 22 B2
La Fouillade F 30 A1
Lafrançaise F 29 B4
La Fulioala E 37 C2
La Gacilly F 15 B3
Lagarde F 36 A2
La Garde-Freinet F 32 B2
La Garnache F 22 B2
La Garriga E 37 C3
La Gaubretière F 22 B2
Lagnieu F 26 B2
Lagny-sur-Marne F 10 C2
La Grand-Combe F 31 A3
La Grande-Croix F 25 B4
La Grande-Motte F 31 B3
Lagrasse F 36 A3
La Grave F 26 B3
La Gravelle F 15 A4
Laguarres E 35 B4
Laguenne F 24 B1
Laguépie F 29 B4
La Guerche-de-Bretagne F 15 B4
La Guerche-sur-l'Aubois F 18 C1
La Guérinière F 22 B1
Laguiole F 24 C2
Laharie F 28 B1
La Haye-du-Puits F 8 A2
La Haye-Pesnel F 8 B2
Lahden D 3 B4
La Herlière F 4 B2
Laheycourt F 11 C5
Lahnstein D 7 B3
Lahr D 13 C3
La Hulpe B 5 B4
La Hutte F 9 B4
L'Aigle F 9 B4
Laignes F 18 B3
Laiguéglia I 33 B4
L'Aiguillon-sur-Mer F 22 B2
Laissac F 30 A1
La Javie F 32 A2
La Jonchère-St Maurice F 24 A1
La Jonquera E 36 B3
Lalbenque F 29 B4
Lalinde F 29 B3
Lalizolle F 24 A3
La Llacuna E 37 C2
Lalley F 26 C2
La Londe-les-Maures F 32 B2
La Loupe F 9 B5
La Louvière B 5 B4
L'Alpe-d'Huez F 26 B3
Laluque F 28 C1
La Machine F 18 C2
Lamagistére F 29 B3
La Mailleraye-sur-Seine F 9 A4
La Malène F 30 A2
La Manresana dels Prats E 37 C2
Lamarche F 19 A4
Lamarche-sur-Saône F 19 B4
Lamargelle F 19 B3
Lamarque F 28 A2
La Masadera E 35 C3
Lamastre F 25 C4
Lamballe F 15 A3
Lambesc F 31 B4
La Meilleraye-de-Bretagne F 15 B4
La Ménitré F 16 B1
La Mole F 32 B2
La Molina E 37 B2
La Monnerie-le-Montel F 25 B3
La Mothe-Achard F 22 B2
Lamothe-Cassel F 29 B4
Lamothe-Montravel F 28 B3
La Mothe-St Héray F 23 B3
Lamotte-Beuvron F 17 B4
La Motte-Chalançon F 31 A4
La Motte-du-Caire F 32 A2
La Motte-Servolex F 26 B2
Lampertheim D 13 B4
La Mure F 26 C2
Lamure-sur-Azergues F 25 A4
Lanaja E 35 C3
Lanarce F 25 C3
Lançon-Provence F 31 B4
Landau D 13 B4
Landen B 5 B5
Landerneau F 14 A1
Landévant F 14 B2
Landévennec F 14 A1
Landivisiau F 14 A1
Landivy F 8 B2
Landos F 25 C3
Landouzy-le-Ville F 11 B4
Landquart CH 21 C4
Landrecies F 11 A3
Landreville F 18 A3
Landscheid D 12 B2
Landstuhl D 13 B3
Lanester F 14 B2
La Neuve-Lyre F 9 B4
La Neuveville CH 20 B2
Langeac F 25 B3
Langeais F 16 B2
Langedijk NL 2 B1
Langemark-Poelkapelle B 4 B2
Langen D 13 B4
Langenberg D 7 A4
Langenbruck CH 20 B2
Langenfeld D 6 A2
Langenlonsheim D 13 B3
Langenthal CH 20 B2
Langeoog D 3 A4
Langförden D 3 B5
Langnau CH 20 C2
Langogne F 25 C3
Langon F 28 B2
Langres F 19 B4
Langueux F 15 A3
Languidic F 14 B2
Langwarden D 3 A5
Langwies CH 21 C4
Lanildut F 14 A1
Lanmeur F 14 A2
Lannéanou F 14 A2
Lannemezan F 35 A4
Lanneuville-sur-Meuse F 11 B5
Lannilis F 14 A1
Lannion F 14 A2
La Nocle-Maulaix F 18 C2
Lanouaille F 23 C5
Lanslebourg-Mont-Cenis F 27 B3
Lanta F 29 C4
Lanton F 28 B1
Lantosque F 33 B3
Lanvollon F 14 A3
Lanzo Torinese I 27 B4
Laon F 11 B3
Laons F 9 B5
La Pacaudière F 25 A3
Lapalisse F 25 A3
La Palme F 36 B4
La Palmyre F 22 C2
La Petit-Pierre F 13 C3
Lapeyrade F 28 B2
Lapeyrouse F 24 A2
La Plagne F 26 B3
Laplume F 29 B3
La Pobla de Lillet E 37 B2
la Porta F 38 A2
La Pouëze F 16 B1
Lapoutroie F 20 A2
La Preste F 36 B3
La Primaube F 30 A1
La Puebla de Roda E 35 B4
La Punt CH 21 C4
Laragne-Montéglin F 32 A1
l'Arboç E 37 C2
L'Arbresle F 25 B4
Larceveau F 34 A2
Larche
Alpes-de-Haute-Provence F 32 A2
Corrèze F 29 A4
La Réole F 28 B2
Largentière F 31 A3
L'Argentière-la-Bessée F 26 C3
La Riera de Gaià E 37 C2
La Rivière-Thibouville F 9 A4
Larmor-Plage F 14 B2
La Roche CH 20 C2
La Rochebeaucourtet-Argentine F 23 C4
La Roche-Bernard F 15 B3
La Roche-Canillac F 24 B1
La Roche-Chalais F 28 A3
La Roche Derrien F 14 A2
La Roche-des-Arnauds F 32 A1
La Roche-en-Ardenne B 6 B1
La Roche-en-Brénil F 18 B3
La Rochefoucauld F 23 C4
La Roche-Guyon F 10 B1
La Rochelle F 22 B2
La Roche-Posay F 23 B4
La Roche-sur-Foron F 26 A3
La Roche-sur-Yon F 22 B2
Larochette L 12 B2
La Rochette F 31 A4
Laroquebrou F 24 C2
La Roquebrussanne F 32 B1
Laroque d'Olmes F 36 B2
La Roque-Gageac F 29 B4
La Roque-Ste Marguerite F 30 A2
Laroque-Timbaut F 29 B3
Larraga E 34 B2
Larrau F 34 A3
Larrazet F 29 C4
Laruns F 35 A3
Lasalle F 31 A2
La Salle F 26 C3
La Salvetat-Peyralés F 30 A1
La Salvetat-sur-Agout F 30 B1
La Sarraz CH 19 C5
Lasarte E 34 A1
La Selva del Camp E 37 C2
La Serra E 37 C2
La Seu d'Urgell E 36 B2
La Seyne-sur-Mer F 32 B1
La Souterraine F 24 A1
Laspaules E 35 B4
Las Planes d'Hostoles E 37 B3
Laspuña E 35 B4
Lassay-les-Châteaux F 9 B3
Lasseube F 35 A3
Lassigny F 10 B2
Lastrup D 3 B4
La Suze-sur-Sarthe F 16 B2
Latasa E 34 B2
La Teste F 28 B1
Lathen D 3 B4
La Thuile I 27 B3
La Torre de Cabdella E 36 B1
La Tour d'Aigues F 32 B1
La Tour de Peilz CH 20 C1
La Tour-du-Pin F 26 B2
La Tranche-sur-Mer F 22 B2
La Tremblade F 22 C2
La Trimouille F 23 B5
La Trinité F 14 B2
La Trinité-Porhoët F 15 A3
Latronquière F 24 C2
Latterbach CH 20 C2
La Turballe F 15 B3
Laubach D 7 B4
Laubert F 25 C3
Laufen CH 20 B2
Lauffen D 13 B5
Launois-sur-Vence F 11 B4

Laurière F 24 A1
Lausanne CH 20 C1
Laussonne F 25 C4
Lauterach A 21 B4
Lauterbach D 7 B5
Lauterbrunnen CH 20 C2
Lauterecken D 13 B3
Lautrec F 30 B1
Lauzerte F 29 B4
Lauzès F 29 B4
Lauzun F 29 B3
Laval F 16 A1
Lavardac F 29 B3
Lavau F 18 B1
Lavaur F 29 C4
Lavelanet F 36 B2
La Vilella Baixa E 37 C1
Lavilledieu F 31 A3
La Villedieu F 23 B3
La Ville Dieu-du-Temple F 29 B4
Lavit F 29 C3
Lavoncourt F 19 B4
La Voulte-sur-Rhône F 25 C4
Lavoûte-Chilhac F 25 B3
La Wantzenau F 13 C3
Lazkao E 34 A1
Lebach D 12 B2
Le Barcarès F 36 B4
Le Barp F 28 B2
Le Bar-sur-Loup F 32 B2
Le Béage F 25 C4
Le Beausset F 32 B1
Lebekke B 5 A4
Le Bessat F 25 B4
Le Blanc F 23 B5
Le Bleymard F 30 A2
Le Boullay-Mivoye F 9 B5
Le Boulou F 36 B3
Le Bourg F 29 B4
Le Bourg-d'Oisans F 26 B3
Le Bourget-du-Lac F 26 B2
Le Bourgneuf-la-Forêt F 15 A5
Le Bousquet d'Orb F 30 B2
Le Brassus CH 19 C5
Le Breuil F 25 A3
Le Breuil-en-Auge F 9 A4
Le Brusquet F 32 A2
Le Bry CH 20 C2
Le Bugue F 29 B3
Le Buisson F 29 B3
Le Caloy F 28 C2
Le Cap d'Agde F 30 B2
Le Cateau Cambrésis F 11 A3
Le Caylar F 30 B2
Le Cayrol F 24 C2
Lech A 21 B5
Le Chambon-Feugerolles F 25 B4
Le Chambon-sur-Lignon F 25 B4
Le Château d'Oléron F 22 C2
Le Châtelard F 26 B3
Le Châtelet F 17 C4
Le Chatelet-en-Brie F 10 C2
Le Chesne F 11 B4
Le Cheylard F 25 C4
Leciñena E 35 C3
Le Collet-de-Deze F 31 A2
Le Conquet F 14 A1
Le Creusot F 18 C3
Le Croisic F 15 B3
Le Crotoy F 4 B1
Lectoure F 29 C3
Lede B 5 B3
Le Deschaux F 19 C4
Lédignan F 31 B3
Le Donjon F 25 A3
Le Dorat F 23 B5
Leek NL 3 A3
Leens NL 3 A3
Leer D 3 A4
Leerdam NL 5 A5
Leerhafe D 3 A4
Leeuwarden NL 2 A2
Le Faou F 14 A1
Le Faoüet F 14 A2
Le Folgoet F 14 A1
Le Fossat F 36 A2
Le Fousseret F 36 A2
Le Fugeret F 32 A2
Legau D 21 B5
Le Gault-Soigny F 11 C3
Legé F 22 B2
Lège-Cap-Ferret F 28 B1
Léglise B 12 B1
Le Grand-Bornand F 26 B3
Le-Grand-Bourg F 24 A1
Le Grand-Lucé F 16 B2
Le Grand-Pressigny F 16 C2
Le Grand-Quevilly F 9 A5
Le Grau-du-Roi F 31 B3
Léguevin F 29 C4
Le Havre F 9 A4
Le Hohwald F 13 C3
Le Houga F 28 C2
Leiden NL 2 B1
Leidschendam NL 2 B1
Leignon B 5 B5
Leimen D 13 B4
Leitza E 34 A2
Lekunberri E 34 A2
Le Lardin-St Lazare F 29 A4
Le Lauzet-Ubaye F 32 A2
Le Lavandou F 32 B2
Le Lion-d'Angers F 16 B1
Le Locle CH 20 B1
Le Loroux-Bottereau F 15 B4
Le Louroux-Béconnais F 15 B5
Le Luc F 32 B2
Le Lude F 16 B2
Lelystad NL 2 B2
Le Malzieu-Ville F 24 C3
Le Mans F 16 A2
Le Mas-d'Azil F 36 A2
Le Massegros F 30 A2
Le Mayet-de-Montagne F 25 A3
Le May-sur-Evre F 15 B5
Lembach F 13 B3
Lemberg F 13 B3
Lembèye F 35 A3
Lemelerveld NL 3 B3
Le Mêle-sur-Sarthe F 9 B4
Le Ménil F 19 A5
Le Merlerault F 9 B4
Le Mesnil-sur-Oger F 11 C4
Lemförde D 3 B5
Le Miroir F 19 C4
Lemmer NL 2 B2
Le Molay-Littry F 8 A3
Le Monastier-sur-Gazeille F 25 C3
Le Monêtier-les-Bains F 26 C3
Le Mont-Dore F 24 B2
Le Montet F 24 A3
Le Mont-St Michel F 8 B2
Lempdes F 24 B3
Le Muret F 28 B2
Le Muy F 32 B2
Lencloître F 16 C2
Le Neubourg F 9 A4
Lengerich
Niedersachsen D 3 B4
Nordrhein-Westfalen D 3 B4
Lenk CH 20 C2
Lennestadt D 7 A4
Le Nouvion-en-Thiérache F 11 A3
Lens
B 5 B3
F 4 B2
Lens Lestang F 25 B5
Lenzburg CH 20 B3
Lenzerheide CH 21 C4
Léon F 28 C1
Leonberg D 13 C5
Léoncel F 26 C2
Leopoldsburg B 5 A5
Le Palais F 14 B2
Le Parcq F 4 B2
Le Péage-de-Roussillon F 25 B4
Le Pellerin F 15 B4
Le Perthus F 36 B3
Le Pertuis F 25 B4
Le Petit-Bornand F 26 B3
L'Epine F 32 A1
Le Poët F 32 A1
Le Poirè-sur-Vie F 22 B2
Le Pont CH 19 C5
Le Pont-de-Montvert F 30 A2
Le Porge F 28 B1
Le Porge-Océan F 28 B1
Le Portel F 4 B1
Le Pouldu F 14 B2
Le Pouliguen F 15 B3
Le Puy-en-Velay F 25 B3
Le Puy-Ste Réparade F 31 B4
Le Quesnoy F 5 B3
Le Rayol F 32 B2
Leré F 17 B4
Lerin E 34 B2
Lerm-et-Musset F 28 B2
Le Roeulx B 5 B4
Le Rouget F 24 C2
Lérouville F 12 C1
Le Rozier F 30 A2
Le Russey F 20 B1
Lés E 35 B4
Les Abrets F 26 B2
Les Aix-d'Angillon F 17 B4
Lesaka E 34 A2
Les Ancizes-Comps F 24 B2
Les Andelys F 10 B1
Les Arcs
Savoie F 27 B3
Var F 32 B2
Les-Aubiers F 16 C1
Les Baux-de-Provence F 31 B3
Les Bézards F 17 B4
Les Bois CH 20 B1
Les Bordes F 17 B4
Les Borges Blanques E 37 C1
Les Borges del Camp E 37 C2
Les Brunettes F 18 C2
Les Cabannes F 36 B2
L'Escala E 37 B4
Lescar F 35 A3
L'Escarène F 33 B3
Lescheraines F 26 B3
Lesconil F 14 B1
Les Contamines-Montjoie F 26 B3
Les Déserts F 26 B2
Les Deux-Alpes F 26 C3
Les Diablerets CH 27 A4
Lesdins F 10 B3
Les Echelles F 26 B2
Le Sel-de-Bretagne F 15 B4
Le Sentier CH 19 C5
Les Escaldes AND 36 B2
Les Essarts F 22 B2
Les Estables F 25 C4
Les Eyzies-de-Tayac F 29 B4
Les Gets F 26 A3
Les Grandes-Ventes F 9 A5
Les Haudères CH 27 A4
Les Herbiers F 22 B2
Les Hôpitaux-Neufs F 19 C5
Les Lucs-sur-Boulogne F 22 B2
Les Mages F 31 A3
Les Mazures F 11 B4
Les Mées F 32 A1
Lesmont F 11 C4
Les Mureaux F 10 C1
Lesneven F 14 A1
Les Omergues F 32 A1
Les Ormes-sur-Voulzie F 10 C3
Les Orres F 32 A2
Le Souquet F 28 C1
Lesparre-Médoc F 28 A2
l'Espérance F 11 B3
l'Esperou F 30 A2
Les Pieux F 8 A2
Lesponne F 35 A4
Les Ponts-de-Cé F 16 B1
Les Ponts-de-Martel CH 20 C1
Les Praz F 27 B3
L'Espunyola E 37 B2
Les Riceys F 18 B3
Les Roches F 25 B4
Les Rosaires F 15 A3
Les Rosiers F 16 B1
Les Rousses F 19 C5
Les Sables-d'Olonne F 22 B2
Lessay F 8 A2
Les Settons F 18 B3
Lessines B 5 B3
L'Estany E 37 C3
Les Ternes F 24 B2
Lesterps F 23 B4
Les Thilliers en-Vexin F 10 B1
Les Touches F 15 B4
Les Trois Moûtiers F 16 B2
Les Vans F 31 A3
Les Verrières CH 19 C5
Les Vignes F 30 A2
Le Teil F 31 A3
Le Teilleul F 8 B3
Le Temple-de-Bretagne F 15 B4
Le Theil F 9 B4
Le Thillot F 20 B1
Le Touquet-Paris-Plage F 4 B1
Le Touvet F 26 B2
Le Translay F 10 B1
Le Tréport F 10 A1
Leucate F 36 B4
Leuglay F 19 B3
Leuk CH 27 A4
Leukerbad CH 27 A4
Leusden NL 2 B2
Leutkirch D 21 B5
Leuven B 5 B4
Leuze-en-Hainaut B 5 B3
Le Val F 32 B2
Le Val-André F 15 A3
Le Val-d'Ajol F 19 B5
Levaré F 8 B3
Le Verdon-sur-Mer F 22 C2
Leverkusen D 6 A2
Le Vernet F 32 A2
Levet F 17 C4
Levie F 38 B2
Levier F 19 C5
Le Vigan F 30 B2
Lévignen F 10 B2
Le Vivier-sur-Mer F 8 B2
Levroux F 17 C3
Leysin CH 27 A4
Lézardrieux F 14 A2
Lézat-sur-Léze F 36 A2
Lezay F 23 B3
Lézignan-Corbières F 30 B1
Lezignan-la-Cèbe F 30 B2
Lézinnes F 18 B3
Lezoux F 25 B3
Lherm F 36 A2
Lhommaizé F 23 B4
L'Hospitalet F 36 B2
L'Hospitalet de l'Infant E 37 D1
L'Hospitalet de Llobregat E 37 C3
L'Hospitalet-du-Larzac F 30 B2
Lhuître F 11 C4
Liancourt F 10 B2
Liart F 11 B4
Libourne F 28 B2
Libramont B 12 B1
Lich D 7 B4
Lichères-près-Aigremont F 18 B2
Lichtenau D 7 A4
Lichtensteig CH 21 B4
Lichtenvoorde NL 3 C3
Lichtervelde B 4 A3
Licques F 4 B1
Liège B 6 B1
Lienen D 3 B4
Lier B 5 A4
Liernais F 18 B3
Liestal CH 20 B2
Lieurac F 36 B2
Lieurey F 9 A4
Liévin F 4 B2
Liffol-le-Grand F 12 C1
Liffré F 15 A4
Ligardes F 29 B3
Ligne F 15 B4
Lignières F 17 C4
Ligny-en-Barrois F 12 C1
Ligny-le-Châtel F 18 B2
Ligueil F 16 B2
L'Île-Bouchard F 16 B2
l'Île-Rousse F 38 A1
Lille
B 5 A4
F 4 B3
Lillebonne F 9 A4
Lillers F 4 B2
Limbourg B 6 B1
Limburg D 7 B4
Limésy F 9 A4
Limoges F 23 C5
Limogne-en-Quercy F 29 B4
Limoise F 18 C2
Limone Piemonte I 33 A3
Limons F 25 B3
Limours F 10 C2
Limoux F 36 A3
Linas de Broto E 35 B3
Lindau D 21 B4
Lindenberg im Allgäu D 21 B4
Lindern D 3 B4
Lindlar D 6 A3
Lingen D 3 B4
Linkenheim D 13 B4
Linnich D 6 B2
Linthal CH 21 C4
Linyola E 37 C1
Linz D 6 B3
Lion-sur-Mer F 9 A3
Liposthey F 28 B2
Lippborg D 7 A4
Lippoldsberg D 7 A5
Lippstadt D 7 A4
Liré F 15 B4
Lisieux F 9 A4
L'Isle CH 19 C5
L'Isle-Adam F 10 B2
L'Isle-de-Noé F 29 C3
L'Isle-en-Dodon F 35 A4
L'Isle-Jourdain
Gers F 29 C4
Vienne F 23 B4
L'Isle-sur-la-Sorgue F 31 B4
L'Isle-sur-le Doubs F 19 B5
L'Isle-sur-Serein F 18 B3
Lisle-sur-Tarn F 29 C4
Lisse NL 2 B1
Listrac-Médoc F 28 A2
Lit-et-Mixe F 28 B1
Livarot F 9 B4
Livernon F 29 B4
Livigno I 21 C5
Livorno Ferraris I 27 B5
Livron-sur-Drôme F 25 C4
Livry-Louvercy F 11 B4
Lixheim F 12 C3
Lizy-sur-Ourcq F 10 B3
Lladurs E 37 B2
Llafranc E 37 C4
Llagostera E 37 C3
Llançà E 36 B4
Llandudec F 14 A1
Llavorsi E 36 B2
Lles E 36 B2
Llessui E 36 B2
Llinars E 37 B2
Llivia E 36 B2
Lloret de Mar E 37 C3
Loano I 33 A4
Loarre E 35 B3
Locana I 27 B4
Lochau A 21 B4
Lochem NL 3 B3
Loches F 16 B2
Locmaria F 14 B2
Locmariaquer F 14 B3
Locminé F 14 B3
Locquirec F 14 A2
Locronan F 14 A1
Loctudy F 14 B1
Lodève F 30 B2
Lodosa E 34 B1
Löhlbach D 7 A4
Löhnberg D 7 B4
Lohne D 3 B5
Lohra D 7 B4
Lokeren B 5 A3
Lollar D 7 B4
Lombez F 36 A1
Lommel B 5 A5
Lommersum D 6 B2
Londerzeel B 5 A4
Londinières F 9 A5
Longchamp-sur-Aujon F 19 A3
Longchaumois F 26 A2
Longeau F 19 B4
Longecourt-en-Plaine F 19 B4
Longeville-les-St Avold F 12 B2
Longeville-sur-Mer F 22 B2
Longny-au-Perche F 9 B4
Longré F 23 B3
Longueau F 10 B2
Longué-Jumelles F 16 B1
Longuyon F 12 B1
Longvic F 19 B4
Longvilly B 12 A1
Longwy F 12 B1
Löningen D 3 B4
Lons-le-Saunier F 19 C4
Loone-Plage F 4 A2
Loon op Zand NL 5 A5
Lopigna F 38 A1
Loppersum NL 3 A3
Lor F 11 B4
Lorch D 13 A3
Lorgues F 32 B2
Lorient F 14 B2
Lorignac F 22 C3
Loriol-sur-Drôme F 25 C4
Lormes F 18 B2
Lörrach D 20 B2
Lorrez-le-Bocage F 17 A4
Lorris F 17 B4
Lorup D 3 B4
Los Arcos E 34 B1
Losheim
Nordrhein-Westfalen D 6 B2
Saarland D 12 B2
Losne F 19 B4
Lossburg D 13 C4
Losse F 28 B2
Losser NL 3 B4
Louargat F 14 A2
Loudéac F 15 A3
Loudun F 16 B2
Loué F 16 B1
Louhans F 19 C4
Loulay F 22 B3
Lourdes F 35 A3
Loures-Barousse F 35 A4
Lourmarin F 31 B4
Loury F 17 B4
Louverné F 16 A1
Louvie-Juzon F 35 A3
Louviers F 9 A5
Louvigné-du-Désert F 8 B2
Louvois F 11 B4
Lövenich D 6 A2
Lubersac F 23 C5
Luc F 25 C3
Luçay-le-Mâle F 17 B3
Lucciana F 38 A2
Lucé F 10 C1
Lucenay-les-Aix F 18 C2
Lucenay-l'Evéque F 18 B3
Luc-en-Diois F 26 C2
Luceni E 34 C2
Lucens CH 20 C1
Luceram F 33 B3
Luçon F 22 B2
Luc-sur-Mer F 9 A3
Lüdenscheid D 7 A3
Lüdinghausen D 6 A3
Ludweiler Warndt D 12 B2
Ludwigshafen D 13 B4
Luesia E 34 B2
Lugny F 19 C3
Lumbier E 34 B2
Lumbres F 4 B2
Lummen B 5 B5
Luna E 34 B3
Lunas F 30 B2
Lunel F 31 B3
Lünen D 7 A3
Lunéville F 12 C2
Lungern CH 20 C3
Lünne D 3 B4
Lunteren NL 2 B2
Lurcy-Lévis F 18 C1
Lure F 19 B5
Luri F 38 A2
Lury-sur-Arnon F 17 B4
Lusignan F 23 B4
Lusigny-sur-Barse F 18 A3
Lussac F 28 B2
Lussac-les-Châteaux F 23 B4
Lussac-les-Eglises F 23 B5
Lussan F 31 A3
Lustenau A 21 B4
Lutry CH 20 C1
Luxembourg L 12 B2
Luxeuil-les-Bains F 19 B5
Luxey F 28 B2
Luzarches F 10 B2
Luzech F 29 B4
Luzern CH 20 B3
Luz-St Sauveur F 35 B3
Luzy F 18 C2
Lyon F 25 B4
Lyons-la-Forêt F 10 B1
Lyss CH 20 B2

M

Maarheeze NL 6 A1
Maaseik B 6 A1
Maastricht NL 6 B1
Mably F 25 A4
Maçanet de Cabrenys E 36 B3
Macau F 28 A2
Machault F 11 B4
Machecoul F 22 B2
Macinaggio F 38 A2
Macon B 11 A4
Mâcon F 25 A4
Macugnaga I 27 B4
Made NL 5 A4
Maël-Carhaix F 14 A2
Magallon E 34 C2
Magaña E 34 C1
Magescq F 28 C1
Magnac-Bourg F 23 C5
Magnac-Laval F 23 B5
Magnieres F 12 C2
Magny-Cours F 18 C2
Magny-en-Vexin F 10 B1
Maia E 34 A2
Maîche F 20 B1
Maienfeld CH 21 B4
Maignelay Montigny F 10 B2
Maillezais F 22 B3
Mailly-le-Camp F 11 C4
Mailly-le-Château F 18 B2
Maintal D 7 B4
Maintenon F 10 C1
Mainvilliers F 10 C1
Mainz D 13 A4
Maison-Rouge F 10 C3
Maisse F 10 C2
Maizières-lès-Vic F 12 C2
Makkum NL 2 A2
Malaucène F 31 A4
Malaunay F 9 A5
Malborn D 12 B2
Malbuisson F 19 C5
Maldegem B 5 A3
Malemort F 29 A4
Malesherbes F 10 C2
Malestroit F 15 B3
Malgrat de Mar E 37 C3
Malicorne-sur-Sarthe F 16 B1
Malijai F 32 A2
Mallemort F 31 B4
Mallén E 34 C2
Malléon F 36 A2
Malmédy B 6 B2
Malpas E 35 B4
Malsch D 13 C4
Maltat F 18 C2
Mamer L 12 B2
Mamers F 9 B4
Mamirolle F 19 B5
Manciet F 28 C3
Mandelieu-la-Napoule F 32 B2
Manderfeld B 6 B2
Manderscheid D 6 B2
Mane
Alpes-de-Haute-Provence F 32 B1
Haute-Garonne F 35 A4
Mañeru E 34 B2
Mangiennes F 12 B1
Manlleu E 37 C3
Männedorf CH 21 B3
Mannheim D 13 B4
Manosque F 32 B1
Manresa E 37 C2
Mansle F 23 C4
Manso F 38 A1
Mantes-la-Jolie F 10 C1
Mantes-la-Ville F 10 C1
Manthelan F 16 B2
Manzat F 24 B2
Manziat F 25 A4
Marans F 22 B2
Marbach F 12 C2
Marboz F 26 A2
Marburg D 7 B4
Marcenat F 24 B2
Marchaux F 19 B5
Marche-en-Famenne B 5 B5
Marchenoir F 17 B3
Marcheprime F 28 B2
Marciac F 28 C3
Marcigny F 25 A4
Marcilla E 34 B2
Marcillac-la-Croisille F 24 B2
Marcillac-Vallon F 30 A1
Marcillat-en-Combraille F 24 A2
Marcille-sur-Seine F 11 C3
Marcilloles F 26 B2
Marcilly-le-Hayer F 11 C3
Marck F 4 B1
Marckolsheim F 20 A2
Marennes F 22 C2
Maresquel F 4 B1
Mareuil F 23 C4
Mareuil-en-Brie F 11 C3
Mareuil-sur-Arnon F 17 C4
Mareuil-sur-Lay F 22 B2
Mareuil-sur-Ourcq F 10 B3
Margaux F 28 A2
Margerie-Hancourt F 11 C4
Margès F 25 B5
Margone I 27 B4
Marguerittes F 31 B3
Margut F 11 B5
Mariembourg B 11 A4
Marienbaum D 6 A2
Marienheide D 7 A3
Marieux F 10 A2
Marignane F 31 B4
Marigny
Jura F 19 C4
Manche F 8 A2

Marigny-le-Châtel F 11 C3
Marine de Sisco F 38 A2
Marines F 10 B1
Maringues F 24 B3
Markdorf D 21 B4
Markelo NL 3 B3
Markgröningen D 13 C5
Markhausen D 3 B4
Marknesse NL 2 B2
Marl D 6 A3
Marle F 11 B3
Marlieux F 25 A5
Marmagne F 18 C3
Marmande F 28 B3
Marmoutier F 13 C3
Marnay F 19 B4
Marnheim D 13 B4
Marolles-les-Braults F 9 B4
Maromme F 9 A5
Marquion F 4 B3
Marquise F 4 B1
Marrum NL 2 A2
Marsac F 29 C5
Marsac-en-Livradois F 25 B3
Marsberg D 7 A4
Marseillan F 30 B2
Marseille = Marseilles F 31 B4
Marseille en Beauvaisis F 10 B1
Marseilles = Marseille F 31 B4
Mars-la-Tours F 12 B1
Marson F 11 C4
Martel F 29 B4
Martelange B 12 B1
Marthon F 23 C4
Martigné-Briand F 16 B1
Martigné-Ferchaud F 15 B4
Martigne-sur-Mayenne F 16 A1
Martigny CH 27 A4
Martigny-les-Bains F 19 A4
Martigues F 31 B4
Martinshöhe D 13 B3
Martinszell D 21 B5
Martorell E 37 C2
Martres Tolosane F 36 A1
Marvejols F 30 A2
Marville F 12 B1
Mas-Cabardès F 36 A3
Masera I 27 A5
Masevaux F 20 B1
Maslacq F 34 A3
Masone I 33 A4
Massat F 36 B2
Massay F 17 B3
Masseret F 24 B1
Masseube F 35 A4
Massiac F 24 B3
Massignac F 23 C4
Massmechelen B 6 B1
Matalebreras E 34 C1
Mataró E 37 C3
Matha F 23 C3
Mathay F 20 B1
Matignon F 15 A3
Matour F 25 A4
Maubert-Fontaine F 11 B4
Maubeuge F 5 B3
Maubourguet F 35 A4
Mauguio F 31 B3
Maulbronn D 13 C4
Maule F 10 C1
Mauléon F 22 B3
Mauléon-Barousse F 35 B4
Mauléon-Licharre F 34 A3
Maulévrier F 22 A3
Maure-de-Bretagne F 15 B4
Maureilhan F 30 B2
Mauriac F 24 B2
Mauron F 15 A3
Maurs F 24 C2
Maury F 36 B3
Maussane-les-Alpilles F 31 B3
Mauvezin F 29 C3
Mauzé-sur-le-Mignon F 22 B3
Maxent F 15 B3
Maxey-sur-Vaise F 12 C1
Mayen D 6 B3
Mayenne F 8 B3
Mayet F 16 B2
Mayres F 25 C4
Mazamet F 30 B1
Mazan F 31 A4
Mazères F 36 A2
Mazères-sur-Salat F 35 A4
Mazières-en-Gâtine F 23 B3
Méan B 5 B5
Meaulne F 17 C4
Meaux F 10 C2
Mechelen B 5 A4
Mechernich D 6 B2
Meckenbeuren D 21 B4
Meckenheim
Rheinland-Pfalz D 6 B3
Rheinland-Pfalz D 13 B4
Meckesheim D 13 B4
Medebach D 7 A4
Medemblik NL 2 B2
Meerle B 5 A4
Meersburg D 21 B4
Meeuwen B 5 A5
Megève F 26 B3
Mehun-sur-Yèvre F 17 B4
Meijel NL 6 A1
Meilen CH 21 B3
Meilhan F 28 C2
Meina I 27 B5
Meinerzhagen D 7 A3
Meiringen CH 20 C3
Meisenheim D 13 B3
Meix-devant-Virton B 12 B1
Melisey F 19 B5
Melle
B 5 A3
D 3 B5
F 23 B3
Mels CH 21 B4
Melun F 10 C2
Memer F 29 B4
Memmingen D 21 B5
Menat F 24 A2
Mendavia E 34 B1
Mendaza E 34 B1
Mende F 30 A2
Menden D 7 A3
Mendig D 6 B3
Ménéac F 15 A3
Menen B 4 B3
Menetou-Salon F 17 B4
Mengen D 21 A4
Menou F 18 B2
Mens F 26 C2
Menslage D 3 B4
Menton F 33 B3
Méobecq F 23 B5
Méounes-les-Montrieux F 32 B1
Meppel NL 2 B3
Meppen D 3 B4
Mer F 17 B3
Merchtem B 5 B4
Merdrignac F 15 A3
Meréville F 10 C2
Merfeld D 6 A3
Méribel F 26 B3
Méribel Motraret F 26 B3
Mérignac F 28 B2
Merksplas B 5 A4
Merlimont Plage F 4 B1
Mersch L 12 B2
Mers-les-Bains F 10 A1
Méru F 10 B2
Mervans F 19 C4
Merville F 4 B2
Méry-sur-Seine F 11 C3
Merzen D 3 B4
Merzig D 12 B2
Meschede D 7 A4
Meschers-sur-Gironde F 22 C3
Meslay-du-Maine F 16 B1
Messac F 15 B4
Messancy B 12 B1
Messei F 8 B3
Messingen D 3 B4
Messkirch D 21 B4
Messtetten D 21 A3
Mesvres F 18 C3
Metelen D 3 B4
Metslawier NL 2 A3
Mettendorf D 12 B2
Mettet B 5 B4
Mettingen D 3 B4
Mettlach D 12 B2
Mettlen CH 20 C2
Mettmann D 6 A2
Metz F 12 B2
Metzervisse F 12 B2
Meulan F 10 B1
Meung-sur-Loire F 17 B3
Meuzac F 23 C5
Meximieux F 26 B2
Meyerhöfen D 3 B5
Meylan F 26 B2
Meymac F 24 B2
Meyrargues F 32 B1
Meyrueis F 30 A2
Meyssac F 29 A4
Meysse F 25 C4
Meyzieu F 25 B4
Mèze F 30 B2
Mézériat F 25 A5
Mézidon-Canon F 9 A3
Mézières-en-Brenne F 23 B5
Mézières-sur-Issoire F 23 B4
Mézilhac F 25 C4
Mézilles F 18 B2
Mézin F 28 B3
Mézos F 28 B1
Michelstadt D 13 B5
Middelburg NL 5 A3
Middelharnis NL 5 A4
Middelkerke B 4 A2
Middelstum NL 3 A3
Midwolda NL 3 A4
Miélan F 35 A4
Mieres E 37 B3
Miesau D 13 B3
Migennes F 18 B2
Migné F 23 B5
Milagro E 34 B2
Millançay F 17 B3
Millas F 36 B3
Millau F 30 A2
Millesimo I 33 A4
Millevaches F 24 B2
Milly-la-Forêt F 10 C2
Mimizan F 28 B1
Mimizan-Plage F 28 B1
Minsen D 3 A4
Mios F 28 B2
Mirabel-aux-Baronnies F 31 A4
Miradoux F 29 B3
Miramas F 31 B3
Mirambeau F 22 C3
Miramont-de-Guyenne F 29 B3
Miranda de Arga E 34 B2
Mirande F 29 C3
Miré F 16 B1
Mirebeau F 16 C2
Mirebeau-sur-Bèze F 19 B4
Mirecourt F 19 A5
Mirepoix F 36 A2
Miribel F 25 B4
Missillac F 15 B3
Mittelberg A 21 B5
Mittersheim F 12 C2
Mitton F 28 B2
Modane F 26 B3
Moëlan-sur-Mer F 14 B2
Moerbeke B 5 A3
Moers D 6 A2
Möhlin CH 20 B2
Moià E 37 C3
Moirans F 26 B2
Moirans-en-Montagne F 26 A2
Moisdon-la-Rivière F 15 B4
Moissac F 29 B4
Mol B 5 A5
Molare I 33 A4
Molaretto I 27 B4
Molas F 35 A4
Molbergen D 3 B4
Molières F 29 B4
Molinet F 18 C2
Molins de Rei E 37 C3
Mollerussa E 37 C1
Mollet de Perelada E 36 B3
Molló E 36 B3
Molompize F 24 B3
Moloy F 19 B3
Molsheim F 13 C3
Mombris D 13 A5
Momo I 27 B5
Monbahus F 29 B3
Monbazillac F 29 B3
Moncalieri I 27 B4
Moncalvo I 27 B5
Moncel-sur-Seille F 12 C2
Mönchengladbach = Munchen-Gladbach D 6 A2
Monclar-de-Quercy F 29 C4
Moncontour F 15 A3
Moncoutant F 22 B3
Mondorf-les-Bains L 12 B2
Mondoubleau F 16 B2
Mondovì I 33 A3
Mondragon F 31 A3
Monein F 35 A3
Mónesi I 33 A3
Monesiglio I 33 A4
Monestier-de-Clermont F 26 C2
Monestiés F 30 A1
Monéteau F 18 B2
Monflanquin F 29 B3
Monflorite E 35 B3
Monforte d'Alba I 33 A3
Monistrol-d'Allier F 25 C3
Monistrol de Montserrat E 37 C2
Monistrol-sur-Loire F 25 B4
Monnaie F 16 B2
Monnerville F 10 C2
Monnickendam NL 2 B2
Monpazier F 29 B3
Monreal
D 6 B3
E 34 B2
Mons B 5 B3
Monschau D 6 B2
Monségur F 28 B3
Monster NL 2 B1
Montabaur D 7 B3
Montafia I 27 C5
Montagnac F 30 B2
Montaigu F 22 B2
Montaigu-de-Quercy F 29 B4
Montaiguët-en-Forez F 25 A3
Montaigut F 24 A2
Montaigut-sur-Save F 29 C4
Montainville F 10 C1
Montalieu-Vercieu F 26 B2
Montalivet-les-Bains F 22 C2
Montana-Vermala CH 27 A4
Montans F 29 C4
Montargis F 17 B4
Montastruc-la-Conseillère F 29 C4
Montauban F 29 B4
Montauban-de-Bretagne F 15 A3
Montbard F 18 B3
Montbarrey F 19 B4
Montbazens F 30 A1
Montbazon F 16 B2
Montbéliard F 20 B1
Montbenoit F 19 C5
Montbeugny F 18 C2
Montblanc E 37 C2
Montbozon F 19 B5
Montbrison F 25 B4
Montbron F 23 C4
Montbrun-les-Bains F 31 A4
Montceau-les-Mines F 18 C3
Montcenis F 18 C3
Montchanin F 18 C3
Montcornet F 11 B4
Montcuq F 29 B4
Montdardier F 30 B2
Mont-de-Marsan F 28 C2
Montdidier F 10 B2
Montebourg F 8 A2
Monte-Carlo MC 33 B3
Montech F 29 C4
Montechiaro d'Asti I 27 B5
Montel-de-Gelat F 24 B2
Montelier F 25 C5
Montélimar F 31 A3
Montella E 36 B2
Montemagno I 27 C5
Montendre F 28 A2
Monteneuf F 15 B3
Montereau-Faut-Yonne F 10 C2
Monterosso Grana I 33 A3
Montesquieu-Volvestre F 36 A2
Montesquiou F 29 C3
Montestruc-sur-Gers F 29 C3
Montfaucon F 15 B4
Montfaucon-d'Argonne F 11 B5
Montfaucon-en-Velay F 25 B4
Montferrat
Isère F 26 B2
Var F 32 B2
Montfort-en-Chalosse F 28 C2
Montfort-l'Amaury F 10 C1
Montfort-le-Gesnois F 16 A2
Montfort-sur-Meu F 15 A4
Montfort-sur-Risle F 9 A4
Montgai E 37 C1
Montgaillard F 35 A4
Montgenèvre F 26 C3
Montgiscard F 36 A2
Montguyon F 28 A2
Monthermé F 11 B4
Monthey CH 27 A3
Monthois F 11 B4
Monthureux-sur-Saône F 19 A4
Montier-en-Der F 11 C4
Montiglio I 27 B5
Montignac F 29 A4
Montigny-le-Roi F 19 B4
Montigny-lès-Metz F 12 B2
Montigny-sur-Aube F 19 B3
Montilly F 18 C2
Montivilliers F 9 A4
Montjaux F 30 A1
Montjean-sur-Loire F 16 B1
Montlhéry F 10 C2
Montlieu-la-Garde F 28 A2
Mont-Louis F 36 B3
Montlouis-sur-Loire F 16 B2
Montluçon F 24 A2
Montluel F 25 B5
Montmarault F 24 A2
Montmartin-sur-Mer F 8 B2
Montmédy F 12 B1
Montmélian F 26 B3
Montmeyan F 32 B2
Montmeyran F 25 C4
Montmirail
Marne F 11 C3
Sarthe F 16 A2
Montmiral F 26 B2
Montmirat F 31 B3
Montmirey-le-Château F 19 B4
Montmoreau-St Cybard F 23 C4
Montmorency F 10 C2
Montmorillon F 23 B4
Montmort-Lucy F 11 C3
Montoir-de-Bretagne F 15 B3
Montoire-sur-le-Loir F 16 B2
Montolieu F 36 A3
Montpellier F 31 B2
Montpezat-de-Quercy F 29 B4
Montpezat-sous-Bouzon F 25 C4
Montpon-Ménestérol F 28 A3
Montpont-en-Bresse F 19 C4
Montréal
Aude F 36 A3
Gers F 28 C3
Montredon-Labessonnié F 30 B1
Montréjeau F 35 A4
Montrésor F 17 B3
Montret F 19 C4
Montreuil
Pas de Calais F 4 B1
Seine St Denis F 10 C2
Montreuil-aux-Lions F 10 B3
Montreuil-Bellay F 16 B1
Montreux CH 20 C1
Montrevault F 15 B4
Montrevel-en-Bresse F 26 A2
Montrichard F 17 B3
Montricoux F 29 B4
Mont-roig del Camp E 37 C1
Montrond-les-Bains F 25 B4
Montsalvy F 24 C2
Montsauche-les-Settons F 18 B3
Montseny E 37 C3
Montsoreau F 16 B2
Mont-sous-Vaudrey F 19 C4
Monts-sur-Guesnes F 16 C2
Mont-St Aignan F 9 A5
Mont-St Vincent F 18 C3
Montsûrs F 16 A1
Monzón E 35 C4
Moordorf D 3 A4
Moorslede B 4 B3
Moos D 21 B3
Morbach D 12 B3
Morbier F 19 C5
Morcenx F 28 B2
Mordelles F 15 A4
Moréac F 14 B3
Morée F 17 B3
Morestel F 26 B2
Moret-sur-Loing F 10 C2
Moretta I 27 C4
Moreuil F 10 B2
Morez F 19 C5
Mörfelden D 13 B4
Morgat F 14 A1
Morges CH 19 C5
Morgex I 27 B4
Morhange F 12 C2
Morhet B 12 B1
Morialmé B 5 B4
Moriani Plage F 38 A2
Morlaàs F 35 A3
Morlaix F 14 A2
Morley F 11 C5
Mormant F 10 C2
Mornant F 25 B4
Mornay-Berry F 17 B4
Morozzo I 33 A3
Morsbach D 7 B3
Mörsch D 13 C4
Mortagne-au-Perche F 9 B4
Mortagne-sur-Gironde F 22 C3
Mortagne-sur-Sèvre F 22 B3
Mortain F 8 B3
Morteau F 19 B5
Mortemart F 23 B4
Mortrée F 9 B4
Mortsel B 5 A4
Morzine F 26 A3
Mosbach D 13 B5
Mössingen D 13 C5
Mostuéjouls F 30 A2
Mouchard F 19 C4
Moudon CH 20 C1
Mougins F 32 B2
Mouilleron-en-Pareds F 22 B3
Mouliherne F 16 B2
Moulinet F 33 B3
Moulins F 18 C2
Moulins-Engilbert F 18 C2
Moulins-la-Marche F 9 B4
Moulismes F 23 B4
Moult F 9 A3
Mourenx F 35 A3
Mouriés F 31 B3
Mourmelon-le-Grand F 11 B4
Mouscron B 4 B3
Moussac F 31 B3
Moussey F 12 C2
Mousteru F 14 A2
Moustey F 28 B2
Moustiers-Ste Marie F 32 B2
Mouthe F 19 C5
Mouthier-Haute-Pierre F 19 B5
Mouthoumet F 36 B3
Moutier CH 20 B2
Moûtiers F 26 B3
Moutiers-les-Mauxfaits F 22 B2
Mouy F 10 B2
Mouzon F 11 B5
Moyenmoutier F 12 C2
Moyenvic F 12 C2
Much D 6 B3
Mudau D 13 B5
Mudersbach D 7 B3
Mugron F 28 C2
Mühlacker D 13 C4
Muhleberg CH 20 C2
Mühleim D 21 A3
Mulegns CH 21 C4
Mülheim D 6 A2
Mulhouse F 20 B2
Müllheim D 20 B2
Munchen-Gladbach = Mönchengladbach D 6 A2
Münchhausen D 7 B4
Munderkingen D 21 A4
Münsingen CH 20 C2
Münster
CH 20 C3
Hessen D 13 B4
Nordrhein-Westfalen D 3 C4
Munster F 20 A2
Muotathal CH 21 C3
Murat F 24 B2
Murato F 38 A2
Murat-sur-Vèbre F 30 B1
Murazzano I 33 A4
Murchante E 34 B2
Mur-de-Barrez F 24 C2
Mur-de-Bretagne F 14 A2
Mur-de-Sologne F 17 B3
Muret F 36 A2
Murg CH 21 B4
Muri CH 20 B3
Murillo el Fruto E 34 B2
Muro F 38 A1
Murol F 24 B2
Muron F 22 B3
Mürren CH 20 C2
Murten CH 20 C2
Murviel-lès-Béziers F 30 B2
Musculdy F 34 A3
Musselkanaal NL 3 B4
Mussidan F 29 A3
Musson B 12 B1
Mussy-sur-Seine F 18 B3
Muzillac F 15 B3
Myennes F 18 B1

N

Naaldwijk NL 5 A4
Näfels CH 21 B4
Nagele NL 2 B2
Nagold D 13 C4
Nagore E 34 B2
Nailloux F 36 A2
Naintré F 23 B4
Najac F 29 B4
Nalliers F 22 B2
Nalzen F 36 B2
Namur B 5 B4
Nançay F 17 B4
Nancy F 12 C2
Nangis F 10 C3
Nant F 30 A2
Nanterre F 10 C2
Nantes F 15 B4
Nanteuil-le-Haudouin F 10 B2
Nantiat F 23 B5
Nantua F 26 A2
Narbonne F 30 B1
Narbonne-Plage F 30 B2
Narzole I 33 A3
Nasbinals F 24 C3
Nassau D 7 B3
Nastätten D 7 B3
Naters CH 27 A5
Naucelle F 30 A1
Naval E 35 B4
Navarclés E 37 C2
Navarrenx F 34 A3
Navás E 37 C2
Navascués E 34 B2
Navés E 37 C2
Navilly F 19 C4
Nay F 35 A3
Neckargemünd D 13 B4
Nederweert NL 6 A1
Neede NL 3 B3
Neermoor D 3 A4
Neeroeteren B 6 A1
Neerpelt B 5 A5
Nègrepelisse F 29 B4
Neheim D 7 A3
Néive I 27 C5
Nemours F 17 A4
Nenzing A 21 B4
Nérac F 29 B3
Néré F 23 C3
Néris-les Bains F 24 A2
Néronde F 25 B4
Nérondes F 17 C4
Nes NL 2 A2
Nesle F 10 B2
Nesslau CH 21 B4
Nessmersiel D 3 A4
Netphen D 7 B4
Netstal CH 21 B4
Nettancourt F 11 C4
Nettetal D 6 A2
Neubeckum D 7 A4
Neuchâtel CH 20 C1
Neudorf D 13 B4
Neuenbürg D 13 C4
Neuenburg D 3 A4
Neuenhaus D 3 B3
Neuenkirchen
Niedersachsen D 3 B5
Nordrhein-Westfalen D 3 B4
Nordrhein-Westfalen D 7 B3
Neuenrade D 7 A3
Neuerburg D 12 A2
Neuf-Brisach F 20 A2
Neufchâteau
B 12 B1
F 12 C1
Neufchâtel-en-Bray F 10 B1
Neufchâtel-sur-Aisne F 11 B4
Neuflize F 11 B4
Neuharlingersiel D 3 A4
Neuhaus D 7 A5
Neuhausen CH 21 B3
Neuhausen ob Eck D 21 B3
Neuillé-Pont-Pierre F 16 B2
Neuilly-en-Thelle F 10 B2

Neuilly-le-Réal F 18 C2
Neuilly-l'Évêque F 19 B4
Neuilly-St Front F 10 B3
Neu-Isenburg D 13 A4
Neukirchen D 7 B5
Neulise F 25 B4
Neumagen D 12 B2
Neung-sur-Beuvron F 17 B3
Neunkirch
Luzern CH 20 B3
Schaffhausen CH 21 B3
Neunkirchen
Nordrhein-Westfalen D 6 B3
Saarland D 12 B3
Neuravensburg D 21 B4
Neureut D 13 B4
Neuss D 6 A2
Neussargues-Moissac F 24 B2
Neustadt
Hessen D 7 B5
Rheinland-Pfalz D 13 B4
Neuves-Maisons F 12 C2
Neuvic
Corrèze F 24 B2
Dordogne F 29 A3
Neuville-aux-Bois F 17 A4
Neuville-de-Poitou F 23 B4
Neuville-les-Dames F 25 A5
Neuville-sur-Saône F 25 B4
Neuvy-le-Roi F 16 B2
Neuvy-Santour F 18 A2
Neuvy-St Sépulchre F 17 C3
Neuvy-sur-Barangeon F 17 B4
Neuwied D 6 B3
Névache F 26 B3
Nevers F 18 C2
Névez F 14 B2
Nexon F 23 C5
Nice F 33 B3
Nidda D 7 B5
Niederbipp CH 20 B2
Niederbronn-les-Bains F 13 C3
Niederfischbach D 7 B3
Niederkrüchten D 6 A2
Nieder-Olm D 13 B4
Niederurnen CH 21 B4
Nieheim D 7 A5
Nierstein D 13 B4
Nieul-le-Dolent F 22 B2
Nieul-sur-Mer F 22 B2
Nieuw-Amsterdam NL 3 B3
Nieuw-Buinen NL 3 B3
Nieuwegein NL 2 B2
Nieuwe Niedorp NL 2 B1
Nieuwe-Pekela NL 3 A3
Nieuwerkerken B 5 B5
Nieuwe-schans NL 3 A4
Nieuwolda NL 3 A3
Nieuwpoort B 4 A2
Nieuw-Weerdinge NL 3 B3
Nijkerk NL 2 B2
Nijlen B 5 A4
Nijmegen NL 6 A1
Nijverdal NL 3 B3
Nîmes F 31 B3
Ninove B 5 B4
Niort F 22 B3
Nissan-lez-Ensérune F 30 B2
Nitry F 18 B2
Nivelles B 5 B4
Nizza Monferrato I 27 C5
Noailles F 10 B2
Noain E 34 B2
Nods F 19 B5
Noé F 36 A2
Noeux-les-Mines F 4 B2
Nogaro F 28 C2
Nogent F 19 A4
Nogent l'Artaud F 10 C3
Nogent-le-Roi F 10 C1
Nogent-le-Rotrou F 9 B4
Nogent-sur-Seine F 11 C3
Nogent-sur-Vernisson F 17 B4
Nohfelden D 12 B3
Nohn D 6 B2
Noirétable F 25 B3
Noirmoutier-en-l'Île F 22 A1
Nolay F 18 C3
Noli I 33 A4
Nomeny F 12 C2
Nomexy F 12 C2
Nonancourt F 9 B5
Nonant-le-Pin F 9 B4
None I 27 C4
Nontron F 23 C4
Nonza F 38 A2
Noordhorn NL 3 A3
Noordwijk NL 2 B1
Noordwijkerhout NL 2 B1
Noordwolde NL 2 B3
Nordausques F 4 B2
Norddeich D 3 A4
Norden D 3 A4
Norderney D 3 A4
Nordhorn D 3 B4
Nordwalde D 3 B4
Norg NL 3 A3
Norrent-Fontes F 4 B2
Nort-sur-Erdre F 15 B4
Nörvenich D 6 B2
Nottuln D 3 C4
Nouan-le-Fuzelier F 17 B4
Nouans-les-Fontaines F 17 B3
Nougaroulet F 29 C3
Nouvion F 4 B1
Nouzonville F 11 B4
Novalaise F 26 B2
Novales E 35 B3
Noves F 31 B3
Novés de Segre E 37 B2
Noville B 12 A1
Novion-Porcien F 11 B4
Novy-Chevrières F 11 B4
Noyalo F 15 B3
Noyal-Pontivy F 14 A3
Noyant F 16 B2
Noyelles-sur-Mer F 4 B1
Noyen-sur-Sarthe F 16 B1
Noyers F 18 B2
Noyers-sur-Cher F 17 B3
Noyers-sur-Jabron F 32 A1
Noyon F 10 B2
Nozay F 15 B4
Nuaillé F 16 B1
Nuaillé-d'Aunis F 22 B3
Nuars F 18 B2
Nuéno E 35 B3
Nuits F 18 B3
Nuits-St Georges F 19 B3
Numansdorp NL 5 A4
Nümbrecht D 7 B3
Nunspeet NL 2 B2
Nus I 27 B4
Nusplingen D 21 A3
Nyon CH 26 A3
Nyons F 31 A4

O

Oberbruck F 20 B1
Oberdiessbach CH 20 C2
Oberdorf CH 20 B2
Oberhausen D 6 A2
Oberkirch D 13 C4
Oberkirchen D 7 A4
Ober-Morlen D 7 B4
Obernai F 13 C3
Obernburg D 13 B5
Oberndorf D 13 C4
Oberriet CH 21 B4
Oberstaufen D 21 B5
Oberstdorf D 21 B5
Oberursel D 7 B4
Oberwesel D 13 A3
Oberwinter D 6 B3
Objat F 29 A4
Obrigheim D 13 B5
Occimiano I 27 B5
Ochagavía E 34 B2
Ochsenhausen D 21 A4
Ochtendung D 6 B3
Ochtrup D 3 B4
Octeville F 8 A2
Oeding D 3 C3
Oegstgeest NL 2 B1
Oelde D 7 A4
Oer-Erkenschwick D 6 A3
Oeventrop D 7 A4
Offenbach D 7 B4
Offenburg D 13 C3
Offranville F 9 A5
Ofterschwang D 21 B5
Ohey B 5 B5
Oiartzun E 34 A2
Oiselay-et-Grachoux F 19 B4
Oisemont F 10 B1
Oisterwijk NL 5 A5
Olagüe E 34 B2
Olargues F 30 B1
Olazagutia E 34 B1
Oldeberkoop NL 2 B3
Oldeboorn NL 2 A2
Oldenbrok D 3 A5
Oldenburg D 3 A5
Oldenzaal NL 3 B3
Oldersum D 3 A4
Olen B 5 A4
Olesa de Montserrat E 37 C2
Oletta F 38 A2
Olette F 36 B3
Olfen D 6 A3
Oliana E 37 B2
Olite E 34 B2
Olivet F 17 B3
Olivone CH 21 C3
Olliergues F 25 B3
Olmeto F 38 B1
Olonne-sur-Mer F 22 B2
Olonzac F 30 B1
Oloron-Ste Marie F 35 A3
Olost E 37 C3
Olot E 37 B3
Olpe D 7 A3
Olsberg D 7 A4
Olsene B 5 B3
Olten CH 20 B2
Olvega E 34 C2
Omegna I 27 B5
Ommen NL 3 B3
On B 5 B5
Onesse-et-Laharie F 28 B1
Onhaye B 5 B4
Onzain F 17 B3
Oostburg NL 5 A3
Oostende B 4 A2
Oosterend NL 2 A2
Oosterhout NL 5 A4
Oosterwolde NL 3 B3
Oosterzele B 5 B3
Oosthuizen NL 2 B2
Oostkamp B 4 A3
Oostmalle B 5 A4
Oost-Vlieland NL 2 A2
Oostvoorne NL 5 A4
Ootmarsum NL 3 B3
Opeinde NL 2 A3
Oper Thalkirchdorf D 21 B5
Opglabbeerk B 6 A1
Opmeer NL 2 B1
Oppenau D 13 C4
Oppenheim D 13 B4
Oradour-sur-Glane F 23 C5
Oradour-sur-Vayres F 23 C4
Oraison F 32 B1
Orange F 31 A3
Orbais F 11 C3
Orbassano I 27 B4
Orbe CH 19 C5
Orbec F 9 A4
Orbigny F 17 B3
Orchamps-Vennes F 19 B5
Orches F 16 C2
Orchies F 4 B3
Orcières F 26 C3
Ordino AND 36 B2
Ordizia E 34 A1
Organyà E 37 B2
Orgelet F 19 C4
Orgères-en-Beauce F 17 A3
Orgibet F 35 B4
Orgnac-l'Aven F 31 A3
Orgon F 31 B4
Origny-Ste Benoite F 11 B3
Orléans F 17 B3
Ormea I 33 A3
Ornans F 19 B5
Oron-la-Ville CH 20 C1
Oropa I 27 B4
Orreaga-Roncesvalles E 34 A2
Orsay F 10 C2
Orscholz D 12 B2
Orsennes F 17 C3
Orsières CH 27 A4
Orthez F 28 C2
Ortilla E 35 B3
Orvault F 15 B4
Osann-Monzel D 12 B2
Osnabrück D 3 B5
Ospedaletti I 33 B3
Oss NL 6 A1
Ossun F 35 A3
Ostbevern D 3 B4
Ostercappeln D 3 B5
Ostheim F 20 A2
Osthofen D 13 B4
Ostiz E 34 B2
Ostrach D 21 B4
Ostrhauderfehn D 3 A4
Oteiza E 34 B2
Ottenhöfen D 13 C4
Otterbach D 13 B3
Otterberg D 13 B3
Ottersweier D 13 C4
Ottignies B 5 B4
Ottmarsheim F 20 B2
Ottobeuren D 21 B5
Ottweiler D 12 B3
Ouanne F 18 B2
Ouarville F 10 C1
Oucques F 17 B3
Oud-Beijerland NL 5 A4
Ouddorp NL 5 A3
Oudemirdum NL 2 B2
Oudenaarde B 5 B3
Oudenbosch NL 5 A4
Oudenburg B 4 A3
Oude-Pekela NL 3 A4
Oude-Tonge NL 5 A4
Oudewater NL 2 B1
Oud Gastel NL 5 A4
Oudon F 15 B4
Ouistreham F 9 A3
Oulchy-le-Château F 11 B3
Oullins F 25 B4
Oulmes F 22 B3
Oulx I 27 B3
Ouroux-en-Morvan F 18 B2
Oust F 36 B2
Outreau F 4 B1
Ouzouer-le-Marché F 17 B3
Ouzouer-sur-Loire F 17 B4
Ovada I 33 A4
Overath D 6 B3
Overdinkel NL 3 B4
Overijse B 5 B4
Overpelt B 5 A5
Oviglio I 27 C5
Oyonnax F 26 A2
Ozzano Monferrato I 27 B5

P

Paal B 5 A5
Pacy-sur-Eure F 9 A5
Paderborn D 7 A4
Paesana I 27 C4
Pagny-sur-Moselle F 12 C2
Pailhès F 36 A2
Paimboeuf F 15 B3
Paimpol F 14 A2
Paimpont F 15 A3
Palafrugell E 37 C4
Palaiseau F 10 C2
Palamós E 37 C4
Palavas-les-Flots F 31 B2
Paliseul B 11 B5
Pallanza I 27 B5
Pallerols E 36 B2
Palluau F 22 B2
Palmerola E 37 B3
Pals E 37 C4
Pamiers F 36 A2
Pamparato I 33 A3
Pamplona E 34 B2
Pancalieri I 27 C4
Pancey F 11 C5
Panissières F 25 B4
Pannes F 17 A4
Panningen NL 6 A1
Panticosa E 35 B3
Papenburg D 3 A4
Paramé F 8 B2
Paray-le-Monial F 18 C3
Parcey F 19 B4
Parennes F 16 A1
Parentis-en-Born F 28 B1
Pargny-sur-Saulx F 11 C4
Pari-Gagné F 25 A4
Parigné-l'Évêque F 16 B2
Paris F 10 C2
Parisot F 29 B4
Parlavà E 37 B4
Parthenay F 16 C1
Passais F 8 B3
Passy F 26 B3
Patay F 17 A3
Paterswolde NL 3 A3
Patrimonio F 38 A2
Pau F 35 A3
Pauillac F 28 A2
Paulhaguet F 25 B3
Paulhan F 30 B2
Pavilly F 9 A4
Payerne CH 20 C1
Payrac F 29 B4
Paziols F 36 B3
Peckelsheim D 7 A5
Pedrola E 34 C2
Peer B 5 A5
Pegli I 33 A4
Peisey-Nancroix F 26 B3
Pélissanne F 31 B4
Pellegrue F 28 B3
Pellevoisin F 17 C3
Pelussin F 25 B4
Pénestin F 15 B3
Penmarch F 14 B1
Penne-d'Agenais F 29 B3
Pepinster B 6 B1
Peralta E 34 B2
Peralta de la Sal E 35 C4
Percy F 8 B2
Perdiguera E 35 C3
Perelada E 37 B4
Périers F 8 A2
Périgueux F 29 A3
Pernes-les-Fontaines F 31 A4
Pérols F 31 B2
Péronne F 10 B2
Péronnes B 5 B4
Perosa Argentina I 27 C4
Perpignan F 36 B3
Perrecy-les-Forges F 18 C3
Perrero I 27 C4
Perrignier F 26 A3
Perros-Guirec F 14 A2
Persan F 10 B2
Pertuis F 31 B4
Péruwelz B 5 B3
Perwez B 5 B4
Pesmes F 19 B4
Pessac F 28 B2
Pétange L 12 B1
Petreto-Bicchisano F 38 B1
Peveragno I 33 A3
Pewsum D 3 A4
Peyrat-le-Château F 24 B1
Peyrehorade F 28 C1
Peyriac-Minervois F 36 A3
Peyrins F 25 B5
Peyrissac F 24 B1
Peyrolles-en-Provence F 32 B1
Peyruis F 32 A1
Pézarches F 10 C2
Pézenas F 30 B2
Pezuls F 29 B3
Pfaffenhoffen F 13 C3
Pfäffikon CH 21 B3
Pfetterhouse F 20 B2
Pforzheim D 13 C4
Pfullendorf D 21 B4
Pfungstadt D 13 B4
Pfyn CH 21 B3
Phalsbourg F 12 C3
Philippeville B 5 B4
Piana F 38 A1
Piana Crixia I 33 A4
Picquigny F 10 B2
Piedicavallo I 27 B4
Piedicroce F 38 A2
Piedimulera I 27 A5
Piera E 37 C2
Pierre-Buffière F 23 C5
Pierrecourt F 19 B4
Pierre-de-Bresse F 19 C4
Pierrefeu-du-Var F 32 B2
Pierrefitte-Nestalas F 35 B3
Pierrefitte-sur-Aire F 12 C1
Pierrefonds F 10 B2
Pierrefontaine-les-Varans F 19 B5
Pierrefort F 24 C2
Pierrelatte F 31 A3
Pierrepont
Aisne F 11 B3
Meurthe-et-Moselle F 12 B1
Pietra Ligure I 33 A4
Pieve di Teco I 33 A3
Pignan F 30 B2
Pijnacker NL 2 B1
Pinas F 35 A4
Pineda de Mar E 37 C3
Pinerolo I 27 C4
Piney F 11 C4
Pino F 38 A2
Pinols F 25 B3
Pionsat F 24 A2
Pipriac F 15 B4
Piré-sur-Seiche F 15 A4
Piriac-sur-Mer F 15 B3
Pirmasens D 13 B3
Pisany F 22 C3
Pissos F 28 B2
Pithiviers F 17 A4
Plabennec F 14 A1
Plaffeien CH 20 C2
Plaisance
Gers F 28 C3
Haute-Garonne F 29 C4
Tarn F 30 B1
Plan E 35 B4
Planchez F 18 B3
Plancoët F 15 A3
Plancy-l'Abbaye F 11 C3
Plan-de-Baix F 26 C2
Plan-d'Orgon F 31 B3
Platja d'Aro E 37 C4
Pléaux F 24 B2
Pleine-Fougères F 8 B2
Plélan-le-Grand F 15 B3
Plémet F 15 A3
Pléneuf-Val-André F 15 A3
Plérin F 15 A3
Plessé F 15 B4
Plestin-les-Grèves F 14 A2
Plettenberg D 7 A3
Pleubian F 14 A2
Pleumartin F 23 B4
Pleumeur-Bodou F 14 A2
Pleurs F 11 C3
Pleyben F 14 A2
Pleyber-Christ F 14 A2
Ploemeur F 14 B2
Ploërmel F 15 B3
Ploeuc-sur-Lie F 15 A3
Plogastel St Germain F 14 B1
Plogoff F 14 A1
Plombières-les-Bains F 19 B5
Plonéour-Lanvern F 14 B1
Plouagat F 14 A2
Plouaret F 14 A2
Plouarzel F 14 A1
Plouay F 14 B2
Ploubalay F 15 A3
Ploubazlanec F 14 A2
Ploudalmézeau F 14 A1
Ploudiry F 14 A1
Plouescat F 14 A1
Plouézec F 14 A3
Plougasnou F 14 A2
Plougastel-Daoulas F 14 A1
Plougonven F 14 A2
Plougonver F 14 A2
Plougrescant F 14 A2
Plouguenast F 15 A3
Plouguerneau F 14 A1
Plouha F 14 A3
Plouhinec F 14 A1
Plouigneau F 14 A2
Ploumanach F 14 A2
Plounévez-Quintin F 14 A2
Plouray F 14 A2
Plouzévédé F 14 A1
Plozévet F 14 B1
Pluméliau F 14 B3
Pluvigner F 14 B3
Pobla de Segur E 35 B4
Podensac F 28 B2
Pogny F 11 C4
Poirino I 27 C4
Poisson F 25 A4
Poissons F 11 C5
Poissy F 10 C2
Poitiers F 23 B4
Poix-de-Picardie F 10 B1
Poix-Terron F 11 B4
Polaincourt-et-Clairefontaine F 19 B5
Polch D 6 B3
Poleñino E 35 C3
Poligny F 19 C4
Polminhac F 24 C2
Pomarez F 28 C2
Pommard F 19 B3
Pompey F 12 C2
Poncin F 26 A2
Pons F 22 C3
Pont I 27 B4
Pont-a-Celles B 5 B4
Pontacq F 35 A3
Pontailler-sur-Saône F 19 B4
Pont-a-Marcq F 4 B3
Pont-à-Mousson F 12 C2
Pontarion F 24 B1
Pontarlier F 19 C5
Pontaubault F 8 B2
Pont-Audemer F 9 A4
Pontaumur F 24 B2
Pont-Aven F 14 B2
Pont Canavese I 27 B4
Pontcharra F 26 B3
Pontcharra-sur-Turdine F 25 B4
Pontchâteau F 15 B3
Pont-Croix F 14 A1
Pont-d'Ain F 26 A2
Pont-de-Beauvoisin F 26 B2
Pont-de-Buis-lès-Quimerch F 14 A1
Pont-de-Chéruy F 26 B2
Pont de Dore F 25 B3
Pont-de-Labeaume F 25 C4
Pont-de-l'Arche F 9 A5
Pont de Molins E 37 B3
Pont-de-Roide F 20 B1
Pont-de-Salars F 30 A1
Pont-d'Espagne F 35 B3
Pont de Suert E 35 B4
Pont-de-Vaux F 25 A4
Pont-de-Veyle F 25 A4
Pont d'Ouilly F 9 B3
Pont-du-Château F 24 B3
Pont-du-Navoy F 19 C4
Pontedássio I 33 B4
Pontedécimo I 33 A4
Ponte di Nava I 33 A3
Ponte-Leccia F 38 A2
Pont-en-Royans F 26 B2
Pontenx-les-Forges F 28 B1
Pont Farcy F 8 B2
Pontfaverger-Moronvillers F 11 B4
Pontgibaud F 24 B2
Pontigny F 18 B2
Pontijou F 17 B3
Pontinvrea I 33 A4
Pontivy F 14 A3
Pont-l'Abbé F 14 B1
Pont-l'Évêque F 9 A4
Pontlevoy F 17 B3
Pontoise F 10 B2
Pontonx-sur-l'Abour F 28 C2
Pontorson F 8 B2
Pont-Remy F 10 A1
Pontresina CH 21 C4
Pontrieux F 14 A2
Ponts E 37 C2
Ponts-aux-Dames F 10 C2
Pont Scorff F 14 B2
Pont-Ste Maxence F 10 B2
Pont-St Esprit F 31 A3
Pont-St Mamet F 29 B3
Pont-St Martin
F 15 B4
I 27 B4
Pont-St Vincent F 12 C2
Pont-sur-Yonne F 18 A2
Pontvallain F 16 B2
Poperinge B 4 B2
Poppel B 5 A5
Pordic F 14 A3
Pornic F 15 B3
Pornichet F 15 B3
Porquerolles F 32 C2
Porrentruy CH 20 B2
Porspoder F 14 A1
Port-a-Binson F 11 B3
Portbail F 8 A2
Portbou E 36 B4
Port-Camargue F 31 B3
Port-de-Bouc F 31 B3
Port-de-Lanne F 28 C1
Port-des-Barques F 22 C2
Port-en-Bessin F 8 A3
Portes-lès-Valence F 25 C4
Portets F 28 B2
Porticcio F 38 B1
Port-Joinville F 22 B1
Port-la-Nouvelle F 30 B2
Port Louis F 14 B2
Port Manech F 14 B2
Port-Navalo F 14 B3
Porto F 38 A1
Porto-Vecchio F 38 B2
Portsall F 14 A1
Port-Ste Marie F 29 B3
Port-St-Louis-du-Rhône F 31 B3
Port-sur-Saône F 19 B5
Port-Vendres F 36 B4
Possesse F 11 C4
Posterholt NL 6 A2
Potigny F 9 B3
Pouancé F 15 B4
Pougues-les-Eaux F 18 B2
Pouilly-en-Auxois F 18 B3
Pouilly-sous Charlieu F 25 A4
Pouilly-sur-Loire F 18 B1
Poujol-sur-Orb F 30 B2
Poullaouen F 14 A2
Pourcy F 11 B3
Pourrain F 18 B2
Pouyastruc F 35 A4
Pouy-de-Touges F 36 A2

Pouzauges F 22 B3
Pozán de Vero E 35 B4
Pradelle F 26 C2
Pradelles F 25 C3
Prades
E 37 C1
F 36 B3
Pragelato I 27 B3
Prahecq F 23 B3
Pralognan-la-Vanoise
F 26 B3
Prat F 36 A1
Pratdip E 37 C1
Prats-de-Mollo-la-Preste F 36 B3
Prauthoy F 19 B4
Prayssac F 29 B4
Prazzo I 32 A3
Préchac F 28 B2
Précy-sur-Thil F 18 B3
Pré-en-Pail F 9 B3
Préfailles F 15 B3
Preignan F 29 C3
Prémery F 18 B2
Prémia I 27 A5
Premiàde Mar E 37 C3
Prémont F 11 A3
Presly F 17 B4
Pressac F 23 B4
Preuilly-sur-Claise
F 23 B4
Prevenchères F 31 A2
Préveranges F 24 A2
Priay F 26 A2
Primel-Trégastel
F 14 A2
Primstal D 12 B2
Privas F 25 C4
Profondeville B 5 B4
Propriano F 38 B1
Provins F 10 C3
Prüm D 6 B2
Prunelli-di-Fiumorbo
F 38 A2
Pruniers F 17 C4
Puchevillers F 10 A2
Puderbach D 7 B3
Puente de Montañana
E 35 B4
Puente la Reina E 34 B2
Puente la Reina de Jaca E 34 B3
Puget-Sur-Argens
F 32 B2
Puget-Théniers F 32 B2
Puget-ville F 32 B2
Puigcerdà E 36 B2
Puig Reig E 37 C2
Puillon F 28 C2
Puimichel F 32 B2
Puimoisson F 32 B2
Puiseaux F 17 A4
Puisieux F 10 A2
Puisserguier F 30 B2
Puivert F 36 B3
Pujols F 28 B2
Pulheim D 6 A2
Purmerend NL 2 B1
Putanges-Pont-Ecrepin F 9 B3
Putte B 5 A4
Puttelange-aux-Lacs
F 12 B2
Putten NL 2 B2
Püttlingen D 12 B2
Puy-Guillaume F 25 B3
Puylaroque F 29 B4
Puylaurens F 36 A3
Puy-l'Évêque F 29 B4
Puymirol F 29 B3
Puyôo F 28 C2
Puyrolland F 22 B3
Pyla-sur-Mer F 28 B1

Q

Quakenbrück D 3 B4
Quargnento I 27 C5
Quarré-les-Tombes
F 18 B2
Quatre-Champs F 11 B4
Queige F 26 B3
Queixans E 36 B2
Quel E 34 B1
Quelaines-St-Gault
F 16 B1
Queralbs E 37 B3
Quérigut F 36 B3
Querqueville F 8 A2
Questembert F 15 B3
Quettehou F 8 A2
Quevauvillers F 10 B2
Quevy B 5 B4
Quiberon F 14 B2
Quiberville F 9 A4
Quiévrain B 5 B3
Quillan F 36 B3
Quillebeuf F 9 A4
Quimper F 14 A1
Quimperlé F 14 B2
Quincampoix F 9 A5
Quincy F 17 B4
Quinéville F 8 A2
Quingey F 19 B4
Quinson F 32 B2
Quinssaines F 24 A2
Quintin F 14 A3
Quissac F 31 B2

R

Raalte NL 3 B3
Raamsdonksveer
NL 5 A4
Rabastens F 29 C4
Rabastens-de-Bigorre
F 35 A4
Racconigi I 27 C4
Rachecourt-sur-Marne F 11 C5
Radevormwald D 6 A3
Radolfzell D 21 B3
Raeren B 6 B2
Raesfeld D 6 A2
Rambervillers F 12 C2
Rambouillet F 10 C1
Rambucourt F 12 C1
Ramerupt F 11 C4
Ramiswil CH 20 B2
Ramonville-St Agne
F 29 C4
Ramsbeck D 7 A4
Ramstein-Meisenbach D 13 B3
Rance B 11 A4
Randan F 25 A3
Rânes F 9 B3
Rankweil A 21 B4
Ransbach-Baumbach
D 7 B3
Raon-l'Étape F 12 C2
Rapperswil CH 21 B3
Rasal E 35 B3
Rastatt D 13 C4
Rastede D 3 A5
Ratingen D 6 A2
Raucourt-et-Flaba
F 11 B4
Raulhac F 24 C2
Rauville-la-Bigot F 8 A2
Rauzan F 28 B2
Ravels B 5 A4
Ravensburg D 21 B4
Razes F 23 B5
Réalmont F 30 B1
Rebais F 10 C3
Recey-sur-Ource F 19 B3
Recke D 3 B4
Recklinghausen D 6 A3
Recogne B 12 B1
Recoules-Prévinquières F 30 A1
Redange L 12 B1
Redon F 15 B3
Rees D 6 A2
Régil E 34 A1
Regniéville F 12 C1
Regny F 25 B4
Reichelsheim D 13 B4
Reichshoffen F 13 C3
Reiden CH 20 B2
Reillanne F 32 B1
Reims F 11 B4
Reinach CH 20 B3
Reinheim D 13 B4
Remagen D 6 B3
Rémalard F 9 B4
Rembercourt-aux-Pots F 11 C5
Remels D 3 A4
Remich L 12 B2
Rémilly F 12 B2
Remiremont F 19 A5
Remolinos E 34 C2
Remoulins F 31 B3
Remscheid D 6 A3
Rémuzat F 31 A4
Renaison F 25 A3
Renazé F 15 B4
Renchen D 13 C4
Rencurel F 26 B2
Renens CH 19 C5
Rennerod D 7 B4
Rennes F 15 A4
Rennes-les-Bains
F 36 B3
Rentería E 34 A2
Réquista F 30 A1
Ressons-sur-Matz
F 10 B2
Rethel F 11 B4
Retie B 5 A5
Retiers F 15 B4
Retournac F 25 B4
Reuilly F 17 B4
Reus E 37 C2
Reusel NL 5 A5
Reuver NL 6 A2
Revel F 36 A2
Revello I 27 C4
Revest-du-Bion F 32 A1
Revigny-sur-Ornain
F 11 C4
Revin F 11 B4
Rezé F 15 B4
Rhaunen D 13 B3
Rheda-Wiedenbrück
D 7 A4
Rhede
Niedersachsen D 3 A4
Nordrhein-Westfalen
D 6 A2
Rheinau D 13 C3
Rheinbach D 6 B2
Rheinberg D 6 A2
Rheine D 3 B4
Rheinfelden D 20 B2
Rhêmes-Notre-Dame
I 27 B4
Rhenen NL 2 C2
Rhens D 7 B3
Rheydt D 6 A2
Riaillé F 15 B4
Rians F 32 B1
Ribaforada E 34 C2
Ribeauvillé F 20 A2
Ribécourt-Dreslincourt F 10 B2
Ribemont F 11 B3
Ribérac F 29 A3
Ribera de Cardós
E 36 B2
Ribes de Freser E 37 B3
Ribiers F 32 A1
Richebourg F 19 A4
Richelieu F 16 B2
Richisau CH 21 B3
Richterswil CH 21 B3
Ridderkerk NL 5 A4
Riddes CH 27 A4
Riec-sur-Bélon F 14 B2
Riedlingen D 21 A4
Riedstadt D 13 B4
Riemst B 6 B1
Rienne B 11 B4
Rietberg D 7 A4
Rieumes F 36 A2
Rieupeyroux F 30 A1
Rieux-Volvestre F 36 A2
Riez F 32 B2
Riggisberg CH 20 C2
Rignac F 30 A1
Rijen NL 5 A4
Rijkevorsel B 5 A4
Rijssen NL 3 B3
Rillé F 16 B2
Rimogne F 11 B4
Rincón de Soto E 34 B2
Riom F 24 B3
Riom-ès-Montagnes
F 24 B2
Rion-des-Landes F 28 C2
Riotord F 25 B4
Rioz F 19 B5
Ripoll E 37 B3
Rischenau D 7 A5
Riscle F 28 C2
Riva Ligure I 33 B3
Rivarolo Canavese
I 27 B4
Rive-de-Gier F 25 B4
Rivedoux-Plage F 22 B2
Rives F 26 B2
Rivesaltes F 36 B3
Rivoli I 27 B4
Rixheim F 20 B2
Roanne F 25 A4
Robertville B 6 B2
Robres E 35 C3
Robres del Castillo
E 34 B1
Rocafort de Queralt
E 37 C2
Rocamadour F 29 B4
Rochechouart F 23 C4
Rochefort
B 5 B5
F 22 C3
Rochefort-en-Terre
F 15 B3
Rochefort-Montagne
F 24 B2
Rochefort-sur-Nenon
F 19 B4
Roche-lez-Beaupré
F 19 B5
Rochemaure F 31 A3
Rocheservière F 22 B2
Rockenhausen D 13 B3
Rocroi F 11 B4
Roda de Bara E 37 C2
Roda de Ter E 37 C3
Rodalben D 13 B3
Roden NL 3 A3
Rödermark D 13 B4
Rodez F 30 A1
Rodoñá E 37 C2
Roermond NL 6 A1
Roesbrugge B 4 B2
Roeschwoog F 13 C4
Roeselare B 4 B3
Roetgen D 6 B2
Roffiac F 24 B3
Rogliano F 38 A2
Rognes F 31 B4
Rogny-les-7-Ecluses
F 17 B4
Rohan F 15 A3
Rohrbach-lès-Bitche
F 12 B3
Roisel F 10 B3
Rolampont F 19 B4
Rolde NL 3 B3
Rolle CH 19 C5
Romagnano Sésia
I 27 B5
Romagné F 8 B2
Romanèche-Thorins
F 25 A4
Romanshorn CH 21 B4
Romans-sur-Isère
F 26 B2
Rombas F 12 B2
Romenay F 19 C4
Romilly-sur-Seine
F 11 C3
Romont CH 20 C1
Romorantin-Lanthenay F 17 B3
Romrod D 7 B5
Roncal E 34 B3
Ronce-les-Bains F 22 C2
Ronchamp F 20 B1
Ronco Canavese I 27 B4
Ronse B 5 B3
Roosendaal NL 5 A4
Roquebilière F 33 A3
Roquebrun F 30 B2
Roquecourbe F 30 B1
Roquefort F 28 B2
Roquemaure F 31 A3
Roquesteron F 32 B3
Roquevaire F 32 B1
Rorschach CH 21 B4
Rosans F 32 A1
Rosbach D 7 B3
Roscoff F 14 A2
Rosel UK 8 A1
Rosenfeld D 13 C4
Rosenthal D 7 A4
Roses E 37 B4
Rosheim F 13 C3
Rosières-en-Santerre
F 10 B2
Rosoy F 18 A2
Rosporden F 14 B2
Rosrath D 6 B3
Rossiglione I 33 A4
Rossignol B 12 B1
Rostrenen F 14 A2
Roth D 7 B3
Rothéneuf F 8 B2
Rottenburg D 13 C4
Rotterdam NL 5 A4
Rottweil D 21 A3
Roubaix F 4 B3
Roudouallec F 14 A2
Rouen F 9 A5
Rouffach F 20 B2
Rougé F 15 B4
Rougemont F 19 B5
Rougemont-le-Château F 20 B1
Rouillac F 23 C3
Rouillé F 23 B4
Roujan F 30 B2
Roulans F 19 B5
Roussac F 23 B5
Roussennac F 30 A1
Rousses F 30 A2
Roussillon F 25 B4
Rouvroy-sur-Audry
F 11 B4
Rouy F 18 B2
Royan F 22 C2
Royat F 24 B3
Roybon F 26 B2
Roye F 10 B2
Royère-de-Vassivière
F 24 B1
Rozay-en-Brie F 10 C2
Rozoy-sur-Serre F 11 B4
Rubí E 37 C3
Ruddervorde B 4 A3
Rüdesheim D 13 B3
Rue F 4 B1
Ruelle-sur-Touvre
F 23 C4
Ruffec F 23 B4
Rugles F 9 B4
Ruhle D 3 B4
Ruillé-sur-le-Loir F 16 B2
Ruinen NL 3 B3
Ruiselede B 4 A3
Rulles B 12 B1
Rülzheim D 13 B4
Rumigny F 11 B4
Rumilly F 26 B2
Rumont F 11 C5
Ruoms F 31 A3
Ruppichteroth D 6 B3
Rupt-sur-Moselle
F 20 B1
Rüsselsheim D 13 B4
Rustrel F 31 B4
Rüthen D 7 A4
Rüti CH 21 B3
Ruurlo NL 3 B3
Ruynes-en-Margeride
F 24 C3

S

Saales F 12 C3
Saanen CH 20 C2
Saarbrücken D 12 B2
Saarburg D 12 B2
Saarlouis D 12 B2
Saas-Fee CH 27 A4
Sabadell E 37 C3
Sabiñánigo E 35 B3
Sables-d'Or-les-Pins
F 15 A3
Sablé-sur-Sarthe F 16 B1
Sabres F 28 B2
Sádaba E 34 B2
Sadernes E 37 B3
Saerbeck D 3 B4
Saeul L 12 B1
S'Agaro E 37 C4
Sagone F 38 A1
Sagy F 19 C4
Saignelégier CH 20 B1
Saignes F 24 B2
Saillagouse F 36 B3
Saillans F 26 C2
Sains Richaumont
F 11 B3
St Affrique F 30 B1
St Agnan F 18 C2
St Agnant F 22 C3
St Agrève F 25 B4
St Aignan F 17 B3
St Aignan-sur-Roë
F 15 B4
St Alban-sur-Limagnole F 25 C3
St Amand-en-Puisaye
F 18 B2
St Amand-les-Eaux
F 5 B3
St Amand-Longpré
F 17 B3
St Amand-Montrond
F 17 C4
St Amans F 25 C3
St Amans-Soult F 30 B1
St Amant-Roche-Savine F 25 B3
St Amarin F 20 B1
St Ambroix F 31 A3
St Amé F 20 A1
St Amour F 26 A2
St André-de-Corcy
F 25 B4
St André-de-Cubzac
F 28 B2
St André-de-l'Eure
F 9 B5
St André-de-Roquepertuis F 31 A3
St André-de-Sangonis
F 30 B2
St Andre-de-Valborgne F 30 A2
St André-les-Alpes
F 32 B2
St Angel F 24 B2
St Anthème F 25 B3
St Antoine F 38 A2
St Antoine-de-Ficalba
F 29 B3
St Antönien CH 21 C4
St Antonin-Noble-Val
F 29 B4
St Août F 17 C3
St Armant-Tallende
F 24 B3
St Arnoult F 10 C1
St Astier F 29 A3
St Auban F 32 B2
St Aubin
CH 20 C1
F 19 B4
UK 8 A1
St Aubin-d'Aubigne
F 15 A4
St Aubin-du-Cormier
F 15 A4
St Aubin-sur-Aire
F 12 C1
St Aubin-sur-Mer F 9 A3
St Aulaye F 28 A3
St Avit F 24 B2
St Avold F 12 B2
St Aygulf F 32 B2
St Bauzille-de-Putois
F 30 B2
St Béat F 35 B4
St Beauzély F 30 A1
St Benim-d'Azy F 18 C2
St Benoît-du-Sault
F 23 B5
St Benoit-en-Woëvre
F 12 C1
St Berthevin F 16 A1
St Blaise-la-Roche
F 12 C3
St Blin F 19 A4
St Bonnet F 26 C3
St Bonnet Briance
F 23 C5
St Bonnet-de-Joux
F 18 C3
St Bonnet-le-Château
F 25 B4
St Bonnet-le-Froid
F 25 B4
St Brévin-les-Pins
F 15 B3
St Briac-sur-Mer F 15 A3
St Brice-en-Coglès
F 8 B2
St Brieuc F 15 A3
St Bris-le-Vineux
F 18 B2
St Broladre F 8 B2
St Calais F 16 B2
St Cannat F 31 B4
St Cast-le-Guildo
F 15 A3
St Céré F 29 B4
St Cergue CH 26 A3
St Cergues F 26 A3
St Cernin F 24 B2
St Chamant F 24 B1
St Chamas F 31 B4
St Chamond F 25 B4
St Chély-d'Apcher
F 24 C3
St Chély-d'Aubrac
F 24 C2
St Chinian F 30 B1
St Christol F 31 A4
St Christol-lès-Alès
F 31 A3
St Christoly-Médoc
F 22 C3
St Christophe-du-Ligneron F 22 B2
St Christophe-en-Brionnais F 25 A4
St Ciers-sur-Gironde
F 28 A2
St Clair-sur-Epte F 10 B1
St Clar F 29 C3
St Claud F 23 C4
St Claude F 26 A2
St Come-d'Olt F 30 A1
St Cosme-en-Vairais
F 9 B4
St Cyprien
Dordogne F 29 B4
Pyrenées-Orientales
F 36 B4
St Cyr-sur-Loire F 16 B2
St Cyr-sur-Mer F 32 B1
St Cyr-sur-Methon
F 25 A4
St Denis F 10 C2
St Denis-d'Oléron
F 22 B2
St Denis d'Orques
F 16 A1
St Didier F 25 A4
St Didier-en-Velay
F 25 B4
St Dié F 12 C2
St Dier-d'Auvergne
F 25 B3
St Dizier F 11 C4
St Dizier-Leyrenne
F 24 A1
Ste Adresse F 9 A4
Ste Anne F 9 B4
Ste Anne-d'Auray
F 14 B3
Ste Croix CH 19 C5
Ste Croix-Volvestre
F 36 A2
Ste Engrâce F 34 A3
Ste Enimie F 30 A2
Ste Efflam F 14 A2
Ste Foy-de-Peyrolières
F 36 A2
Ste Foy-la-Grande
F 28 B3
Ste Foy l'Argentiere
F 25 B4
Ste Gauburge-Ste Colombe F 9 B4
Ste Gemme la Plaine
F 22 B2
Ste Geneviève F 10 B2
St Égrève F 26 B2
Ste Hélène F 28 B2
Ste Hélène-sur-Isère
F 26 B3
Ste Hermine F 22 B2
Ste Jalle F 31 A4
Ste Livrade-sur-Lot
F 29 B3
St Eloy-les-Mines
F 24 A2
Ste Marie-aux-Mines
F 20 A2
Ste Marie-du-Mont
F 8 A2
Ste Maure-de-Touraine F 16 B2
Ste Maxime F 32 B2
Ste Ménéhould F 11 B4
Ste Mère-Église F 8 A2
St Emiland F 18 C3
St Émilion F 28 B2
Sainteny F 8 A2
Ste Ode B 12 A1
Saintes F 22 C3
Ste Savine F 11 C4
Ste Sévère-sur-Indre
F 17 C4
Ste Sigolène F 25 B4
St Esteben F 34 A2
St Estèphe F 28 A2
Ste Suzanne F 16 A1
St Étienne F 25 B4
St Etienne-de-Baigorry F 34 A2
St Étienne-de-Cuines
F 26 B3
St Etienne-de-Fursac
F 24 A1
St Etienne-de-Montluc
F 15 B4
St Etienne-de-St Geoirs F 26 B2
St Étienne-de-Tinée
F 32 A2
St Étienne-du-Bois
F 26 A2
St Étienne-du-Rouvray
F 9 A5
St Etienne-les-Orgues
F 32 A1
Ste Tulle F 32 B1
St Fargeau F 18 B2
St Félicien F 25 B4
St Felix-de-Sorgues
F 30 B1
St Félix-Lauragais
F 36 A2
St Firmin F 26 C3
St Florent F 38 A2
St Florentin F 18 B2
St Florent-le-Vieil
F 15 B4
St Florent-sur-Cher
F 17 C4
St Flour F 24 B3
St Flovier F 17 C3
St Fort-sur-le-Né F 23 C3
St Fulgent F 22 B2
St Galmier F 25 B4
St Gaudens F 35 A4
St Gaultier F 23 B5
St Gély-du-Fesc F 30 B2
St Genest-Malifaux
F 25 B4
St Gengoux-le-National F 18 C3
St Geniez F 32 A2
St Geniez-d'Olt F 30 A1
St Genis-de-Saintonge
F 22 C3
St Genis-Pouilly F 26 A3
St Genix-sur-Guiers
F 26 B2
St Georges Buttavent
F 8 B3
St Georges-d'Aurac
F 25 B3
St Georges-de-Commiers F 26 B2
St Georges-de-Didonne F 22 C3
St Georges-de-Luzençon F 30 A1
St Georges-de Mons
F 24 B2
St Georges-de-Reneins F 25 A4
St Georges d'Oléron
F 22 C2
St Georges-en-Couzan
F 25 B3
St Georges-lès-Baillargeaux F 23 B4
St Georges-sur-Loire
F 16 B1
St Georges-sur-Meuse
B 5 B5
St Geours-de-Maremne F 28 C1

St Gérand-de-Vaux F 25 A3
St Gérand-le-Puy F 25 A3
St Germain F 19 B5
St Germain-Chassenay F 18 C2
St Germain-de-Calberte F 30 A2
St Germain-de-Confolens F 23 B4
St Germain-de-Joux F 26 A2
St Germain-des-Fossés F 25 A3
St Germain-du-Bois F 19 C4
St Germain-du-Plain F 19 C3
St Germain-du Puy F 17 B4
St Germain-en-Laye F 10 C2
St Germain-Laval F 25 B4
St Germain-Lembron F 24 B3
St Germain-les-Belles F 24 B1
St Germain-Lespinasse F 25 A3
St Germain-l'Herm F 25 B3
St Gervais-d'Auvergne F 24 A2
St Gervais-les-Bains F 26 B3
St Gervais-sur-Mare F 30 B2
St Gildas-de-Rhuys F 14 B3
St Gildas-des-Bois F 15 B3
St Gilles
  Gard F 31 B3
  Ille-et-Vilaine F 15 A4
St Gilles-Croix-de-Vie F 22 B2
St Gingolph F 27 A3
St Girons
  Ariège F 36 B2
  Landes F 28 C1
St Girons-Plage F 28 C1
St Gobain F 11 B3
St Gorgon-Main F 19 B5
St Guénolé F 14 B1
St Helier UK 8 A1
St Herblain F 15 B4
St Hilaire
  Allier F 18 C2
  Aude F 36 A3
St Hilaire-de-Riez F 22 B2
St Hilaire-des-Loges F 22 B3
St Hilaire-de-Villefranche F 22 C3
St Hilaire-du-Harcouët F 8 B2
St Hilaire-du-Rosier F 26 B2
St Hippolyte
  Aveyron F 24 C2
  Doubs F 20 B1
St Hippolyte-du-Fort F 30 B2
St Honoré-les-Bains F 18 C2
St Hubert B 12 A1
St Imier CH 20 B2
St Izaire F 30 B1
St Jacques-de-la-Lande F 15 A4
St Jacut-de-la-Mer F 15 A3
St James F 8 B2
St Jean-Brévelay F 15 B3
St Jean-d'Angély F 22 C3
St Jean-de-Belleville F 26 B3
St Jean-de-Bournay F 26 B2
St Jean-de-Braye F 17 B3
St Jean-de-Côle F 23 C4
St Jean-de-Daye F 8 A2
St Jean de Losne F 19 B4
St Jean-de-Luz F 34 A2
St Jean-de-Maurienne F 26 B3
St Jean-de-Monts F 22 B1
St Jean-d'Illac F 28 B2
St Jean-du-Bruel F 30 A2
St Jean-du-Gard F 31 A2
St Jean-en-Royans F 26 B2
St Jean-la-Riviere F 33 B3
St Jean-Pied-de-Port F 34 A2
St Jean-Poutge F 29 C3
St Jeoire F 26 A3
St Joachim F 15 B3
St Jorioz F 26 B3
St Joris Winge B 5 B4
St Jouin-de-Marnes F 16 C1
St Juéry F 30 B1
St Julien F 26 A2
St Julien-Chapteuil F 25 B4
St Julien-de-Vouvantes F 15 B4
St Julien-du-Sault F 18 A2
St Julien-du-Verdon F 32 B2
St Julien-en-Born F 28 B1
St Julien-en-Genevois F 26 A3
St Julien-l'Ars F 23 B4
St Julien la-Vêtre F 25 B3
St Julien-Mont-Denis F 26 B3
St Julien-sur-Reyssouze F 26 A2
St Junien F 23 C4
St Just F 31 A3
St Just-en-Chaussée F 10 B2
St Just-en-Chevalet F 25 B3
St Justin F 28 C2
St Just-St Rambert F 25 B4
St Lary-Soulan F 35 B4
St Laurent-d'Aigouze F 31 B3
St Laurent-de-Chamousset F 25 B4
St Laurent-de-Condel F 9 A3
St Laurent-de-la-Cabrerisse F 36 A3
St Laurent-de-la-Salanque F 36 B3
St Laurent-des-Autels F 15 B4
St Laurent-du-Pont F 26 B2
St Laurent-en-Caux F 9 A4
St Laurent-en-Grandvaux F 19 C4
St Laurent-Médoc F 28 A2
St Laurent-sur-Gorre F 23 C4
St Laurent-sur-Mer F 8 A3
St Laurent-sur-Sèvre F 22 B3
St Leger B 12 B1
St Léger-de-Vignes F 18 C2
St Léger-sous-Beuvray F 18 C3
St Léger-sur-Dheune F 18 C3
St Léonard-de-Noblat F 24 B1
St Lô F 8 A2
St Lon-les-Mines F 28 C1
St Louis F 20 B2
St Loup F 25 A3
St Loup-de-la-Salle F 19 C3
St Loup-sur-Semouse F 19 B5
St Lunaire F 15 A3
St Lupicin F 26 A2
St Lyphard F 15 B3
St Lys F 36 A2
St Macaire F 28 B2
St Maclou F 9 A4
St Maixent-l'École F 23 B3
St Malo F 8 B1
St Mamet-la-Salvetat F 24 C2
St Mandrier-sur-Mer F 32 B1
St Marcel
  Drôme F 25 C4
  Saône-et-Loire F 19 C3
St Marcellin F 26 B2
St Marcellin sur Loire F 25 B4
St Marcet F 35 A4
St Mards-en-Othe F 18 A2
St Mars-la-Jaille F 15 B4
St Martin-d'Ablois F 11 C3
St Martin-d'Auxigny F 17 B4
St Martin-de-Belleville F 26 B3
St Martin-de-Bossenay F 11 C3
St Martin-de-Crau F 31 B3
St Martin-de-Londres F 30 B2
St Martin-d'Entraunes F 32 A2
St Martin-de-Queyrières F 26 C3
St Martin-de-Ré F 22 B2
St Martin des Besaces F 8 A3
St Martin-d'Estreaux F 25 A3
St Martin-de-Valamas F 25 C4
St Martin-d'Hères F 26 B2
St Martin-du-Frêne F 26 A2
St Martin-en-Bresse F 19 C4
St Martin-en-Haut F 25 B4
St Martin-la-Méanne F 24 B1
St Martin-Osmonville F 10 B1
St Martin-sur-Ouanne F 18 B2
St Martin-Valmeroux F 24 B2
St Martin-Vésubie F 33 A3
St Martory F 35 A4
St Mathieu F 23 C4
St Mathieu-de-Tréviers F 31 B2
St Maurice CH 27 A3
St Maurice-Navacelles F 30 B2
St Maurice-sur-Moselle F 20 B1
St Maximin-la-Ste Baume F 32 B1
St Méard-de-Gurçon F 28 B3
St Médard-de-Guizières F 28 A2
St Médard-en-Jalles F 28 B2
St Méen-le-Grand F 15 A3
St Menges F 11 B4
St M'Hervé F 15 A4
St Michel
  Aisne F 11 B4
  Gers F 35 A4
St Michel-Chef-Chef F 15 B3
St Michel-de-Castelnau F 28 B2
St Michel-de-Maurienne F 26 B3
St Michel-en-Grève F 14 A2
St Michel-enl'Herm F 22 B2
St Michel-Mont-Mercure F 22 B3
St Mihiel F 12 C1
St Montant F 31 A3
St Moritz CH 21 C4
St Nazaire F 15 B3
St Nazaire-en-Royans F 26 B2
St Nazaire-le-Désert F 31 A4
St Nectaire F 24 B2
St Nicolas-de-Port F 12 C2
St Nicolas-de-Redon F 15 B3
St Nicolas-du-Pélem F 14 A2
St Niklaas B 5 A4
St Omer F 4 B2
St Pair-sur-Mer F 8 B2
St Palais F 34 A2
St Palais-sur-Mer F 22 C2
St Pardoux-la-Rivière F 23 C4
St Paul-Cap-de-Joux F 29 C4
St Paul-de-Fenouillet F 36 B3
St Paul-de-Varax F 26 A2
St Paulien F 25 B3
St Paul-le-Jeune F 31 A3
St Paul-lès-Dax F 28 C1
St Paul-Trois-Châteaux F 31 A3
St Pé-de-Bigorre F 35 A3
St Pée-sur-Nivelle F 34 A2
St Péravy-la-Colombe F 17 B3
St Péray F 25 C4
St Père-en-Retz F 15 B3
St Peter Port UK 8 A1
St Philbert-de-Grand-Lieu F 22 A2
St Pierre F 30 B1
St Pierre-d'Albigny F 26 B3
St Pierre-d'Allevard F 26 B3
St Pierre-de-Chartreuse F 26 B2
St Pierre-de-Chignac F 29 A3
St Pierre-de-la-Fage F 30 B2
St Pierre-d'Entremont F 26 B2
St Pierre-d'Oléron F 22 C2
St Pierre-Eglise F 8 A2
St Pierre-en-Port F 9 A4
St Pierre-le-Moûtier F 18 C2
St Pierre Montlimart F 15 B4
St Pierre-Quiberon F 14 B2
St Pierre-sur-Dives F 9 A3
St Pierreville F 25 C4
St Pieters-Leeuw B 5 B4
St Plancard F 35 A4
St Poix F 15 B4
St Pol-de-Léon F 14 A2
St Polgues F 25 B3
St Pol-sur-Ternoise F 4 B2
St Pons-de-Thomières F 30 B1
St Porchaire F 22 C3
St Pourçain-sur-Sioule F 24 A3
St Priest F 25 B4
St Privat F 24 B2
St Quay-Portrieux F 14 A3
St Quentin F 10 B3
St Quentin-la-Poterie F 31 A3
St Quentin-les-Anges F 16 B1
St Rambert-d'Albon F 25 B4
St Rambert-en-Bugey F 26 B2
St Raphaël F 32 B2
St Rémy-de-Provence F 31 B3
St Rémy-du-Val F 9 B4
St Remy-en-Bouzemont F 11 C4
St Renan F 14 A1
St Révérien F 18 B2
St Riquier F 10 A1
St Romain-de-Colbosc F 9 A4
St Rome-de-Cernon F 30 A1
St Rome-de-Tarn F 30 A1
St Sadurní-d'Anoia E 37 C2
St Saëns F 9 A5
St Sampson UK 8 A1
St Samson-la-Poterie F 10 B1
St Saturnin-de-Lenne F 30 A2
St Saturnin-lès-Apt F 31 B4
St Sauflieu F 10 B2
St Saulge F 18 B2
St Sauveur
  Finistère F 14 A2
  Haute-Saône F 19 B5
St Sauveur-de-Montagut F 25 C4
St Sauveur-en-Puisaye F 18 B2
St Sauveur-en-Rue F 25 B4
St Sauveur-Lendelin F 8 A2
St Sauveur-le-Vicomte F 8 A2
St Sauveur-sur-Tinée F 32 A3
St Savin
  Gironde F 28 A2
  Vienne F 23 B4
St Savinien F 22 C3
St Savournin F 31 B4
St Seine-l'Abbaye F 19 B3
St Sernin-sur-Rance F 30 B1
St Sevan-sur-Mer F 8 B1
St Sever F 28 C2
St Sever-Calvados F 8 B2
St Sorlin-d'Arves F 26 B3
St Soupplets F 10 B2
St Sulpice F 29 C4
St Sulpice-Laurière F 24 A1
St Sulpice-les-Feuilles F 23 B5
St Symphorien F 28 B2
St Symphoriende-Lay F 25 B4
St Symphorien d'Ozon F 25 B4
St Symphoriensur-Coise F 25 B4
St Thégonnec F 14 A2
St Thiébault F 19 A4
St Trivier-de-Courtes F 26 A2
St Trivier-sur-Moignans F 25 A4
St Trojan-les-Bains F 22 C2
St Tropez F 32 B2
St Truiden B 5 B5
St Vaast-la-Hougue F 8 A2
St Valérien F 18 A2
St Valery-en-Caux F 9 A4
St Valéry-sur-Somme F 4 B1
St Vallier
  Drôme F 25 B4
  Saône-et-Loire F 18 C3
St Vallier-de-Thiey F 32 B2
St Varent F 16 C1
St Vaury F 24 A1
St Venant F 4 B2
St Véran F 27 C3
St Vincent I 27 B4
St Vincent-de-Tyrosse F 28 C1
St Vit F 19 B4
St Vith B 6 B2
St Vivien-de-Médoc F 22 C2
St Yan F 25 A4
St Ybars F 36 A2
St Yorre F 25 A3
St Yrieix-la-Perche F 23 C5
Saissac F 36 A3
Salardú E 35 B4
Salau F 36 B2
Salavaux CH 20 C2
Salbertrand I 27 B3
Salbris F 17 B4
Salem D 21 B4
Salernes F 32 B2
Salers F 24 B2
Salies-de-Béarn F 34 A3
Salies-du-Salat F 35 A4
Salignac-Eyvigues F 29 B4
Saligney-sur-Roudon F 18 C2
Salinas E 35 B4
Salindres F 31 A3
Salins-les-Bains F 19 C4
Sallanches F 26 B3
Sallent E 37 C2
Sallent de Gállego E 35 B3
Salles F 28 B2
Salles-Curan F 30 A1
Salles-sur-l'Hers F 36 A2
Salmiech F 30 A1
Salon-de-Provence F 31 B4
Salornay-sur-Guye F 18 C3
Salou E 37 C2
Salses-le-Chateau F 36 B3
Salt E 37 C3
Salussola I 27 B5
Saluzzo I 27 C4
Salvagnac F 29 C4
Salviac F 29 B4
Salzkotten D 7 A4
Samadet F 28 C2
Samatan F 36 A1
Samedan CH 21 C4
Samer F 4 B1
Samnaun CH 21 C5
Samoëns F 26 A3
Samogneux F 12 B1
Sampéyre I 33 A3
Sampigny F 12 C1
San Adrián E 34 B2
Sanary-sur-Mer F 32 B1
San Carlo CH 27 A5
Sancergues F 18 B1
Sancerre F 17 B4
Sancey-le-Long F 19 B5
Sancoins F 18 C1
San Damiano d'Asti I 27 C5
San Damiano Macra I 33 A3
Sande D 3 A5
Sandhorst D 3 A4
Sandillon F 17 B4
San Esteban de Litera E 35 C4
Sangatte F 4 B1
San Germano Vercellese I 27 B5
Sangüesa E 34 B2
Sanguinet F 28 B1
Sankt Anton am Arlberg A 21 B5
Sankt Augustin D 6 B3
Sankt Blasien D 20 B3
Sankt Gallen CH 21 B4
Sankt Gallenkirch A 21 B4
Sankt Georgen D 20 A3
Sankt Goar D 7 B3
Sankt Goarshausen D 7 B3
Sankt Ingbert D 12 B3
Sankt Margrethen CH 21 B4
Sankt Niklaus CH 27 A4
Sankt Paul F 32 A2
Sankt Peter D 20 A3
Sankt Wendel D 12 B3
San Lorenzo al Mare I 33 B3
San Martin de Unx E 34 B2
San-Martino-di-Lota F 38 A2
San Mateo de Gallego E 34 C3
San Michele Mondov ì I 33 A3
San Pedro Manrique E 34 B1
San Remo I 33 B3
Santacara E 34 B2
Santa Coloma de Farners E 37 C3
Santa Coloma de Gramenet E 37 C3
Santa Coloma de Queralt E 37 C2
Sant Agust ìde Lluçanès E 37 B3
Santa Lucia-de-Porto-Vecchio F 38 B2
Santa Margaridao de Montbui E 37 C2
Santa Maria E 34 B3
Santa Maria de Corco E 37 B3
Santa Maria Maggiore I 27 A5
Sant Antoni de Calonge E 37 C4
Santa Pau E 37 B3
Santa Severa F 38 A2
Sant Boi de Llobregat E 37 C3
Sant Celoni E 37 C3
Sant Felíu E 37 C3
Sant Feliu de Codines E 37 C3
Sant Feliu de Guíxols E 37 C4
Sant Feliu Sasserra E 37 C3
Santhià I 27 B5
Sant Hilari Sacalm E 37 C3
Sant Hipòlit de Voltregà E 37 B3
Sant Jaume dels Domenys E 37 C2
Sant Joan de les Abadesses E 37 B3
Sant Juliáde Loria AND 36 B2
Sant Llorençde Morunys E 37 B2
Sant Llorenç Savall E 37 C3
Sant Mart ide Llemaná E 37 B3
Sant Marti de Maldá E 37 C2
Sant Marti Sarroca E 37 C2
Santo-Pietro-di-Tenda F 38 A2
Sant Pau de Seguries E 37 B3
Santpedor E 37 C2
Sant Pere de Riudebitlles E 37 C2
Sant Pere Pescador E 37 B4
Sant Pere Sallavinera E 37 C2
Sant Quirze de Besora E 37 B3
Sant Ramon E 37 C2
Sant Vincençde Castellet E 37 C2
San Vicente de Arana E 34 B1
Saorge F 33 B3
Saramon F 29 C3
Sarcelles F 10 B2
Sare F 34 A2
Sargans CH 21 B4
Sari-d'Orcino F 38 A1
Sariñena E 35 C3
Sarlat-la-Canéda F 29 B4
Sarliac-sur-l'Isle F 29 A3
Sarnen CH 20 C3
Sarpoil F 25 B3
Sarral E 37 C2
Sarralbe F 12 B3
Sarrancolin F 35 B4
Sarras F 25 B4
Sarre I 27 B4
Sarrebourg F 12 C3
Sarreguemines F 12 B3
Sarre-Union F 12 C3
Sarriàde Ter E 37 B3
Sarron F 28 C2
Sartène F 38 B1
Sartilly F 8 B2
Sarzeau F 15 B3
Sassello I 33 A4
Sassenberg D 3 C5
Sas van Gent NL 5 A3
Satillieu F 25 B4
Satteins A 21 B4
Saucats F 28 B2
Saugues F 25 C3
Saujon F 22 C3
Saulces Monclin F 11 B4
Saulgau D 21 A4
Saulieu F 18 B3
Saulnot F 20 B1
Sault F 31 A4
Sault-Brénaz F 26 B2
Sault-de-Navailles F 28 C2
Saulx F 19 B5
Saulxures-sur-Moselotte F 20 B1
Saulzais-le-Potier F 17 C4
Saumos F 28 B1
Saumur F 16 B1
Saurat F 36 B2
Sausset-les-Pins F 31 B4
Sauteyrargues F 31 B2
Sauvagnat F 24 B2
Sauve F 31 B2
Sauveterre-de-Béarn F 34 A3
Sauveterre-de-Guyenne F 28 B2
Sauviat-sur-Vige F 24 B1
Sauxillanges F 25 B3
Sauzet
  Drôme F 25 C4
  Lot F 29 B4
Sauzé-Vaussais F 23 B4
Sauzon F 14 B2
Savenay F 15 B4
Saverdun F 36 A2
Saverne F 13 C3
Savières F 11 C3
Savigliano I 27 C4
Savignac-les-Eglises F 29 A3
Savigny-sur-Braye F 16 B2
Savines-le-lac F 32 A2
Savognin CH 21 C4
Savona I 33 A4
Savournon F 32 A1
Scaër F 14 A2
Scey-sur-Saône et St Albin F 19 B4
Schaffhausen CH 21 B3
Schagen NL 2 B1
Schangnau CH 20 C2
Schapbach D 13 C4
Scharrel D 3 A4
Scheemda NL 3 A3
Scheidegg D 21 B4
Scherfede D 7 A5
Schermbeck D 6 A2
Scherpenzeel NL 2 B2
Scheveningen NL 2 B1
Schiedam NL 5 A4
Schiers CH 21 C4
Schillingen D 12 B2
Schiltach D 13 C4
Schiltigheim F 13 C3
Schirmeck F 12 C3
Schlangen D 7 A4
Schleiden D 6 B2
Schliengen D 20 B2

Schlitz D 7 B5
Schloss Neuhans D 7 A4
Schluchsee D 20 B3
Schlüchtern D 7 B5
Schmallenberg D 7 A4
Schmelz D 12 B2
Schoenburg B 6 B2
Schöllkrippen D 7 B5
Schomberg D 21 A3
Schönau D 20 B2
Schönecken-D. 6 B2
Schönhagen D 7 A5
Schoondijke NL 5 A3
Schoonebeek NL 3 B3
Schoonhoven NL 5 A4
Schopfheim D 20 B2
Schortens D 3 A4
Schotten D 7 B5
Schramberg D 20 A3
Schrecksbach D 7 B5
Schröcken A 21 B5
Schruns A 21 B4
Schüpfheim CH 20 C3
Schüttorf D 3 B4
Schwagstorf D 3 B4
Schwaigern D 13 B5
Schwalmstadt D 7 B5
Schwanden CH 21 C4
Schwarzenburg
CH 20 C2
Schwei D 3 A5
Schweich D 12 B2
Schweighausen D 20 A2
Schwelm D 6 A3
Schwenningen D 21 A3
Schwerte D 7 A3
Schwetzingen D 13 B4
Schwyz CH 21 B3
Scionzier F 26 A3
Scopello I 27 B5
Scuol CH 21 C5
Sebazac-
Concourès F 30 A1
Seborga I 33 B3
Séchault F 11 B4
Seclin F 4 B3
Secondigny F 22 B3
Sedan F 11 B4
Séderon F 31 A4
Seebach F 13 C3
Seefeld D 3 A5
Seeheim-
Jugenheim D 13 B4
Seelbach D 13 C3
Sées F 9 B4
Segonzac F 23 C3
Segré F 15 B5
Segura E 34 B1
Ségur-les-Villas F 24 B2
Seiches-sur-
le-Loir F 16 B1
Seignelay F 18 B2
Seilhac F 24 B1
Seilles B 5 B5
Seissan F 35 A4
Sélestat F 20 A2
Selgua E 35 C4
Seligenstadt D 13 A4
Selles-St Denis F 17 B3
Selles-sur-Cher F 17 B3
Sellières F 19 C4
Selm D 6 A3
Selongey F 19 B4
Selonnet F 32 A2
Selters D 7 B3
Seltz F 13 C4
Semide F 11 B4
Semur-en-Auxois
F 18 B3
Sena E 35 C3
Senarpont F 10 B1
Sénas F 31 B4
Senden D 6 A3
Sendenhorst D 7 A3
Seneffe B 5 B4
Senez F 32 B2
Sengouagnet F 35 B4
Sengwarden D 3 A5
Senlis F 10 B2
Sennecey-le-Grand
F 19 C3
Sennwald CH 21 B4
Senonches F 9 B5
Senones F 12 C2
Sens F 18 A2
Sens-de-Bretagne
F 15 A4
Senterada E 35 B4
Seon CH 20 B3
Sépeaux F 18 B2
Sépey CH 27 A4
Seppenrade D 6 A3
Seppois F 20 B2
Septeuil F 10 C1
Seraincourt F 11 B4
Seraing B 6 B1
Sérent F 15 B3
Sérifontaine F 10 B1
Sérignan F 30 B2
Sermaises F 10 C2
Sermaize-les-Bains
F 11 C4
Serooskerke NL 5 A3
Serravalle I 27 B5
Serres F 32 A1
Serrières F 25 B4
Serrières-de-Briord
F 26 B2
Sertig Dörfli CH 21 C4
Servance F 20 B1
Serverette F 25 C3
Servian F 30 B2
Serviers F 31 A3
Sesma E 34 B1
Sestriere I 27 C3
Setcases E 36 B3
Sète F 30 B2
Séttimo Torinese I 27 B4
Settimo Vittone I 27 B4
Seurre F 19 C4
Sévérac-le-Château
F 30 A2
Sévigny F 11 B4
Sevrier F 26 B3
Seyches F 29 B3
Seyne F 32 A2
Seynes F 31 A3
Seyssel F 26 B2
Sézanne F 11 C3
's-Gravendeel NL 5 A4
's-Gravenhage = The
Hague NL 2 B1
's-Gravenzande NL 5 A4
's-Heerenberg NL 6 A2
's-Hertogenbosch
NL 5 A5
Siauges-St Romain
F 25 B3
Siddeburen NL 3 A3
Siedlinghausen D 7 A4
Siegburg D 6 B3
Siegen D 7 B4
Sierck-les-Bains F 12 B2
Sierentz F 20 B2
Sierra de Luna E 34 B3
Sierre CH 27 A4
Sietamo E 35 B3
Sigean F 30 B1
Sigmaringen D 21 A4
Signes F 32 B1
Signy-l'Abbaye F 11 B4
Signy-le-Petit F 11 B4
Sigogne F 23 C3
Sigües E 34 B2
Sillé-le-Guillaume
F 16 A1
Sillenstede D 3 A4
Sils E 37 C3
Silvaplana CH 21 C4
Simandre F 19 C3
Simard F 19 C4
Simmerath D 6 B2
Simmerberg D 21 B4
Simmern D 13 B3
Simplon CH 27 A5
Sindelfingen D 13 C5
Singen D 21 B3
Sinn D 7 B4
Sins CH 20 B3
Sinsheim D 13 B4
Sint Annaland NL 5 A4
Sint Annaparochie
NL 2 A2
Sint Athonis NL 6 A1
Sint Nicolaasga NL 2 B2
Sint Oedenrode NL 5 A5
Sinzheim D 13 C4
Sinzig D 6 B3
Sion CH 27 A4
Siorac-en-Périgord
F 29 B3
Sissach CH 20 B2
Sissonne F 11 B3
Sisteron F 32 A1
Sitges E 37 C2
Sittard NL 6 A1
Sixt-Fer-á-Cheval
F 27 A3
Sizun F 14 A1
Slagharen NL 3 B3
Slochteren NL 3 A3
Slootdorp NL 2 B1
Sluis NL 4 A3
Smilde NL 3 B3
Sneek NL 2 A2
Sobernheim D 13 B3
Soest
D 7 A4
NL 2 B2
Sögel D 3 B4
Sohren D 13 B3
Soignies B 5 B4
Soissons F 10 B3
Soleils F 32 B2
Solenzara F 38 B2
Solesmes F 5 B3
Solgne F 12 C2
Solignac F 23 C5
Solingen D 6 A3
Solivella E 37 C2
Solliès-Pont F 32 B2
Solomiac F 29 C3
Solothurn CH 20 B2
Solre-le-Château F 5 B4
Solsona E 37 C2
Somain F 4 B3
Sombernon F 18 B3
Sombreffe B 5 B4
Someren NL 6 A1
Sommariva del Bosco
I 27 C4
Sommeilles F 11 C4
Sommepy-Tahure
F 11 B4
Sommesous F 11 C4
Somme-Tourbe F 11 B4
Sommières F 31 B3
Sommières-du-Clain
F 23 B4
Sompuis F 11 C4
Sonceboz CH 20 B2
Son en Breugel NL 6 A1
Songeons F 10 B1
Sonsbeck D 6 A2
Sonthofen D 21 B5
Sore F 28 B2
Sörenberg CH 20 C3
Sorèze F 36 A3
Sorges F 23 C4
Sorgues F 31 A3
Sornac F 24 B2
Sort E 36 B2
Sos F 28 B3
Sos del Rey Católico
E 34 B2
Sospel F 33 B3
Sotta F 38 B2
Souain F 11 B4
Soual F 36 A3
Soucy F 18 A2
Soudron F 11 C4
Souesmes F 17 B4
Soufflenheim F 13 C3
Souillac F 29 B4
Souilly F 11 B5
Soulac-sur-Mer F 22 C2
Soulaines-Dhuys
F 11 C4
Soulatgé F 36 B3
Soultz-Haut-Rhin
F 20 B2
Soultz-sous-Forêts
F 13 C3
Soumagne B 6 B1
Soumoulou F 35 A3
Souppes-sur-Loing
F 17 A4
Souprosse F 28 C2
Sourdeval F 8 B3
Sournia F 36 B3
Sours F 10 C1
Sousceyrac F 24 C2
Soustons F 28 C1
Souvigny F 18 C2
Souzay-Champigny
F 16 B1
Soyaux F 23 C4
Spa B 6 B1
Spaichingen D 21 A3
Spakenburg NL 2 B2
Speicher D 12 B2
Speyer D 13 B4
Spézet F 14 A2
Spiekeroog D 3 A4
Spiez CH 20 C2
Spigno Monferrato
I 33 A4
Spijk NL 3 A3
Spijkenisse NL 5 A4
Spincourt F 12 B1
Splügen CH 21 C4
Spohle D 3 A5
Spotorno I 33 A4
Sprimont B 6 B1
Stabroek B 5 A4
Staden B 4 B3
Stadskanaal NL 3 B3
Stadtallendorf D 7 B5
Stadtkyll D 6 B2
Stadtlohn D 3 C3
Stäfa CH 21 B3
Stainville F 11 C5
Stalden CH 27 A4
Stans CH 20 C3
Staphorst NL 2 B3
Staufen D 20 B2
Stavelot B 6 B1
Stavenisse NL 5 A4
Stavoren NL 2 B2
Stechelberg CH 20 C2
Steckborn CH 21 B3
Stede Broek NL 2 B2
Steeg A 21 B5
Steenbergen NL 5 A4
Steenvoorde F 4 B2
Steenwijk NL 2 B3
Steffisburg CH 20 C2
Steinach D 20 A3
Stein an Rhein CH 21 B3
Steinau D 7 B5
Steinen D 20 B2
Steinfeld D 3 B5
Steinfurt D 3 B4
Steinheim
Bayern D 21 A5
Nordrhein-Westfalen
D 7 A5
Stekene B 5 A4
Stellendam NL 5 A4
Stenay F 11 B5
Stes Maries-
de-la-Mer F 31 B3
Stiens NL 2 A2
Stockach D 21 B4
Stöckalp CH 20 C3
Stolberg D 6 B2
Stollhamm D 3 A5
Stompetoren NL 2 B1
Strackholt D 3 A4
Straelen D 6 A2
Strasbourg F 13 C3
Stresa I 27 B5
Strijen NL 5 A4
Stromberg
Nordrhein-Westfalen
D 7 A4
Rheinland-Pfalz D 13 B3
Stroppiana I 27 B5
Strücklingen D 3 A4
Stuben A 21 B5
Stukenbrock D 7 A4
Suchteln D 6 A2
Sugères F 25 B3
Sugny B 11 B4
Suippes F 11 B4
Sulgen CH 21 B4
Sully-sur-Loire F 17 B4
Sülz D 13 C4
Sulzbach
Bayern D 13 B5
Saarland D 12 B3
Sumiswald CH 20 B2
Sunbilla E 34 A2
Sundern D 7 A4
Super Sauze F 32 A2
Surgères F 22 B3
Surhuisterveen NL 2 A3
Sùria E 37 C2
Surin F 23 B4
Sursee CH 20 B3
Surwold D 3 B4
Sury-le-Comtal F 25 B4
Susa I 27 B4
Susch CH 21 C5
Suze-la-Rousse F 31 A3
Swifterbant NL 2 B2

T

Tafalla E 34 B2
Tággia I 33 B3
Tagnon F 11 B4
Tailfingen D 21 A4
Taillis F 15 A4
Tain-l'Hermitage
F 25 B4
Talant F 19 B3
Talizat F 24 B3
Tallard F 32 A2
Talloires F 26 B3
Talmay F 19 B4
Talmont-St Hilaire
F 22 B2
Talmont-sur-Gironde
F 22 C3
Tamarit de Mar E 37 C2
Tamarite de Litera
E 35 C4
Tamariu E 37 C4
Tancarville F 9 A4
Taninges F 26 A3
Tannay
Ardennes F 11 B4
Nièvre F 18 B2
Tanus F 30 A1
Tapio F 36 A2
Taradell E 37 C3
Tarare F 25 B4
Tarascon F 31 B3
Tarascon-sur-Ariège
F 36 B2
Tarazona E 34 C2
Tarbes F 35 A4
Tardets-Sorholus
F 34 A3
Tardienta E 35 C3
Targon F 28 B2
Tarnos F 28 C1
Tarragona E 37 C2
Tàrrega E 37 C2
Tartas F 28 C2
Täsch CH 27 A4
Taulé F 14 A2
Taulignan F 31 A3
Taunusstein D 7 B4
Tauste E 34 C2
Tauves F 24 B2
Tavannes CH 20 B2
Tavaux F 19 B4
Taverny F 10 B2
Tavescan E 36 B2
Tecklenburg D 3 B4
Teillay F 15 B4
Teillet F 30 B1
Telgte D 3 C4
Temse B 5 A4
Tenay F 26 B2
Ten Boer NL 3 A3
Tence F 25 B4
Tende F 33 A3
Tenneville B 12 A1
Ter Apel NL 3 B4
Terborg NL 3 C3
Tergnier F 10 B3
Terme di Valdieri I 33 A3
Termens E 35 C4
Termes F 24 C3
Terneuzen NL 5 A3
Terrassa E 37 C3
Terrasson-
Lavilledieu F 29 A4
Tervuren B 5 B4
Tessy-sur-Vire F 8 B2
Teterchen F 12 B2
Tettnang D 21 B4
Thalfang D 12 B2
Thalkirch CH 21 C4
Thalwil CH 21 B3
Thann F 20 B2
Thaon-les-Vosges
F 19 A5
Thayngen CH 21 B3
The Hague = 's-
Gravenhage NL 2 B1
Thénezay F 16 C1
Thenon F 29 A4
Therouanne F 4 B2
Theux B 6 B1
Thézar-les-Corbières
F 36 A3
Thèze F 35 A3
Thiberville F 9 A4
Thibie F 11 C4
Thiéblemont-
Farémont F 11 C4
Thierrens CH 20 C1
Thiers F 25 B3
Thiezac F 24 B2
Thionville F 12 B2
Thiron-Gardais F 9 B4
Thivars F 10 C1
Thiviers F 23 C4
Thizy F 25 A4
Tholen NL 5 A4
Tholey D 12 B3
Thônes F 26 B3
Thonnance-les-
Joinville F 11 C5
Thonon-les-Bains
F 26 A3
Thorame-Basse F 32 A2
Thorame-Haute F 32 A2
Thorens-Glières F 26 A3
Thorigny-sur-Oreuse
F 11 C3
Thouarcé F 16 B1
Thouars F 16 C1
Thueyts F 25 C4
Thuin B 5 B4
Thuir F 36 B3
Thun CH 20 C2
Thuret F 24 B3
Thurey F 19 C4
Thüringen A 21 B4
Thurins F 25 B4
Thury-Harcourt F 9 B3
Thusis CH 21 C4
Tiefencastel CH 21 C4
Tiel NL 5 A5
Tielt B 4 A3
Tienen B 5 B4
Tiengen D 20 B3
Tiercé F 16 B1
Tiermas E 34 B2
Tierrantona E 35 B4
Tignes F 27 B3
Tigy F 17 B4
Tijnje NL 2 A2
Tilburg NL 5 A5
Til Châtel F 19 B4
Tilh F 28 C2
Tillac F 35 A4
Tille F 10 B2
Tilloy Bellay F 11 B4
Tilly F 23 B5
Tilly-sur-Seulles F 8 A3
Tinchebray F 8 B3
Tincques F 4 B2
Tinlot B 5 B5
Tinténiac F 15 A4
Tintigny B 12 B1
Titisee-Neustadt
D 20 B3
Titz D 6 A2
Tocane-St Apre F 29 A3
Todtmoos D 20 B3
Todtnau D 20 B2
Tolosa E 34 A1
Tolva E 35 B4
Tombeboeuf F 29 B3
Tona E 37 C3
Tongeren B 5 B5
Tönisvorst D 6 A2
Tonnay-Boutonne
F 22 C3
Tonnay-Charente
F 22 C3
Tonneins F 29 B3
Tonnerre F 18 B2
Torà E 37 C2
Torcy-le-Petit F 9 A5
Tordera E 37 C3
Torellò E 37 B3
Torfou F 22 A2
Torhout B 4 A3
Torigni-sur-Vire F 8 A3
Torino = Turin I 27 B4
Torla E 35 B3
Torredembarra E 37 C2
Torregrosa E 37 C1
Torre la Ribera E 35 B4
Torre Péllice I 27 C4
Torroella de Montgrì
E 37 B4
Tossa de Mar E 37 C3
Tosse F 28 C1
Tôtes F 9 A5
Toucy F 18 B2
Toul F 12 C1
Toulon F 32 B1
Toulon-sur-Allier
F 18 C2
Toulon-sur-Arroux
F 18 C3
Toulouse F 29 C4
Tourcoing F 4 B3
Tour de la Parata
F 38 B1
Tourlaville F 8 A2
Tournai B 4 B3
Tournan-en-Brie F 10 C2
Tournay F 35 A4
Tournon-d'Agenais
F 29 B3
Tournon-St Martin
F 23 B4
Tournon-sur-Rhône
F 25 B4
Tournus F 19 C3
Tourouvre F 9 B4
Tourriers F 23 C4
Tours F 16 B2
Tourteron F 11 B4
Tourves F 32 B1
Toury F 17 A3
Touvois F 22 B2
Traben-Trarbach
D 12 B3
Trainel F 11 C3
Tramacastilla de Tena
E 35 B3
Tramelan CH 20 B2
Trampot F 12 C1
Trana I 27 B4
Trans-en-Provence
F 32 B2
Trappes F 10 C2
Travo F 38 B2
Treban F 24 A3
Trébeurden F 14 A2
Treffort F 26 A2
Trégastel-Plage F 14 A2
Tréguier F 14 A2
Trégunc F 14 B2
Treignac F 24 B1
Treignat F 24 A2
Treignes B 11 A4
Treis-Karden D 6 B3
Trélazé F 16 B1
Trélissac F 29 A3
Trélon F 11 A4
Trélou-sur-Marne
F 11 B3
Tremblay-le-Vicomte
F 9 B5
Tremp E 35 B4
Trendelburg D 7 A5
Trensacq F 28 B2
Trept F 26 B2
Trets F 32 B1
Trévoux F 25 B4
Treysa D 7 B5
Trézelles F 25 A3
Triaize F 22 B2
Triaucourt-en-
Argonne F 11 C5
Triberg D 20 A3
Trier D 12 B2
Trie-sur-Baïse F 35 A4
Trignac F 15 B3
Trilport F 10 C2
Trino I 27 B5
Triora I 33 B3
Triste E 34 B3
Trivero I 27 B5
Troarn F 9 A3
Troisdorf D 6 B3
Trois-Ponts B 6 B1
Troisvierges L 12 A2
Tronget F 24 A3
Tronzano-Vercellese
I 27 B5
Trôo F 16 B2
Trosly-Breuil F 10 B3
Trossingen D 21 A3
Trouville-
sur-Mer F 9 A4
Troyes F 18 A3
Trun
CH 21 C3
F 9 B4
Tschagguns A 21 B4
Tubbergen NL 3 B3
Tübingen D 13 C5
Tubize B 5 B4
Tuchan F 36 B3
Tudela E 34 B2
Tuffé F 16 A2
Tulette F 31 A3
Tulle F 24 B1
Tullins F 26 B2
Turbenthal CH 21 B3
Turckheim F 20 A2
Turin = Torino I 27 B4
Turnhout B 5 A4
Turries F 32 A2
Turtmann CH 27 A4
Tuttlingen D 21 B3
Twello NL 2 B3
Twist D 3 B4
Tzummarum NL 2 A2

U

Überlingen D 21 B4
Uchaud F 31 B3
Uckerath D 6 B3
Uden NL 6 A1
Uedem D 6 A2
Uelsen D 3 B3
Uetendorf CH 20 C2
Ugine F 26 B3
Uitgeest NL 2 B1
Uithoorn NL 2 B1
Uithuizen NL 3 A3
Uithuizermeeden
NL 3 A3
Ujué E 34 B2
Ulldemolins E 37 C1
Ulmen D 6 B2
Ulrichstein D 7 B5
Ulrum NL 3 A3
Uncastillo E 34 B2
Unkel D 6 B3
Unna D 7 A3
Unterägeri CH 21 B3
Unteriberg CH 21 B3
Unterschächen
CH 21 C3
Ur F 36 B2
Urçay F 17 C4
Urdax E 34 A2
Urdos F 35 B3
Urk NL 2 B2
Urnäsch CH 21 B4
Urries E 34 B2
Urroz E 34 B2
Ury F 10 C2
Useldange L 12 B1
Usingen D 7 B4
Usquert NL 3 A3
Ussé F 16 B2
Usséglio I 27 B4
Ussel
Cantal F 24 B2
Corrèze F 24 B2
Usson-du-Poitou
F 23 B4
Usson-en-Forez F 25 B3
Usson-les-Bains F 36 B3
Ustaritz F 34 A2
Uster CH 21 B3
Utrecht NL 2 B2
Uttenweiler D 21 A4
Uza F 28 B1
Uzein F 35 A3
Uzel F 14 A3
Uzerche F 24 B1
Uzès F 31 A3
Uznach CH 21 B3

V

Vaas F 16 B2
Vaasen NL 2 B2
Vabre F 30 B1
Vacqueyras F 31 A3
Vado Ligure I 33 A4
Vaduz FL 21 B4
Vagney F 20 A1
Vaiges F 16 A1
Vaihingen D 13 C4
Vaillant F 19 B4
Vailly-sur-Aisne F 11 B3

Vailly-sur Sauldre
F 17 B4
Vaison-la-Romaine
F 31 A4
Vaite F 19 B4
Valberg F 32 A2
Valbonnais F 26 C2
Valdahon F 19 B5
Val d'Esquières F..32 B2
Valdieri I 33 A3
Val-d'Isère F 27 B3
Valençay F 17 B3
Valence
  Charente F 23 C4
  Drôme F 25 C4
Valence d'Agen F .26 B3
Valence d'Albigeois
F 30 A1
Valence-sur-Baïse
F 29 C3
Valenciennes F 5 B3
Valensole F 32 B1
Valentigney F 20 B1
Valentine F 35 A4
Valflaunes F 31 B2
Valgorge F 31 A3
Valgrisenche I ...27 B4
Valkenburg NL 6 B1
Valkenswaard NL ...5 A5
Valle Mosso I 27 B5
Vallendar D 7 B3
Valleraugue F 30 A2
Vallet F 15 B4
Vallfogona de Riucorb
E 37 C2
Valloire F 26 B3
Vallon-Pont-d'Arc
F 31 A3
Vallorbe F 19 C5
Vallouise F 26 C3
Valls E 37 C2
Valmont F 9 A4
Valognes F 8 A2
Valpelline I 27 B4
Valras-Plage F 30 B2
Valréas F 31 A3
Vals CH 26 C1
Valsavarenche I ..27 B4
Vals-les-Bains F .25 C4
Valsonne F 25 B4
Val-Suzon F 19 B3
Val Thorens F 26 B3
Valtierra E 34 B2
Valtournenche I ..27 B4
Valverde E 34 C2
Vanault-les-Dames
F 11 C4
Vandenesse F 18 C2
Vandenesse-en-
Auxois F 18 B3
Vannes F 15 B3
Vaour F 29 B4
Varacieux F 26 B2
Varades F 15 B4
Varages F 32 B1
Varallo I 27 B5
Varazze I 33 A4
Varel D 3 A5
Varengeville-sur-Mer
F 9 A4
Varennes-en-Argonne
F 11 B5
Varennes-le-Grand
F 19 C3
Varennes-St Sauveur
F 19 C4
Varennes-sur-Allier
F 25 A3
Varennes-sur-Amance
F 19 B4
Varilhes F 36 A2
Varreddes F 10 C2
Vars F 26 C3
Varsseveld NL 3 C3
Varzo I 27 A5
Varzy F 18 B2
Vassieux-en-Vercors
F 26 C2
Vassy F 8 B3
Vatan F 17 B3
Vatry F 11 C4
Vättis CH 21 C4
Vauchamps F 11 C3
Vauchassis F 18 B2
Vaucouleurs F 12 C1
Vaudoy-en-Brie F .10 C3
Vaulruz CH 20 C2
Vaulx Vraucourt F .10 A2
Vaumas F 18 C2
Vausseroux F 23 B3
Vauvenargues F ..32 B1
Vauvert F 31 B3
Vauvillers F 19 B5
Vaux-sur-Sûre B ..12 B1
Vayrac F 29 B4
Vechta D 3 B5
Veendam NL 3 A3

Veenendaal NL 2 B2
Veghel NL 6 A1
Velbert D 6 A3
Velen D 6 A2
Velles F 17 C3
Vellmar D 7 A5
Velp NL 2 B2
Venaco F 38 A2
Venaria-Laumes
F 18 B3
Venaria I 27 B4
Venasca I 33 A3
Vence F 32 B3
Vendays-Montalivet
F 22 C2
Vendeuil F 11 B3
Vendeuvre-sur-Barse
F 18 A3
Vendoeuvres F ...23 B5
Vendôme F 17 B3
Venelles F 31 B4
Vénissieux F 25 B4
Venlo NL 6 A2
Vennezey F 12 C2
Venray NL 6 A1
Ventavon F 32 A1
Ventimiglia I 33 B3
Venzolasca F 38 A2
Vera de Bidasoa E .34 A2
Vera de Moncayo
E 34 C2
Verbánia I 27 B5
Verberie F 10 B2
Verbier CH 27 A4
Vercelli I 27 B5
Vercel-Villedieu-le-
Camp F 19 B5
Vercheny F 26 C2
Verclause F 31 A4
Verdille F 23 C3
Verdú E 37 C2
Verdun F 12 B1
Verdun-sur-Garonne
F 29 C4
Verdun-sur-le-Doubs
F 19 C4
Verfeil F 29 C4
Verges E 37 B4
Vergt F 29 A3
Veringenstadt D ..21 A4
Verl D 7 A4
Vermand F 10 B3
Vermenton F 18 B2
Vernante I 33 A3
Vernantes F 16 B2
Vernayaz CH 27 A4
Vern-d'Anjou F ...16 B1
Vernet F 36 A2
Vernet-les-Bains F .36 B3
Verneuil F 11 B3
Verneuil-sur-Avre F .9 B4
Vernier CH 26 A3
Vernon F 10 B1
Vernoux-en-Vivarais
F 25 C4
Verrès I 27 B4
Verrey-sous-Salmaise
F 18 B3
Verrières F 23 B4
Versailles F 10 C2
Versam CH 21 C4
Versmold D 3 B5
Versoix CH 26 A3
Verteillac F 23 C4
Vertou F 15 B4
Vertus F 11 C3
Verviers B 6 B1
Vervins F 11 B3
Verzuolo I 33 A3
Verzy F 11 B4
Vescovato F 38 A2
Vésime I 27 C5
Vesoul F 19 B5
Vétroz CH 27 A4
Veules-les-Roses F .9 A4
Veulettes-sur-Mer
F 9 A4
Veurne B 4 A2
Vevey CH 20 C1
Vex CH 27 A4
Veynes F 32 A1
Veyre-Monton F ..24 B3
Veyrier F 26 B3
Vézelay F 18 B2
Vézelise F 12 C2
Vézenobres F 31 A3
Vezins F 16 A1
Vézins-de-Lévézou
F 30 A1
Vezzani F 38 A2
Vianden L 12 B2
Viane F 30 B1
Viaréggio I 34 A1
Vic E 37 C3
Vicdessos F 36 B2
Vic-en-Bigorre F .35 A4
Vic-Fézensac F ...29 C3
Vichy F 25 A3
Vic-le-Comte F ...24 B3
Vico F 38 A1
Vic-sur-Aisne F ...10 B3

Vic-sur-Cère F 24 C2
Vidauban F 32 B2
Vieille-Brioude F .25 B3
Vielha E 35 B4
Vielle-Aure F 35 B4
Viellespesse F 24 B3
Viellevigne F 22 B2
Vielmur-sur-Agout
F 30 B1
Viels Maison F ...11 C3
Vienenburg D 7 B5
Vienne F 25 B4
Vierhouten NL 2 B2
Vierraden D 6 B1
Viernheim D 13 B4
Viersen D 6 A2
Vierville-sur-Mer F ..8 A3
Vierzon F 17 B4
Vieteren B 4 B2
Vieux-Boucau-les-
Bains F 28 C1
Vif F 26 B2
Vigeois F 24 B1
Vigevano I 27 B5
Vigneulles-
Hattonchâtel F ..12 C1
Vignevieille F 36 B3
Vignory F 19 A4
Vignoux-sur-
Barangeon F 17 B4
Vigone I 27 C4
Vihiers F 16 B1
Viladamat E 37 C3
Viladrau E 37 C3
Vilafranca del
Penedès E 37 C2
Vilajuïga E 37 B4
Vilanova de Sau E ..37 C3
Vilanova i la Geltrú
E 37 C2
Vila-Rodona E 37 C2
Vilaseca E 37 C2
Vilassar de Mar E ..37 C3
Vfilabona E 34 A1
Vildóssola I 27 A5
Villa E 31 C3
Villafranca E 34 B2
Villaines-
la-Juhel F 9 B3
Villamblard F 29 A3
Villandraut F 28 B2
Villanova d'Asti I ..27 C4
Villanova Mondovi
I 33 A3
Villanueva de Gállego
E 34 C2
Villard-de-Lans F .26 B2
Villaretto I 27 B4
Villar Perosa I 27 C4
Villars-les-Dombes
F 25 A5
Villastellone I 27 C4
Villé F 13 C3
Villebois-Lavalette
F 23 C4
Villecerf F 10 C2
Villecomtal F 30 A1
Villedieu-les-Poêles
F 8 B2
Villedieu-sur-Indre
F 17 B3
Ville-di-Pietrabugno
F 38 A2
Villefagnan F 23 B4
Villefontaine F ...26 B2
Villefort F 31 A2
Villefranche-
d'Albigeois F 30 B1
Villefranche-d'Allier
F 24 A2
Villefranche-de-
Lauragais F 36 A2
Villefranche-de-
Lonchat F 28 B3
Villefranche-de-Panat
F 30 A1
Villefranche-de-
Rouergue F 30 A1
Villefranche-du-
Périgord F 29 B4
Villefranche-sur-
Cher F 17 B3
Villefranche-sur-
Mer F 33 B3
Villegenon F 17 B4
Villemaur-sur-Vanne
F 18 A2
Villemontais F ...25 B3
Villemur-sur-Tarn
F 29 C4
Villenauxe-la-Grande
F 11 C3
Villeneuve-d'Ornon
F 28 B2
Villeneuve
  CH 27 A4
Villeneuve-d'Ascq
F 4 B3

Villeneuve-de-Berg
F 31 A3
Villeneuve-de-Marsan
F 28 C2
Villeneuve-de-Rivière
F 35 A4
Villeneuve-la-Guyard
F 10 C3
Villeneuve-
l'Archevêque F ..18 A2
Villeneuve-le-Comte
F 10 C2
Villeneuve-lès-
Avignon F 31 B3
Villeneuve-les-
Corbières F 36 B3
Villeneuve-St Georges
F 10 C2
Villeneuve-sur-Allier
F 18 C2
Villeneuve-sur-Lot
F 29 B3
Villeneuve-sur-Yonne
F 18 A2
Villeréal F 29 B3
Villeromain F 17 B3
Villers-Bocage
  Calvados F 8 A3
  Somme F 10 B2
Villers-Bretonneux
F 10 B2
Villers-Carbonnel
F 10 B2
Villers-Cotterêts F ..10 B3
Villers-Farlay F ...19 B5
Villers-le-Gambon
B 5 B4
Villers-le-Lac F ...20 B1
Villers-sur-Mer F ..9 A3
Villerupt F 12 B1
Villerville F 9 A4
Villeseneux F 11 C4
Ville-sous-la-Ferté
F 19 A3
Ville-sur-Illon F ..19 A5
Ville-sur-Tourbe F .11 B4
Villetrun F 17 B3
Villeurbanne F ...25 B4
Villevêque F 16 B2
Villevocance F ...25 B4
Villiers-St Benoit
F 18 B2
Villiers-St-Georges
F 11 C3
Villingen
  D 20 A3
Villmar D 7 B4
Villmergen CH ...20 B3
Villoldo E 34 B2
Viloorde B 5 B4
Vimoutiers F 9 B4
Vimy F 4 B2
Vinadio I 33 A3
Vinaixa E 37 C1
Vinay F 26 B2
Vinça F 36 B3
Vineuil F 17 B3
Vinets F 11 C4
Vingrau F 36 B3
Vinon F 17 B4
Vinon-sur-Verdon
F 32 B1
Vins-sur-Caramy F ..32 B2
Vinstra N 32 A1
Viöl D 13 C2
Vöhringen D 22 A3
Void-Vacon F 12 C1
Voiron F 26 B2
Voise F 10 C1
Voisey F 19 B4

Voiteur F 19 C4
Volendam NL 2 B2
Völklingen D 12 B2
Volkmarsen D 7 A5
Vollenhove NL 2 B2
Vollore-Montagne
F 25 B3
Voltri I 33 A4
Volvic F 24 B3
Voorschoten NL ...2 B1
Vorden
  D 3 B5
  NL 3 B3
Voreppe F 26 B2
Vorey F 25 B3
Voué F 11 C4
Vouillé F 23 B4
Voulx F 10 C2
Voussac F 24 A3
Vouvray F 16 B2
Vouvry CH 27 A3
Vouziers F 11 B4
Voves F 17 A3
Vreden D 3 B3
Vriezenveen NL ...3 B3
Vrigne-aux-Bois F .11 B4
Vron F 4 B1
Vroomshoop NL ...3 B3
Vught NL 5 A5
Vuillafans F 19 B5
Vy-lès Lure F 19 B5

Waalwijk NL 5 A5
Waarschoot B 5 A3
Wabern D 7 A5
Wächtersbach D ...7 B5
Wädenswil CH ...21 B3
Wadern D 12 B2
Wadersloh D 7 A4
Wageningen NL ...2 C2
Waghäusel D 13 B4
Waimes B 6 B2
Wald CH 21 B3
Waldböckelheim
F 13 B3
Waldbröl D 7 A3
Waldeck D 7 A5
Waldfischbach-
Burgalben D 13 B3
Waldkirch D 20 A2
Waldkirchen D 21 C4
Waldkraiburg D ..21 A3
Wald-Michelbach
D 13 B4
Waldmohr D 13 B3
Waldshut D 20 B3
Waldstatt CH 21 B4
Waldwisse F 12 B2
Walenstadt CH ...21 B4
Walincourt F 10 A3
Wallenhorst D 3 B5
Walldorf D 13 B4
Walldürn D 13 B5
Wallenfels D 18 A1
Wallhausen D 7 B4
Wallsbüll D 13 C3
Walldürn E 13 C3
Walkenried D 7 A5
Wallenhorst D 3 B5
Walsrode D 7 A5
Waltenhofen D ...21 B5
Wangen im Allgäu
D 21 B4
Wangerooge D 3 A4
Wängi CH 21 B3
Warburg D 7 A5
Wardenburg D 3 A5
Waregem B 5 B3
Waremme B 5 B5
Warendorf D 3 C4
Warga NL 2 A2
Warnsveld NL 2 B3
Warsingsfehn D ...3 A4
Warstein D 7 A4
Warth A 21 B5
Wasbister B 5 B5
Wasselonne F 13 C3
Wassen CH 21 C3
Wassenaar NL 2 B1
Wasserauen CH ..21 B4
Wassy F 11 C4
Waterloo B 5 B4
Watten F 4 B2
Wavignies F 10 B2
Wavre B 5 B4
Weener D 3 A4
Weesp NL 2 B2
Weeze D 6 A2
Weggis CH 20 B3
Wehr D 20 B2
Weierbach D 13 B3
Weil am Rhein D ..20 B2
Weilburg D 7 B4
Weil der Stadt D ..13 C4
Weilheim D 21 B6
Weilmünster D 7 B4
Weiltingen D 20 A4
Weinfelden CH ...21 B4
Weingarten
  Baden-Württemberg
  D 13 B4
Weinheim D 13 B4
Weinstadt CH 21 C4
Weissannen CH ..21 C4

Weitnau D 21 B5
Welkenraedt B 6 B1
Wellin B 11 A5
Welschenrohr CH .20 B2
Welver D 7 A3
Wenden D 7 B3
Wengen CH 20 C2
Werdohl D 7 A3
Werkendam NL 5 A4
Werl D 7 A3
Werlte D 3 B4
Wermelskirchen D ..6 B3
Werne D 7 A3
Weseke D 6 A2
Wesel D 6 A2
Wesseling D 6 B2
Westerburg D 7 B3
Westerbork NL 3 B3
Westerburg D 7 B3
Westerhaar NL 3 B3
Westerholt D 3 A4
Westerkappeln D ...3 B4
Westerlo B 5 A4
Westerstede D 3 A4
Westkapelle
  B 4 A3
  NL 5 A3
West-Terschelling
  NL 2 A2
Wetter
  Hessen D 7 B4
  Nordrhein-Westfalen
  D 6 A3
Wetteren B 5 A3
Wettringen D 3 B4
Wetzikon CH 21 B3
Wetzlar D 7 B4
Weyerbusch D 7 B3
Weyer Markt
  CH 13 C3
Weyersheim F 13 C3
Wickede D 7 A3
Wiefelstede D 3 A5
Wiehl D 7 B3
Wierden NL 3 B3
Wiesbaden D 13 A4
Wiesen CH 21 C4
Wiesloch D 13 B4
Wiesmoor D 3 A4
Wietmarschen D ..3 B4
Wiggen CH 20 C2
Wijchen NL 6 A1
Wijhe NL 2 B3
Wijk bij Duurstede
NL 2 C2
Wil CH 21 B4
Wildalpen A 9 A5
Wildberg D 13 C4
Wildbad D 13 C4
Wildeck D 7 B5
Wildegg CH 20 B3
Wilhelmsdorf D ...21 B4
Wilhelmshaven D ..3 A5
Wilhermsdorf D ...20 A2
Wilkau-Haßlau D ..20 A2
Willebadessen D ...7 A5
Willebroek B 5 A4
Willgottheim F ...13 C3
Willich D 6 A2
Willingen D 7 A4
Willisau CH 20 B3
Wilsum D 3 B3
Wiltz L 12 B1
Wimereux F 4 B1
Wimmenau F 13 C3
Wimmenau F 13 C3
Wimmis CH 20 C2
Wincheringen D ..12 B2
Windermere
  CH 20 B2
Baden-Württemberg
  D 13 C4
Windischgarsten
  A 9 A5

Wörth
  Bayern D 13 B5
  Rheinland-Pfalz D 13 B4
Woudsend NL 2 B2
Woumen B 4 A2
Wulfen D 6 A3
Wünnenberg D 7 A4
Wuppertal D 6 A3
Würselen D 6 B2
Wuustwezel B 5 A4

X

Xanten D 6 A3
Xertigny F 19 A5

Y

Ydes F 24 B2
Yebra de Basa E ..35 B3
Yenne F 26 B2
Yerseke NL 5 A4
Yerville F 9 A4
Ygos-St-Saturnin
F 28 C2
Ygrande F 18 C1
Ymonville F 17 A3
Yport F 9 A4
Ypres = Ieper B ...4 B2
Yssingeaux F 25 B4
Yverdon-les-Bains
  CH 20 C1
Yvetot F 9 A4
Yvignac F 15 A3
Yvoir B 5 B4
Yvonand CH 20 C1
Yzeure F 18 C2

Z

Zaamslag NL 5 A3
Zaanstad NL 2 B1
Zaltbommel NL 5 A5
Zandhoven B 5 A4
Zandvoort NL 2 B1
Zarautz E 34 A1
Zarren B 4 A2
Zeebrugge B 4 A3
Zeist NL 2 B2
Zele B 5 A4
Zelhem NL 3 B3
Zell
  CH 20 B2
  Baden-Württemberg
  D 13 C4
  Rheinland-Pfalz D 12 A3
Zelzate B 5 A3
Zemst B 5 B4
Zerf D 12 B2
Zermatt CH 27 A4
Zernez CH 21 C5
Zestoa E 34 A1
Zetel D 3 A4
Zevenaar NL 2 C3
Zevenbergen NL ..5 A4
Zicavo F 38 B2
Zierenberg D 7 A5
Zierikzee NL 5 A3
Zinal CH 27 A4
Zoetermeer NL 2 B1
Zofingen CH 20 B2
Zomergem B 5 A3
Zonhoven B 5 B5
Zonza F 38 B2
Zottegem B 5 B3
Zoutkamp NL 3 A3
Zubieta E 34 A2
Zubiri E 34 B2
Zuera E 34 C3
Zug CH 21 B3
Zuidhorn NL 3 A3
Zuidlaren NL 3 A3
Zujar E 30 B3
Zundert NL 5 A4
Zunderdt NL 5 A4
Zürich CH 21 B3
Zurzach CH 20 B3
Zutphen NL 2 B3
Zwartsluis NL 2 B3
Zweibrücken D 13 B3
Zweisimmen CH ..20 C2
Zwiefalten D 21 A4
Zwolle NL 2 B3